Knowing God's Divine Love Through Jesus

Second Edition

A Workbook by

James J. Stewart

All Biblical quotations are from the text file of:
The Project Gutenberg eBook of The New Testament of our Lord and Savior Jesus Christ.
Editor: American Bible Union

This ebook is for the use of anyone anywhere in the United States and most
other parts of the world at no cost and with almost no restrictions whatsoever.

Release date: August 19, 2008 [eBook #26361]
Most recently updated: January 3, 2021

Language: English

3

<u>Table of Contents</u>

Introduction

The other gospels are centered around people with very little formal education. The author of Luke and Acts is different in this regard. Luke, the author of both Luke's Gospel and Acts in the Bible, although not well-known except for his name, he is known that he was both a doctor and the only Gentile to have written anything in the New Testament. In Paul's letter to the Colossians, he draws a distinction between Luke and other colleagues who were "of the circumcision," meaning Jews (Colossians 4:11). Luke is the only non-Jewish writer in the New Testament, and he is explicitly identified as such.

Luke wrote both the gospel of Luke and the book of Acts, making 27.5% of the New Testament. Paul mentions him in three epistles. Both Luke and Acts address the same person, named Theophilus (Luke 1:3; Acts 1:1). Perhaps Theophilus, had already received the basics of Christian doctrine, but had not yet fully mastered them. No one knows exactly who Theophilus was, but we know that Luke's purpose in writing the two companion books was so that Theophilus would know with certainty about the person and work of Jesus Christ (Luke 1:4). The name, Theophilus, means 'lover of God.' God's divine love shines through both books.

Paul had a close relationship with Luke, and Paul called him 'the beloved physician' (Colossians 4:14). Luke's interest in medicine may be the reason why his gospel puts a high emphasis on Jesus' healing acts. Luke is referred to as a 'fellow laborer' by Paul in Philemon 1:24. During Paul's second missionary journey (Acts 16:6–11), Luke accompanied Paul to Troas, which is in Asia Minor, which is currently Turkey. Luke was with Paul when he traveled to Jerusalem and Rome, and also when he was imprisoned there (2 Timothy 4:11). Luke's vivid description of his travels with Paul in Acts 27 suggests that he was skilled in navigation and probably traveled extensively.

Luke's expertise in the Greek language has been noted by many scholars. His vocabulary is extensive and rich in classical Greek, as illustrated in the preface of his Gospel (Luke 1:1–4). Sailing was something he was familiar with, and he had a special affinity for documenting geographic details. Luke was a well-educated, observant, and carefully accurate writer.

This workbook is written with four features:

1. The Guttenberg New Testament is an old translation that is free of copyright restrictions. The users may use their preferred translation if necessary. Care must be taken to use a translation and not a paraphrase however, as a paraphrase is not useful for serious Bible study and spiritual growth.

2. Notes are provided to clarify each passage. Similar notes are often found in other Bibles.

3. Questions for reflection are provided to stimulate the thinking of the workbook user and to provide opportunities for spiritual growth. There are no "right" or "wrong" answers.

4. There are sample prayers provided to suggest ways to pray beyond simple expressions of thanks and requests.

At the end of this workbook there are samples of other books that are available exclusively on Amazon by the author of this workbook. May God dwell in your heart as your proceed with this workbook! Amen.

> *The prayers are optional for the readers and students to pray as part of their spiritual growth.*

THE GOSPEL ACCORDING TO LUKE

Introduction: Luke 1:1-4

FORASMUCH as many have taken in hand to set forth in order a narration concerning the things fully believed among us[1:1], (2) as they, who from the beginning were eyewitnesses and ministers of the word, delivered them to us; (3) it seemed good to me also, having accurately traced all from the very first, to write to thee in order, most excellent Theophilus; (4) that thou mightest know the certainty concerning those things[1:4] wherein thou wast instructed.

Compare:

John 20:30-31

Notes

1. Notice that this is not a religious statement. There is no religious language here.
2. Theophilus is mentioned both here and at the beginning of Acts, the second volume of this narrative witness.

Questions for Reflection

1. What is implied by the phrase, eyewitnesses and servants of the word?

2. Since Luke's audience is both Gentile and Jewish, what do you anticipate about the remainder of the Gospel in light of his approach here?

Birth of John the Baptist: Luke 1:5-25

(5) There was in the days of Herod, the king of Judaea, a certain priest, Zachariah by name, of the course of Abijah; and his wife was of the daughters of Aaron, and her name was Elisabeth. (6) And they were both righteous before God, walking in all the commandments and ordinances of the Lord blameless. (7) And they had no child, because Elisabeth was barren; and they both were now far advanced in years.

(8) And it came to pass, that while he executed the priest's office before God, in the order of his course, (9) it fell to his lot, according to the custom of the priest's office, to burn incense, going into the temple of the Lord. (10) And the whole multitude of the people were praying without, at the hour of incense. (11) And there appeared to him an angel of the Lord, standing on the right side of the altar of incense. (12) And Zachariah seeing him was troubled, and fear fell upon him. (13) But the angel said to him: Fear not, Zachariah; for thy prayer was heard, and thy wife Elisabeth shall bear thee a son, and thou shalt call his name John. (14) And thou shalt have joy and gladness; and many shall rejoice at his birth. (15) For he shall be great before the Lord; and he shall not drink wine nor strong drink; and he shall be filled with the Holy Spirit, even from his mother's womb. (16) And many of the sons of Israel shall he turn to the Lord their God. (17) And he shall go before him in the spirit and power of Elijah, to turn the hearts of the fathers to the children, and the disobedient to the wisdom of the just; to make ready a prepared people for the Lord.

(18) And Zachariah said to the angel: Whereby shall I know this? For I am an old man, and my wife is far advanced in years. (19) And the angel answering said to him: I am Gabriel, that stands in the presence of God; and I was sent to speak to thee, and to bring thee these glad tidings. (20) And, behold, thou shalt be dumb, and

not able to speak, until the day that these things shall be performed, because thou didst not believe thy words, which shall be fulfilled in their season.

(21) And the people were waiting for Zachariah; and they were wondering at his long tarrying in the temple. (22) And when he came out he was not able to speak to them, and they perceived that he had seen a vision in the temple; and he was making signs to them, and remained speechless.

(23) And it came to pass, when the days of his ministration were completed, that he departed to his own house.

(24) And after those days his wife Elisabeth conceived; and she hid herself five months, saying: (25) Thus has the Lord dealt with me, in the days wherein he looked on me to take away my reproach among men.

The Birth of Jesus Foretold: Luke 1:26-38

(26) And in the sixth month the angel Gabriel was sent from God to a city of Galilee, named Nazareth, (27) to a virgin betrothed to a man whose name was Joseph, of the house of David; and the virgin's name was Mary. (28) And the angel coming in to her, said: Hail, highly favored! The Lord is with thee. Blessed art thou among women. (29) And she was troubled at the saying; and was considering what manner of salutation this might be. (30) And the angel said to her: Fear not, Mary; for thou didst find favor with God. (31) And, behold, thou shalt conceive in thy womb, and bring forth a son, and shalt call his name Jesus. (32) He shall be great, and shall be called Son of the Highest; and the Lord God will give to him the throne of David his father; (33) and he shall reign over the house of Jacob forever; and of his kingdom there shall be no end. (34) Then said Mary to the angel: How shall this be, seeing that I know not a man? (35) And the angel answering said to her: The Holy Spirit will come upon thee, and the power of the Highest will overshadow thee; therefore also the Holy One that is born shall be called the Son of God. (36) And, behold, Elisabeth thy kinswoman, she also has conceived a son in her old age; and this is the sixth month with her who is called barren. (37) For with God nothing shall be[1:37] impossible.

(38) And Mary said: Behold the handmaid of the Lord; let it be to me according to thy word. And the angel departed from her.

Notes

1. We have the two words, marriage' and 'wedding' in our language because in the ancient world they were two different things. 'Marriage' referred to the contract between families for the purpose of procreation. Mary was, therefore, married in the sense that the legal bond could only be broken by divorce. 'Wedding' referred to the day that they began living together because the girl/woman was physically ready to bear children.

2. Many other religions through the ages have claimed their leaders to have been born of a virgin mother. Consequently, some scholars do not consider Mary's virginity an important issue.

Questions for Reflection

1. What would happen to our divorce rate if marriages were based mostly on contract and commitment?

2. Would you feel any less close to Jesus if you had never heard the stories of His birth? Why?

Elizabeth Receives Mary: Luke 1:39-56

(39) And Mary arose in those days, and went into the hill-country with haste, into a city of Judah; (40) and entered into the house of Zachariah, and saluted Elisabeth. (41) And it came to pass, as Elisabeth heard the salutation of Mary, that the babe leaped in her womb; and Elisabeth was filled with the Holy Spirit. (42) And she spoke out with a loud voice and said: Blessed art thou among women, and blessed is the fruit of thy womb. (43) And whence is this to me, that the mother of my Lord should come to me? (44) For, behold, as the voice of thy salutation came into my ears, the babe leaped in my womb for joy. (45) And happy is she, who believed that there shall be[1:45] a fulfillment of the things told her from the Lord.

(46) And Mary said: My soul magnifies the Lord; (47) and my spirit rejoiced in God my Savior. (48) Because he looked upon the low estate of his handmaid; for, behold, henceforth all generations will call me happy. (49) Because the Mighty One did great things for me; and holy is his name. (50) And his mercy is from generation to generation, to those who fear him. (51) He wrought might with his arm; he scattered the proud in the imagination of their hearts. (52) He cast down princes from thrones, and exalted those of low degree. (53) The hungry he filled with good, and the rich he sent empty away. (54) He helped Israel, his servant; to remember mercy, (55) as he spoke to our fathers, for Abraham and for his seed forever.

(56) And Mary abode with her about three months, and returned to her own house. 39 Mary arose in those days and went into the hill country with haste, into a city of Judah, 40 and entered into the house of Zacharias and greeted Elizabeth. 41 It happened, when Elizabeth heard Mary's greeting, that the baby leaped in her womb, and Elizabeth was filled with the Holy Spirit. 42 She called out with a loud voice, and said, "Blessed are you among women, and blessed is the fruit of your womb! 43 Why am I so favored, that the mother of my Lord should come to me? 44 For behold, when the voice of your greeting came into my ears, the baby leaped in my womb for joy! 45 Blessed is she who believed, for there will be a fulfillment of the things which have been spoken to her from the Lord!"

46 Mary said, "My soul magnifies the Lord. 47 My spirit has rejoiced in God my Savior, 48 for he has looked at the humble state of his handmaid. For behold, from now on, all generations will call me blessed. 49 For he who is mighty has done great things for me. Holy is his name. 50 His mercy is for generations of generations on those who fear him. 51 He has shown strength with his arm. He has scattered the proud in the imagination of their hearts. 52 He has put down princes from their thrones. And has exalted the lowly. 53 He has filled the hungry with good things. He has sent the rich away empty. 54 He has given help to Israel, his servant, that he might remember mercy, 55 As he spoke to our fathers, to Abraham and his seed forever."

56 Mary stayed with her about three months, and then returned to her house.

Notes

1. The recurring theme of joy is predominant for Luke. Subtle feelings of joy and salvation, often felt by expectant parents, are skillfully extended throughout the story of Jesus. Notice the universality of the conversation not just the undertones of God's salvation.

2. Speaking of God as Savior {47} is theologically sound. God's saving act is a living act in Jesus.

Questions for Reflection

1. What are the predominant things said in Mary's song?

2. What kind of person, male or female has this kind of faith? Do you known anyone like this?

The Birth of John the Baptist: Luke 1:57-80

(57) Now Elisabeth's full time came that she should be delivered; and she brought forth a son. (58) And her neighbors and her kindred heard that the Lord showed great mercy toward her; and they rejoiced with her.

(59) And it came to pass, that on the eighth day they came to circumcise the child; and they called him Zachariah, after the name of his father. (60) And his mother answered and said: Nay; but he shall be called John. (61) And they said to her: There is none of thy kindred that is called by this name. (62) And they made signs to his father, how he would have him called. (63) And asking for a writing-tablet, he wrote, saying: His name is John. And they all wondered. (64) And his mouth was opened immediately, and his tongue was loosed; and he spoke, blessing God. (65) And fear came on all that dwelt around them. And all these things[1:65] were told abroad in all the hill-country of Judaea. (66) And all who heard laid them up in their hearts, saying: What then will this child be! And the hand of the Lord was with him.

(67) And Zachariah his father was filled with the Holy Spirit, and prophesied, saying: (68) Blessed be the Lord, the God of Israel, that he visited and wrought redemption for his people; (69) and raised up a horn of salvation for us, in the house of David his servant, (70) (as he spoke by the mouth of his holy prophets of old,) (71) salvation from our enemies, and from the hand of all that hate us; (72) to show mercy to our fathers, and to remember his holy covenant; (73) the oath which he swore to Abraham our father, (74) to grant to us, that without fear, being rescued from the hand of our enemies, we should serve him, (75) in holiness and righteousness before him all our days.

(76) And also thou, O child, shalt be called Prophet of the Highest; for thou shalt go before the face of the Lord, to prepare his ways, (77) in order to give knowledge of salvation to his people in remission of their sins; (78) through the tender mercies of our God, whereby the dayspring from on high visited us, (79) to give light to those sitting in darkness and the shadow of death, in order to guide our feet into the way of peace.

(80) And the child grew, and became strong in spirit, and was in the deserts till the day of his manifestation to Israel.

Notes

1. Since this gospel is addressed partially to a Gentile audience, prophecy is not often introduced by Luke. Although this is a prophecy coming from a Jew, it is not a quotation of Hebrew Scripture.
2. Zechariah's prophecy can be seen as closely tied to the theme of fulfillment that was introduced in the prologue {Verses 1-4}.

Questions for Reflection

1. When this passage was used as part of the liturgy of the early church, how do you suppose it moved the congregation? Is that different from reactions today?

2. What do you suppose is the significance of Zechariah's confirming the name for the baby as supplied by Elizabeth and going on to say much more?

> Just as I am, I offer myself to You, Gracious God. Pease help me make, mature, and multiply more faithful disciples of Jesus that are born again. In His name I pray. Amen.

The Birth of Jesus: Luke 2:1-40

AND it came to pass in those days, that there went out a decree from Caesar Augustus, that all the world should be registered. (2) This registering was the first made when Cyrenius was governor of Syria. (3) And all went to be registered, each one to his own city. (4) And Joseph also went up from Galilee, out of the city of Nazareth, into Judaea, to the city of David which is called Bethlehem (because he was of the house and family of David) , (5) to be registered with Mary his betrothed wife, who was with child. (6) And so it was, that, while they were there, the days were completed that she should bring forth. (7) And she brought forth her first-born son, and wrapped him n swathing bands, and laid him in a manger; because there was no room for them in the inn.

(8) And there were in the same country shepherds abiding in the field, and keeping watch over their flock by night. (9) And, behold, an angel of the Lord came upon them, and the glory of the Lord shone around them; and they were sore afraid. (10) And the angel said to them: Fear not; for, behold, I bring you good tidings of great joy, which shall be to all the people. (11) For to you is born this day in the city of David a Savior, who is Christ the Lord. (12) And this shall be to you the sign: Ye will find a babe wrapped in swathing bands, lying in a manger. (13) And suddenly there was with the angel a multitude of the heavenly host, praising God and saying: (14) Glory to God in the highest, and on earth peace, good will among men.

(15) And it came to pass, when the angels were gone away from them into heaven, that the shepherds said one to another: Let us go now unto Bethlehem, and see this thing that is come to pass, which the Lord made known to us. (16) And they came with haste, and found both Mary and Joseph, and the babe lying in the manger. (17) And having seen it, they made known abroad the saying which was told them concerning this child. (18) And all that heard wondered at the things which were told them by the shepherds. (19) And Mary kept all these things[2:19], pondering them in her heart. (20) And the shepherds returned, glorifying and praising God for all that they heard and saw, as it was told to them.

(21) And when eight days were completed for circumcising him, his name was called Jesus; the name given by the angel before he was conceived in the womb.

(22) And when the days of their purification, according to the law of Moses, were completed, they brought him up to Jerusalem, to present him to the Lord, (23) (as it is written in the law of the Lord: Every male that opens the womb shall be called holy to the Lord;) (24) and to offer a sacrifice according to what is said in the law of the Lord: A pair of turtle-doves, or two young pigeons.

(25) And, behold, there was a man in Jerusalem, whose name was Simeon; and this man was just and devout, waiting for the consolation of Israel; and the Holy Spirit was upon him, (26) And it was revealed to him by the Holy Spirit, that he should not see death, before he had seen the Christ of the Lord. (27) And he came by the Spirit into the temple; and when the parents brought in the child Jesus, to do for him after the custom of the law, (28) then he took him into his arms, and blessed God, and said: (29) Now, Lord, thou lettest thy servant depart in peace, according to thy word; (30) because my eyes saw thy salvation, (31) which thou preparedst before the face of all the peoples, (32) a light for a revelation to the Gentiles, and the glory of thy people Israel.

(33) And his father and mother wondered at the things spoken of him. (34) And Simeon blessed them, and said to Mary his mother: Behold, this child is set for the fall and rising of many in Israel, and for a sign that shall be spoken against, (35) (and a sword shall pierce through thine own soul also) , that thoughts from many hearts may be revealed.

(36) And there was Anna, a prophetess, daughter of Phanuel, of the tribe of Asher. She was of great age, and had lived with a husband seven years from her virginity; (37) and she was a widow of about fourscore and four years, who departed not from the temple, serving day and night with fastings and prayers. (38) And she, coming up at that very time, likewise gave thanks to the Lord, and spoke of him to all that were looking for the redemption of Jerusalem.

(39) And when they had performed all things according to the law of the Lord, they returned into Galilee, to their own city Nazareth. (40) And the child grew, and became strong, being filled with wisdom; and the favor of God was upon him.

Compare:
Matthew 1:18-2:23.

Notes
1. The Emperor, Augustus, reigned from 27 BC to 14 AD. Quirinius was a military governor sent to put down a rebellion.
2. Simeon and Anna are not otherwise known in the Bible. Simeon's "Nunc Dimittis" {29-32} is an important benediction in the Roman Catholic Mass.

Questions for Reflection
1. Why do you think it is important for the writer to identify Jesus as Savior, Christ, and Lord here at the beginning of his testimony to Gentiles?

2. Why do you suppose Luke, a Gentile, includes the testimonies of Anna and Simeon in his testimony?

3. If you were one of Jesus' parents, what would you think of the testimonies of Anna and Simeon?

A Story from Jesus' Childhood: Luke 2:41-52

(41) And his parents went to Jerusalem every year at the feast of the passover. (42) And when he was twelve years old, they having gone up according to the custom of the feast, (43) and completed the days, as they returned, Jesus the child remained behind in Jerusalem. And his parents knew it not, (44) but supposing that he was in the company, went a day's journey, and sought him among their kindred and acquaintance; (45) and not finding him, they returned to Jerusalem, seeking him.

(46) And it came to pass, that after three days they found him in the temple, sitting in the midst of the teachers, both hearing them, and asking them questions. (47) And all that heard him, were astonished at his understanding and answers. (48) And seeing him they were amazed. And his mother said to him: Child, why didst thou thus deal with us? Behold, thy father and I sought thee, sorrowing. (49) And he said to them: How is it that ye sought me? Did ye not know, that I must be in my Father's house[2:49]? (50) And they understood not the saying which he spoke to them.

(51) And he went down with them, and came to Nazareth, and was subject to them. And his mother kept all these sayings in her heart. (52) And Jesus increased in wisdom and stature, and in favor with God and men.

Notes
1. This is the only information in the Bible about Jesus? childhood. They were not required by law to go to Passover because they lived so far from Jerusalem, but they may have gone out of pious motives.
2. Women and children often traveled separately from the men because they had to travel more slowly. The temporary loss as to Jesus' whereabouts was understandable.

<u>Question for Reflection</u>

> ➤ Do you think that Mary and Joseph fully understood the implications of who Jesus was? Why?

> Heavenly Father, as a child Jesus submitted to the authority of His parents. I know I must submit to your authority as your child. I also love you, Father, as you love me. In the name of Jesus my risen Savior I pray. Amen.

John the Baptist Introduced: Luke 3:1-20

NOW in the fifteenth year of the reign of Tiberius Caesar, when Pontius Pilate was governor of Judaea, and Herod tetrarch of Galilee, and his brother Philip tetrarch, of Iturea and of the region of Trachonitis, and Lysanias tetrarch of Abilene, (2) when Annas was high priest and Caiaphas, the word of God came to John, the son of Zachariah, in the wilderness. (3) And he came into all the country about the Jordan, preaching the immersion of repentance, unto remission of sins, (4) as it is written in the book of the words of Isaiah the prophet:

The voice of one crying in the wilderness,

Prepare the way of the Lord,

Make straight his paths.

(5) Every valley shall be filled,

And every mountain and hill shall be brought low;

And the crooked shall be straight,

And the rough ways smooth;

(6) And all flesh shall see the salvation of God.

(7) He said therefore to the multitudes that came out to be immersed by him: Brood of vipers, who warned you to flee from the coming wrath? (8) Bring forth therefore fruits worthy of repentance; and begin not to say within yourselves, We have Abraham for our father; for I say to you, that God is able of these stones to raise up children to Abraham. (9) And now also the axe is laid to the root of the trees. Every tree therefore, that brings not forth good fruit, is cut down and cast into the fire.

(10) And the multitudes asked him, saying: What then shall we do? (11) He answering says to them: He that has two coats, let him impart to him that has none; and he that has food, let him do likewise.

(12) And there came also publicans to be immersed; and they said to him: Teacher, what shall we do? (13) And he said to them: Exact no more than that which is appointed you. (14) And soldiers also asked him, saying: What shall we also do? And he said to them: Do violence to no one, neither accuse any falsely; and be content with your wages[3:14].

(15) And while the people were in expectation, and all were reasoning in their hearts concerning John, whether he himself were not the Christ, (16) John answered them all, saying: I indeed immerse you in water; but there comes he that is mightier than I, the latchet of whose sandals I am not worthy to loose; he will immerse you in the Holy Spirit and fire; (17) whose fan is in his hand, and he will thoroughly cleanse his threshing-floor, and will gather the wheat into his garner; but the chaff he will burn up with fire unquenchable.

(18) And with many other exhortations he published the good tidings to the people.

(19) But Herod the tetrarch, being reproved by him on account of Herodias, the wife of his brother, and for all the evils which Herod did, (20) added to all this also, that he shut up John in prison.

Compare:
Matthew 3:1-12
Mark 1:1-8.

Notes

1. The year is about 26 or 27 AD. Pilate, as procurator of Rome, was the authority for all of Judea, but the remainder of the kingdom of Herod the Great had been divided between his sons Herod Antipas and Philip.

2. Caiaphas, as High Priest, was the authority over all religious and most civil matters in the region.

3. Before the ministry of John, baptism in Judea was for conversion to Judaism, hence baptism for repentance was a radical departure that no doubt upset the authorities in Jerusalem.

4. There are still people in the Middle East who believe that John the Baptist was the Messiah.

<u>**Questions for Reflection**</u>

1. Since most thought John to be a prophet, what difficulty do you think the temple authorities had with him?

2. Why do you think Jesus' relationship with a Jewish prophet important to Luke's Gentile audience?

<u>**The Baptism of Jesus: Luke 3:21-22**</u>

(21) Now it came to pass, when all the people had been immersed, that as Jesus, having also been immersed, was praying, the heaven was opened, (22) and the Holy Spirit descended in a bodily shape as a dove upon him; and there came a voice out of heaven: Thou art my beloved Son; in thee I am well pleased.

<u>**Compare:**</u>
Matthew 3:13-17
Mark 1:9-11
John 1:29-34

<u>**Notes**</u>

1. Prayer is associated with the most important events in Jesus' life. It is interesting to note that His praying is not mentioned for the Jewish audience of the other gospels.
2. The words from heaven, as testified to in the other gospels, are slightly different, but the message is the same.
3. Jesus' baptism provides an illustration of what is called the Trinity:
   (1) God's voice from heaven,
   (2) Jesus in the river with John, and
   (3) The Holy Spirit as a dove.

<u>**Questions for Reflection**</u>

1. Why do you suppose this writer uses the phrase 'in bodily form' for this Gentile audience?

2. If you had just been baptized and heard the voice while watching Jesus, would you follow Him? Why?

<u>**The Family Heritage of Jesus: Luke 3:23-38**</u>

(23) And Jesus himself was, when he began[3:23], about thirty years of age; being the son (as was supposed) of Joseph, the son of Heli, (24) the son of Matthat, the son of Levi, the son of Melchi, the son of Janna, the son of Joseph, (25) the son of Matthias, the son of Amos, the son of Nahum, the son of Esli, the son of Naggai, (26) the son of Maath, the son of Mattathias, the son of Shimei, the son of Joseph, the son of Judah, (27) the son of Joanna, the son of Reza, the son of Zerubbabel, the son of Salathiel, the son of Neri, (28) the son of Melchi, the son of Addi, the son of Cosam, the son of Elmodam, the son of Er, (29) the son of Joses, the son of Eliezer,

the son of Jorim, the son of Matthat, the son of Levi, (30) the son of Simeon, the son of Judah, the son of Joseph, the son of Jonan, the son of Eliakim, (31) the son of Meleah, the son of Mainan, the son of Mattatha, the son of Nathan, the son of David, (32) the son of Jesse, the son of Obed, the son of Boaz, the son of Salmon, the son of Nahon, (33) the son of Amminadab, the son of Ram, the son of Hezron, the son of Pharez, the son of Judah, (34) the son of Jacob, the son of Isaac, the son of Abraham, the son of Terah, the son of Nahor, (35) the son of Serug, the son of Reu, the son of Peleg, the son of Eber, the son of Salah, (36) the son of Cainan, the son of Arphaxad, the son of Shem, the son of Noah, the son of Lamech, (37) the son of Methuselah, the son of Enoch, the son of Jared, the son of Mehalaleel, the son of Cainan, (38) the son of Enos, the son of Seth, the son of Adam, the son of God.

<u>Compare:</u>
Matthew 1:1-17

<u>Notes</u>
1. While the Matthew account of Jesus? genetic heritage stresses his Jewish roots from Matthew's primarily Jewish male audience, Luke's tracing of Jesus' heritage stresses His universal ties to all of humanity.
2. Some have tried to argue that Luke traces Jesus' heritage through Mary, while Matthew traces Jesus' heritage through Joseph, but this position is not entirely defendable.
3. In ancient times, one's family heritage was crucially important to one's identity.

<u>Questions for Reflection</u>
1. Is Jesus' heritage helpful to you? Why?

2. Are there any reasons your own ancestral roots could be important?

Christ my King, You rule my community of faith with mercy and grace. I am surrounded with temptations and depend upon You to save me. I am devoted to You and adore You, Lord Jesus, for it is in Your name I pray. Amen.

Jesus Tempted in the Wilderness: Luke 4:1-13

AND Jesus, full of the Holy Spirit, returned from the Jordan; and he was led in the Sprit into the wilderness (2) forty days, tempted by the Devil. And he ate nothing in those days; and when they were ended, he hungered.

(3) And the Devil said to him: If thou art the Son of God, command this stone that it become bread. (4) And Jesus answered him, saying: It is written, Man shall not live on bread alone.

(5) And the Devil, leading him up into a high mountain, showed him all the kingdoms of the world in a moment of time. (6) And the Devil said to him: All this power will I give thee, and the glory of them; because it has been delivered to me, and I give it to whomsoever I will. (7) If thou therefore wilt worship me, all shall be thine. (8) And Jesus answering said to him: It is written, Thou shalt worship the Lord thy God, and him only shalt thou serve.

(9) And he brought him to Jerusalem, and set him on the pinnacle of the temple, and said to him: If thou art the Son of God, cast thyself down from hence. (10) For it is written: He will give his angels command concerning thee, to keep thee; (11) and on their hands they shall bear thee up, lest haply thou dash thy foot against a stone. (12) And Jesus answering said to him: It is said, Thou shalt not tempt the Lord thy God.

(13) And having finished every temptation, the Devil departed from him for a season.

Compare:
Matthew 4:1-11
Mark 1:12-13

Notes
1. Even though Matthew offers a different order of the temptations, the basic content is the same.
2. The idea of being filled with the Holy Spirit is Christian in perspective not to be heard in a Jewish context.
3. It is implied that Jesus will be tempted at a later time, something to remember.

Questions for Reflection
1. Since all of us face temptations, how do you feel, knowing that Jesus Himself faced temptations similar to ours?

2. Do you believe that our hungers affect how much we are tempted, as you consider Jesus' temptations?

Jesus Begins Ministry: Luke 4:14-30

(14) And Jesus returned in the power of the Spirit into Galilee; and there went out a report concerning him through all the surrounding country. (15) And he taught in their synagogues, being honored by all.

(16) And he came to Nazareth, where he had been brought up. And, as his custom was, he went into the synagogue on the sabbath day; and he stood up to read. (17) And there was delivered to him the book of the prophet Isaiah. And unrolling the book, he found the place where it was written:

(18) The Spirit of the Lord is upon me;

Because he anointed me to publish good tidings to the poor;

He has sent me to proclaim deliverance to the captives,

And recovering of sight to the blind,

To send the oppressed away free,

(19) To proclaim the acceptable year of the Lord.

(20) And rolling up the book he gave it again to the servant, and sat down. And the eyes of all in the synagogue were fastened on him. (21) And he began to say to them: To-day is this scripture fulfilled in your ears. (22) And all bore witness to him, and wondered at the words of grace which proceeded out of his mouth. And they said: Is not this Joseph's son? (23) And he said to them: Ye will surely say to me this proverb, Physician, heal thyself. Whatever we heard done in Capernaum, do also here in thy country. (24) And he said: Verily I say to you, no prophet is accepted in his own country. (25) But I tell you of a truth, there were many widows in Israel in the days of Elijah, when the heaven was shut up three years and six months, when there was a great famine throughout all the land; (26) and to none of them was Elijah sent, but unto Zarephath of Sidonia, to a woman that was a widow. (27) And there were many lepers in Israel, in the time of Elisha the prophet; and none of them was cleansed, but only Naaman the Syrian. (28) And all in the synagogue, when they heard these things, were filled with wrath. (29) And they rose up, and thrust him out of the city, and led him to the brow of the hill whereon their city was built, to cast him down headlong. (30) But he, passing through the midst of them, went away.

<u>Compare:</u>
Matthew 13:53-58
Mark 6:1-6

<u>Notes</u>
1. It is implied that it was Jesus' practice to not only go to the synagogue for worship but to also convey his message.
2. The passage read from Isaiah concerned the Year of Jubilee, which although prescribed by Jewish law, was consistently avoided because of its provisions: Forgiving all loans, setting free all slaves, and spending 10% of one's assets on a party of fatted portions and strong drink at the foot of Mt. Sinai.
3. Sitting down to teach was the practice of fully qualified teachers, hence certain schools have 'chairs' for certain subjects.

<u>Questions for Reflection</u>
1. If you owned slaves or held loan papers, and you were sitting in that synagogue, how would you react if The Teacher told you that His teaching about it meant that The Year of Jubilee was about to be fulfilled?

2. If you were a slave or had a mortgage, how would you react?

<u>Jesus Goes to Capernaum: Luke 4:31-37</u>

(31) And he came down to Capernaum, a city of Galilee. And he was teaching them on the sabbath; (32) and they were astonished at his teaching, because his word was with power.

(33) And in the synagogue there was a man having a spirit of an unclean demon; and he cried out with a loud voice, (34) saying: Ah! what have we to do with thee, Jesus of Nazareth? Didst thou come to destroy us? I

know thee who thou art, the Holy One of God. (35) And Jesus rebuked him, saying: Hold thy peace, and come out from him. And the demon throwing him in the midst came out from him, doing him no harm. (36) And amazement came on all; and they spoke with one another, saying: What is this word, that with authority and power he commands the unclean spirits, and they come out? (37) And there went out a rumor concerning him into every place of the country around.

Compare:
Matthew 7:28-29
Mark 1:21-28

Notes
1. Demons were thought to be both personal and antagonistic to one's well-being. Jesus is frequently seen as someone who can deliver people from such possession. In modern psychiatry, those we label as schizophrenic often describe their feelings of being controlled or possessed by something other than themselves.
2. Capernaum would soon begin to function as Jesus' base of operations in the area around the Sea of Galilee.

Question for Reflection
> What are the differences Jesus deals with evil and the way most people do?

Further Healings: Luke 4:38-44

(38) And he rose up and went from the synagogue, and entered into the house of Simon. And the mother-in-law of Simon was seized with a violent fever[4:38]; and they besought him for her. (39) And standing over her he rebuked the fever, and it left her; and immediately she arose and ministered to them.

(40) Now when the sun was setting, all that had any sick with diverse diseases brought them to him; and he laid his hands on each one of them, and healed them. (41) And demons also came out from many, crying out, and saying: Thou art the Son of God. And he, rebuking them, suffered them not to speak, because they knew that he was the Christ.

(42) And when it was day he went out, and went into a desert place. And the multitudes sought him, and came to him, and stayed him, that he should not depart from them. (43) And he said to them: I must publish

the good news of the kingdom of God to other cities also; because for this I was sent forth. (44) And he preached in the synagogues of Galilee.

Compare:
Matthew 8:14-17
Mark 1:29-39

Notes
1. In some ancient sources, the region in verse 44 is Galilee, as agreed upon by Matthew and Mark. If the writer originally referred to Judea, it is the only time outside of John's Gospel that Jesus' early ministry in Judea is mentioned.
2. The writer specifies Jesus giving people individual attention.

<u>Question for Reflection</u>

➢ Would you feel comfortable with someone laying hands upon you so that you can be healed? Why?

> Thank You, Heavenly Father, for healing beyond hurt, for Your divine love beyond measure, for life beyond life, and for the mysteries beyond comprehending that You provide for me. I offer my prayers and myself in Jesus' name. Amen.

A Catch of Fish: Luke 5:1-11

AND it came to pass, as the multitude pressed upon him to hear the word of God, and he was standing by the lake of Gennesaret, (2) that he saw two ships standing by the lake; but the fishermen had gone out of them, and were washing the nets. (3) And entering into one of the ships, which was Simon's, he asked him to put out a little from the land. And sitting down, he taught the multitudes out of the ship.

(4) And when he ceased speaking, he said to Simon: Put out into the deep; and do ye let down your nets for a draught. (5) And Simon answering said to him: Master, we toiled all night and took nothing; but at thy word I will let down the net. (6) And having done this, they inclosed a great multitude of fishes; and their net began to break. (7) And they beckoned to their partners in the other ship, to come and help them. And they came, and filled both the ships, so that they began to sink. (8) And Simon Peter, seeing it, fell down at the knees of Jesus, saying: Depart from me; for I am a sinful man, O Lord. (9) For astonishment had seized him, and all that were with him, at the draught of the fishes which they had taken; (10) and likewise also James and John, sons of Zebedee, who were partners with Simon.

And Jesus said to Simon: Fear not; from henceforth thou shalt catch men. (11) And having brought their ships to land, they forsook all, and followed him.

Compare:
Matthew 4:18-22
Mark 1:16-20

Notes
1. Although Luke does not describe it as a miracle, Simon Peter seems to think that it is.
2. The Lake of Gennesaret is also known as the Sea of Tiberias or the Sea of Galilee.

Questions for Reflection
1. What kind of person would give up their livelihood on a moment's notice to serve Christ? Have you met such a person?

2. What would it take for you to drop everything and serve God full time?

3. Why do you suppose Jesus asked them to put down their nets, when he was planning to call them into His service?

Jesus Cures a Leper: Luke 5:12-16

(12) And it came to pass, when he was in one of the cities, that there was a man full of leprosy. And seeing Jesus he fell on his face, and besought him, saying: Lord, if thou wilt, thou canst cleanse me. (13) And stretching forth his hand he touched him, saying: I will; be thou cleansed. And immediately the leprosy departed from him. (14) And he charged him to tell no one: But go, and show thyself to the priest, and offer for thy cleansing as Moses commanded, for a testimony to them.

(15) But all the more went abroad the report concerning him; and great multitudes came together to hear, and to be healed of their infirmities. (16) And he was wont to retire into the solitary places, and pray.

<u>**Compare:**</u>
Matthew 8:1-4
Mark 1:40-45

<u>**Notes**</u>
1. When the Bible refers to leprosy, it can be one of any number of skin disorders. A person with such a skin disorder could not live within town or city limits. In Jerusalem, lepers lived outside the wall in Gehenna [translated: hell], where people lived among smolder garbage and wild dogs in 'the outer darkness.'
2. Jewish law required that a leper be certified by a priest as clean before he or she could return to normal society. Once certified as clean, the former leper was to give a prescribed offering of thanksgiving.

<u>**Questions for Reflection**</u>
1. Some people believe that people with AIDS should be quarantined, as were the lepers. What does this passage say to you about Jesus' attitude towards such people?

2. If you were very ill, how would you feel being confined to 'the outer darkness?'

<u>Sin and Forgiveness: Luke 5:17-26</u>

(17) And it came to pass, on a certain day, that he was teaching; and there were Pharisees and teachers of the law sitting by, who had come out of every village of Galilee, and Judaea, and Jerusalem; and there was power of the Lord for healing them. (18) And, behold, men brought on a bed a man who was palsied; and they sought to bring him in, and to lay him before him. (19) And not finding by what way they might bring him in, because of the multitude, they went upon the housetop, and let him down through the tiling with the couch into the midst before Jesus. (20) And seeing their faith he said: Man, thy sins are forgiven thee. (21) And the scribes and the Pharisees began to reason, saying: Who is this that speaks blasphemies? Who can forgive sins, but God alone? (22) But Jesus, perceiving their thoughts, answering said to them: What reason ye in your hearts? (23) Which is easier, to say, Thy sins are forgiven thee; or to say, Arise and walk? (24) But that ye may know that the Son of man has power on the earth to forgive sins, (he said to the palsied man,) I say to thee, arise, and taking up thy couch go to thy house. (25) And immediately standing up before them, he took up that whereon he lay, and departed to his house, glorifying God. (26) And they were all amazed; and they glorified God, and were filled with fear, saying: We have seen strange things to-day.

<u>**Compare:**</u>
Matthew 9:1-8
Mark 2:1-12

<u>**Notes**</u>
1. The fact that 'Pharisees and teachers of the law' came from such distances indicates that this is late in the three-year public career of Jesus. We can expect that from this point on his ministry will be seen as increasingly disruptive of the status quo in the religious power structure.
2. The Christ of faith is seen here in comparison to the faith of others – those who brought the man needing healing, the man in need, and the other faith leaders of the time.

<u>**Questions for Reflection**</u>

1. Are you the kind of person who would go to a great deal of trouble to acquire healing for someone?

2. Do you tend to be supportive of those who accomplish the unexpected or astounding? If so, how?

<u>**Jesus & a Tax Collector: Luke 5:27-32**</u>

(27) And after these things he went forth, and saw a publican, named Levi, sitting at the place of receiving custom; and he said to him: Follow me. (28) And leaving all, he arose and followed him.

(29) And Levi made him a great feast in his own house; and there was a great company of publicans and of others who reclined at the table with them. (30) And the Pharisees, and their scribes[5:30], murmured against his disciples, saying: Why do ye eat and drink with the publicans and sinners? (31) And Jesus answering said to them: They who are well need not a physician, but they who are sick. (32) I have not come to call righteous men, but sinners to repentance.

<u>**Compare:**</u>
Matthew 9:9-13
Mark 2:13-17

<u>**Notes**</u>

1. Jesus' charisma is demonstrated here by his simply saying to Matthew, 'Follow me,' and he does.
2. Jesus demonstrates his radical call to ministry by 'calling' or inviting those who the religious leaders considered either outcasts or detached from 'the true faith.'

<u>**Questions for Reflection**</u>

1. Would your friends be critical of you if you gave your life to someone you just met? Why?

2. Would you rather spend time discussing your faith experiences with someone who is already a Christian or with someone who doesn't really know your Christ of faith?

<u>**Jesus Teaches About Fasting: Luke 5:33-39**</u>

(33) And they said to him: Why do the disciples of John fast often, and make prayers, and likewise those of the Pharisees, but thine eat and drink? (34) And he said to them: Can ye make the sons of the bridechamber fast, [5:34] while the bridegroom is with them? (35) But days will come, when the bridegroom will be taken away from them; then shall they fast in those days. (36) And he spoke also a parable to them: No one rends a piece from a new garment, and puts it on an old garment; else both the new will make a rent, and the piece from the new agrees not with the old. (37) And no one puts new wine into old skins; else the new wine will burst the skins, and will itself be poured out, and the skins will perish. (38) But new wine must be put into new skins, and both

are preserved together[5:38]. (39) And no one having drunk old wine straightway desires new; for he says: The old is better[5:39].

<u>Compare:</u>
Matthew 9:14-17
Mark 2:19-20

<u>Notes</u>

1. The reference to old wine in old wineskins gives us insight as to why the religious leaders, as well as his cousin John, had trouble accepting Jesus' new teaching.
2. Fasting does not necessarily mean total abstinence from food and drink. Fluids were almost always taken, and extended fasts often included limited amounts of fruit.

<u>Questions for Reflection</u>

1. Have you ever fasted for purposes of spiritual reflection? Do you know others who do so?

2. Have you found spiritual reflection to be totally satisfying without fasting?

> Nothing calms me or gives my souls rest, O Lord, like spending time alone with you. May those be times when I can both seek and find you, Lord. In Jesus' name I pray. Amen.

Laws Concerning Sabbath: Luke 6:1-11

AND it came to pass on the second sabbath after the first[6:1], that he was going through grain-fields; and his disciples plucked and ate the ears of grain, rubbing them with their hands. (2) And some of the Pharisees said: Why do ye that which it is not lawful to do on the sabbath? (3) And Jesus answering them said: And have ye not read this, what David did when he hungered, himself and they who were with him; (4) how he went into the house of God, and took and ate the show-bread, and gave to those who were with him, which it is not lawful to eat except for the priests alone? (5) And he said to them: The Son of man is Lord also of the sabbath.

(6) And it came to pass also on another sabbath, that he entered into the synagogue and taught. And there was a man whose right hand was withered. (7) And the scribes and Pharisees were watching, whether he would heal on the sabbath; that they might find an accusation against him. (8) But he knew their thoughts, and said to the man having the withered hand: Arise, and stand forth in the midst. And he rose up, and stood. (9) Then said Jesus to them: I will ask you what is lawful[6:9] on the sabbath, to do good, or to do evil; to save life, or to destroy it? (10) And looking round on them all, he said to him: Stretch forth thy hand. And he did so, and his hand was restored. (11) And they were filled with madness, and conferred one with another, as to what they should do to Jesus.

Compare:
Matthew 12:1-14
Mark 2:23-3:6

Notes
1. Over many years, the Scribes had created many laws to specifically interpret the observance of the Sabbath. Since there is a moral obligation to honor and keep the Sabbath properly, these additional laws were seen as extremely important.
2. Repeatedly curing people on the Sabbath was probably the greatest irritation for the Temple authorities.

Questions for Reflection
1. Do you set aside one day each week to limit physical activity as prescribed by the Ten Commandments? If not, try it for a few months and focus on God.

2. Do you believe you can accomplish more in six days than in seven days if you rest one day each week?

An Inner Circle Chosen: Luke 6:12-16

(12) And it came to pass in those days, that he went out into the mountain to pray, and continued all night in prayer to God. (13) And when it was day, he called to him his disciples. And having chosen from them twelve (whom he named also apostles) ; (14) Simon, whom he also named Peter, and Andrew his brother, and James and John, and Philip and Bartholomew, (15) and Matthew and Thomas, James the son of Alpheus, and Simon called Zelotes, (16) and Judas brother of James, and Judas Iscariot, who became a betrayer;

Compare:
Matthew 10:1-4
Mark 3:13-19

Notes

1. Jesus chooses twelve for close companionship. The term apostle literally means appointed representative.' After the resurrection and ascension, the term is given a specialized Christian meaning, as witness to the resurrection.

2. Slight variations in the list of the twelve are evidently due to differences in Aramaic, Hebrew, and Greek naming.

3. This is one of many instances where Jesus finds privacy for extended periods of prayer.

Questions for Reflection

1. Who are the people that you consider your closest friends and companions? Does their quality of faith matter to you? Why?

2. What in their faith had a role in your becoming close to them?

Jesus Preaches on a Plain: Luke 6:17-49

(17) and having come down with them, he stood on a plain, and a company of his disciples, and a great multitude of people from all Judaea and Jerusalem and the sea-coast of Tyre and Sidon, who came to hear him, and to be healed of their diseases; (18) and those vexed by unclean spirits were healed; (19) and all the multitude sought to touch him, because power went out from him and healed them all.

(20) And he, lifting up his eyes on his disciples, said: Happy are ye poor; for yours is the kingdom of God. (21) Happy are ye that hunger now; for ye shall be filled. Happy are ye that weep now; for ye shall laugh.

(22) Happy are ye, when men shall hate you, and when they shall separate you from them, and shall reproach you, and cast out your name as evil, for the sake of the Son of man. (23) Rejoice in that day, and leap for joy; for, behold, your reward is great in heaven; for in the same manner did their fathers to the prophets.

(24) But woe to you that are rich; for ye have received your consolation. (25) Woe to you that are full; for ye shall hunger. Woe to you that laugh now; for ye shall mourn and weep. (26) Woe! when all men shall speak well of you; for in the same manner did their fathers to the false prophets.

(27) But I say to you who hear: Love your enemies, do good to those who hate you, (28) bless those who curse you, pray for those who abuse you[6:28]. (29) To him who smites thee on the cheek offer also the other; and him who takes away thy cloak forbid not to take thy coat also.

(30) Give to every one that asks of thee; and of him who takes away thy goods demand them not again. (31) And as ye would that men should do to you, do ye also in like manner to them.

(32) For if ye love those who love you, what thanks have ye? For even the sinners love those who love them. (33) And if ye do good to those who do good to you, what thanks have ye? For even the sinners do the same. (34) And if ye lend to those of whom ye hope to receive, what t hanks have ye? And sinners lend to sinners, that they may receive as much in return.

(35) But love your enemies, and do good, and lend, hoping for nothing in return; and your reward shall be great, and ye shall be sons of the Highest; for he is kind to the unthankful and evil. (36) Be ye merciful, as your Father also is merciful.

(37) And judge not, and ye shall not be judged; condemn not, and ye shall not be condemned; acquit, and ye shall be acquitted.

(38) Give, and it shall be given to you; good measure, pressed down, shaken together, running over, shall

they give into your bosom. For with the same measure with which ye mete it shall be measured to you again.

(39) And he spoke also a parable to them: Can the blind lead the blind? Shall they not both fall into the ditch? (40) A disciple is not above the teacher; but every one shall be perfected as his teacher.

(41) And why beholdest thou the mote that is in thy brother's eye, but perceivest not the beam that is in thine own eye?

(42) How canst thou say to thy brother: Brother, let me cast out the mote that is in thine eye, when thou thyself beholdest not the beam that is in thine own eye? Hypocrite! cast out first the beam out of thine eye, and then thou shalt see clearly to cast out the mote that is in thy brother's eye.

(43) For there is no good tree that bears corrupt fruit, nor corrupt tree that bears good fruit. (44) For every tree is known from its own fruit. For from thorns they do not gather figs, nor from a bramble bush do they harvest grapes. (45) The good man out of the good treasure of his heart brings forth that which is good; and the evil, out of the evil, brings forth that which is evil; for out of the abundance of the heart his mouth speaks.

(46) And why call ye me, Lord, Lord, and do not the things which I say?(47) Every one that comes to me, and hears my sayings, and does them, I will show you to whom he is like. (48) He is like a man building a house, who digged deep, and laid a foundation on the rock. And when a flood arose, the stream burst upon that house, and could not shake it; because it was well builded. (49) But he that hears, and does not, is like a man that built a house upon the earth without a foundation; on which the stream burst, and immediately it fell[6:49]; and the ruin of that house was great.

Compare:
Matthew 5-7

Notes
1. Sermons in the gospel testimonies are generally believed to be collections of things that Jesus taught, put together to inspire, evangelize, and encourage.
2. Verses 24-26 are unique to this gospel testimony.

Questions for Reflection
1. What are your impressions of the Jesus of your faith as you read this sermon?

2. What parts of this sermon would you use to share your faith with someone who does not know Jesus?

> Eternal and humbling God, I love You. My faith is often weak, but You are my strength. I ask for Your healing and redemption for those I know to be sick or in pain. I surrender them and myself to Your power and divine love and ask that you heal me and redeem me in Jesus' name. Amen.

Jesus Heals a Roman Soldier's Slave: Luke 7:1-10

WHEN he completed all his sayings in the hearing of the people, he entered into Capernaum. (2) And a certain centurion's servant, who was dear to him, was sick and about to die. (3) And having heard concerning Jesus, he sent to him elders of the Jews, asking him that he would come and heal his servant. (4) And they, coming to Jesus, besought him earnestly, saying: He is worthy that thou shouldst do this for him; (5) for he loves our nation, and himself built our synagogue.

(6) And Jesus went with them. And when he was now not far from the house, the centurion sent friends to him, saying to him: Lord, trouble not thyself; for I am not worthy that thou shouldst enter under my roof. (7) Wherefore neither thought I myself worthy to come to thee; but say with a word, and my servant will be healed. (8) For I am a man placed under authority, having soldiers under me, and I say to this one, Go, and he goes, and to another, Come, and he comes; and to my servant, Do this, and he does it. (9) And Jesus hearing these things, marveled at him; and turning said to the multitude that followed him: I say to you, I found not so great faith, even in Israel.

(10) And they who were sent, returning to the house, found the servant whole that had been sick.

Compare:
Matthew 8:5-13
John 4:46-53

Notes
1. This story is similar to the one in Matthew, though it is not exactly the same.
2. For Luke's audience, the faith of a Gentile is as important as that of a Jew.

Questions for Reflection
1. Why do you think the Centurion send Jewish leaders to Jesus rather than one of his slaves or a member of his family?

2. Since the Centurion saw Jesus as having the authority to heal, even at a distance, do you have that same kind of confidence in Jesus and trust Him with His answer? Do you thank Him immediately without waiting for His answer?

Jesus Resurrects a Man: Luke 7:11-17

(11) And it came to pass the day after, that he went into a city called Nain; and many of his disciples went with him, and a great multitude. (12) And as he came near to the gate of the city, behold, a dead man was carried out, the only son of his mother, and she was a widow; and a great multitude of the city was with her. (13) And seeing her, the Lord had compassion on her, and said to her: Weep not. (14) And he came and touched the bier; and they who bore it stood still. And he said: Young man, I say to thee, arise. (15) And the dead sat up, and began to speak. And he gave him to his mother. (16) And fear seized on all; and they glorified God, saying: A great prophet has arisen among us; and, God has visited his people. (17) And this report went forth in all Judaea concerning him, and in all the country around.

<u>**Compare:**</u>
Mark 5:21-24
John 11:1-44

<u>**Notes**</u>
1. Nain is about 25 miles Southwest of Capernaum.
2. Jewish law proscribed against burying anyone within a town.

<u>**Questions for Reflection**</u>
1. Since death is part of life, what might be some reasons Jesus decided to raise this particular man from death?

2. Have you ever talked with anyone about having a so-called near-death experience? What thoughts do you have when you hear these stories?

<u>**John the Baptist Inquires: Luke 7:18-35**</u>

(18) And the disciples of John reported to him concerning all these things. (19) And John calling to him two of his disciples sent them to Jesus, saying: Art thou he that comes, or look we for another? (20) And coming to him, the men said: John the Immerser has sent us to thee, saying: Art thou he that comes, or look we for another? (21) And in that very hour he cured many, of diseases and plagues, and evil spirits; and on many blind he bestowed sight. (22) And answering he said to them: Go, and report to John what ye saw and heard; that the blind receive sight, the lame walk, the lepers are cleansed, the deaf hear, the dead are raised, to the poor good tidings are published. (23) And happy is he, whoever shall not be offended at me.

(24) And when the messengers of John had departed, he began to say to the multitudes concerning John: What went ye out into the wilderness to behold? A reed shaken by the wind? (25) But what went ye out to see? A man clothed in soft raiment? Behold, they who are gorgeously appareled, and live delicately, are in kings' palaces.

(26) But what went ye out to see? A prophet? Yea, I say to you, and much more than a prophet. (27) This is he, of whom it is written:

Behold, I send forth my messenger before thy face, Who shall prepare thy way before thee.

(28) For I say to you, among those born of women, no one is a greater prophet than John; but he that is least in the kingdom of God is greater than he.

(29) And all the people, hearing it, and the publicans, justified God, having been immersed with John's immersion. (30) But the Pharisees and the lawyers rejected the counsel of God toward themselves, not having been immersed by him.

(31) To what then shall I liken the men of this generation? And to what are they like? (32) They are like to children sitting in the market, and calling to one another, saying: We piped to you, and ye danced not; we sang the lament to you, and ye wept not. (33) For John the Immerser has come, neither eating bread nor drinking wine; and ye say: He has a demon. (34) The Son of man has come eating and drinking; and ye say: Behold a glutton, and a wine-drinker, a friend of publicans and sinners. (35) But wisdom was justified on the part of all her children.

<u>Compare:</u>
Matthew 11:2-19

<u>Notes</u>

1. At this time John is in prison in Machaerus because of Herodias and Herod.
2. John may be asking these questions to help his disciples make a transition to Jesus. This is confirmed by Jesus' response. John knew very well who Jesus was.

<u>Questions for Reflection</u>

1. What is the basis of Jesus? appeal to John, to answer John's questions?

2. Why do you suppose these questions are of particular concern for Luke's testimony?

<u>Jesus Bonds with a Sinner: Luke 7:36-50</u>

(36) And one of the Pharisees asked him to eat with him. And entering into the house of the Pharisee, he reclined at table. (37) And, behold, a woman who was a sinner in the city, learning that he is reclining at table in the house of the Pharisee, brought an alabaster box of ointment; (38) and standing behind at his feet weeping, began to wet his feet with tears, and wipe them with the hairs of her head, and kissed his feet, and anointed them with the ointment.

(39) And seeing it, the Pharisee who had bidden him spoke within himself, saying: This man, if he were a prophet, would know who and what sort of woman this is that touches him; for she is a sinner. (40) And Jesus answering said to him: Simon, I have somewhat to say to thee. And he says: Teacher, say on. (41) A certain money-lender had two debtors. The one owed five hundred denaries[7:41], and the other fifty. (42) And they having nothing to pay, he forgave them both. Which of them therefore, tell me, will love him most? (43) Simon answering said: I suppose he to whom he forgave most. And he said to him: Thou didst rightly judge. (44) And turning to the woman, he said to Simon: Seest thou this woman? I entered into thy house, thou gavest me no water for my feet; but she has wet my feet with tears, and wiped them with her hair. (45) Thou gavest me no kiss; but she, from the time I came in, ceased not to kiss my feet. (46) My head with oil thou didst not anoint; but she anointed my feet with ointment. (47) Wherefore I say to thee, her many sins are forgiven; for she loved much. But to whom little is forgiven, the same loves little. (48) And he said to her: Thy sins are forgiven. (49) And they who reclined with him began to say within themselves: Who is this that also forgives sins? (50) And he said to the woman: Thy faith has saved thee; go in peace.

<u>Compare:</u>
Matthew 26:6-13
Mark 14:3-9
John 12:1-8

<u>Notes</u>

1. Outside of the Passion narratives, this is one of the few stories found in all four of the gospels.
2. Evidently the house was quite open, making the woman's entry possible.

3. Although such an anointing would be usually on the head, evidently humility moves her to anoint his feet.

4. Jesus' perspective on the woman is very different from that of the Pharisee, who had not followed all of the traditions of a good host towards Jesus and his followers.

<u>Questions for Reflection</u>

1. When you invite someone to your home, what are some of your requirements as host (ess) ?

2. What lessons are to be learned here in such areas as:
   * Humility?

   * Honor?

   * Compassion?

   * Forgiveness?

> Heavenly Father, I realize that this world is not my eternal home, but my life here lasts only as long as my flesh body endures. Then I will put on my spiritual body. I praise You for the divine love that is always ready to welcome me and bring me home. In Jesus' name I pray. Amen.

Itinerant Preaching and Healing: Luke 8:1-3

AND it came to pass afterward, that he journeyed through every city and village, preaching, and publishing the good news of the kingdom of God; and with him the twelve, (2) and certain women who had been healed of evil spirits and infirmities, Mary called the Magdalene, from whom had gone out seven demons, (3) and Joanna wife of Chuza, Herod's steward, and Susanna, and many others, who ministered to them of their substance.

Compare:
Matthew 4:23, 9:35, 27:55-56
Mark 3:14, 15:40-41
Luke 23:49

Notes
1. Mary is evidently from the town of Magdala, on the edge of the Sea of Galilee. She cannot be directly tied to the woman described at the end of the last chapter.
2. The steward in this case was undoubtedly a household administrator of some kind.

Questions for Reflection
1. What do you suppose are Jesus' thoughts and feelings having people He has healed following Him so closely?

2. What are some of the consequences of living on the road and sharing resources with friends?

The Parable of the Sower: Luke 8:4-15

(4) And a great multitude coming together, of those also who came to him out of every city, he spoke by a parable: (5) The sower went forth to sow his seed. And as he sowed, one fell by the way-side; and it was trodden down, and the fowls of the air devoured it. (6) And another fell upon the rock; and springing up, it withered away, because it had no moisture. (7) And another fell among the thorns; and the thorns sprang up with it, and choked it. (8) And another fell into the good ground, and sprang up, and bore fruit a hundredfold. And saying these things, he cried: He that has ears to hear, let him hear.

(9) And his disciples asked him, what this parable was. (10) And he said: To you it is given to know the mysteries of the kingdom of God; but to the rest in parables, that seeing they may not see, and hearing they may not understand.

(11) Now the parable is this: The seed is the word of God. (12) Those by the way-side are they that hear; after that comes the Devil, and takes away the word from their heart, that they may not believe and be saved. (13) Those on the rock are they who, when they hear, with joy receive the word; and these have no root, who for a while believe, and in time of temptation fall away. (14) And that which fell among the thorns, these are they who have heard, and going forth are choked with the cares and riches and pleasures of life, and bring no fruit to perfection. (15) But that in the good ground, these are they who, in an honest and good heart, having heard, hold fast the word, and bring forth fruit with patience.

<u>**Compare:**</u>
Matthew 13:1-23
Mark 4:1-20

<u>**Notes**</u>
1. A parable is not to be confused with an allegory or extended metaphor. A parable is told to illustrate or convey a single truth. Their lengths are highly varied.
2. The phrase, 'honest and good' is idiomatic of Greco-Roman culture, describing the classic fine gentleman.
3. Jesus' parables are frequently centered on agricultural settings because of His audience.

<u>**Questions for Reflection**</u>
1. Do parables enable Jesus to communicate with us more intimately? Why?

2. Can you comprehend His teaching, even if you have never sown seed yourself?

3. How does this parable help us to learn from Him apart from or within our daily struggles?

<u>**Disciplined Learning: Luke 8:16-18**</u>
(16) No one, having lighted a lamp, covers it with a vessel, or puts it under a bed; but puts it on a lamp-stand, that they who enter in may behold the light. (17) For nothing is secret that shall not be made manifest, nor hidden, that shall not be known and come abroad. (18) Take heed therefore how ye hear. For whoever has, to him shall be given; and whoever has not, even what he seems to have shall be taken from him.

<u>**Compare:**</u>
Mark 4:21-25

<u>**Questions for Reflection**</u>
1. **Does this accurately describe** the learning process for you? How so?

2. Does this parable affect your hunger to learn from Him? Why?

<u>**The Meaning of Family: Luke 8:19-21**</u>
(19) And his mother and his brothers came to him; and they could not come near him on account of the multitude. (20) And it was told him, saying: Thy mother and thy brothers are standing without, desiring to see

thee. (21) And he answering, said to them: My mother and my brothers are these, who hear and do the word of God.

<u>Compare:</u>
Matthew 12:46-50
Mark 3:31-35

<u>Notes</u>
1. **<u>Traditi</u>on** says that Jesus' brothers were children from Joseph's earlier marriage to a wife who had died, probably in childbirth.
2. So long as a father was alive, he had authority over all his family, including grown children. When a woman of childbearing years was widowed, she was either immediately remarried or was chaperoned by her adult children.

<u>Questions for Reflection</u>
1. What attitude do you detect in Jesus as he responds to the question being raised?

2. What does His answer tell about you and other followers of Jesus?

<u>Unexpected Power: Luke 8:22-25</u>

(22) And it came to pass on a certain day, that he went into a ship with his disciples. And he said to them: Let us go over to the other side of the lake. And they launched forth. (23) And as they were sailing, he fell asleep. And there came down a storm of wind on the lake; and they began to be filled, and were in jeopardy. (24) And coming to him, they awoke him, saying: Master, Master, we perish. And he, rising, rebuked the wind and the raging of the water; and they ceased, and there was a calm. (25) And he said to them: Where is your faith? And they, fearing, wondered; saying one to another: Who then is this, that he commands even the winds and the water, and they obey him!

<u>Compare:</u>
Matthew 8:23-27
Mark 4:35-41

<u>Notes</u>
1. The varying titles with which Jesus is addressed in this incident show the varying backgrounds of the disciples and their varying attitudes.
2. In hindsight it is easy for us to not be surprised by the power displayed in this story. It is well to remember that a miracle is simply any event in which the observer experiences the presence of God.
3. Sudden storms on this body of water were and are quite common.

<u>**Questions for Reflection**</u>

1. How do you think Jesus see his followers in this experience?

2. How do you suppose Jesus experiences miracles like this happening through Him?

<u>**Healing a 'Mental Illness:' Luke 8:26-39**</u>

(26) And they sailed to the country of the Gerasenes, which is over against Galilee. (27) And when he had gone forth upon the land, there met him a certain man out of the city, who had demons a long time, and wore no clothing, and abode not in a house, but in the tombs. (28) And seeing Jesus, he cried out, and fell down before him, and with a loud voice said: What have I to do with thee, Jesus, Son of the most high God? I beseech thee, do not torment me. (29) For he commanded the unclean spirit to come out from the man. For of a long time it had seized him, and he was bound, being secured with chains and fetters; and bursting the bands, he was driven by the demon into the deserts.

(30) And Jesus asked him, saying: What is thy name? And he said, Legion; because many demons had entered into him. (31) And he besought him that he would not command them to go away into the abyss. (32) And there was a herd of many swine feeding in the mountain; and they besought him that he would permit them to enter into them. And he permitted them. (33) And going out of the man, the demons entered into the swine; and the herd rushed down the steep into the lake, and were choked. (34) And seeing what was done the herdsmen fled, and reported it in the city and in the country, (35) And they went out to see what was done. And they came to Jesus, and found the man from whom the demons had gone out, sitting at the feet of Jesus, clothed and in his right mind; and they were afraid. (36) They also who saw it reported to them how he that was possessed by demons was healed. (37) And the whole multitude of the surrounding country of the Gerasenes besought him to depart from them; for they were seized with great fear.

And he, entering into the ship, returned. (38) And the man, out of whom the demons had gone, besought him that he might be with him. But he sent him away, saying: (39) Return into thy house, and relate how great things God did for thee. And he departed, and published through the whole city how great things Jesus did for him.

<u>**Compare:**</u>
Matthew 8:28-34
Mark 5:1-20

<u>**Notes**</u>

1. The description of the area varies -- the Gerasenes, the Gadarenes, or the Gergensenes, -- depending upon the source.
2. The description of the man's affliction closely resembles that of a schizophrenic.

<u>**Questions for Reflection**</u>

1. Describe Jesus' attitude towards the man and his illness?

2. How would you feel if after observing the healing, you had to listen to the complaints of the swineherds?

<u>**A Girl's Resurrection: Luke 8:40-56**</u>

(40) And it came to pass, when Jesus returned, that the multitude received him; for they were all waiting for him. (41) And, behold, there came a man whose name was Jairus, and he was a ruler of the synagogue; and falling at the feet of Jesus, he besought him that he would come into his house; (42) for he had an only daughter, about twelve years of age, and she was dying. And as he went the multitudes thronged him.

(43) And a woman having a flow of blood twelve years, who had spent all her living on physicians, and could not be healed by any one, (44) came up behind, and touched the fringe of his garment; and immediately her flow of blood ceased. (45) And Jesus said: Who is it that touched me? And when all denied it, Peter and those with him said: Master, the multitudes throng thee and press thee, and sayest thou: Who is it that touched me? (46) And Jesus said: Some one touched me; for I perceived that power has gone out from me.

(47) And the woman, seeing that she was not concealed, came trembling, and falling down before him, declared before all the people for what cause she touched him, and how she was healed immediately. (48) And he said to her: Daughter, thy faith has made thee whole; go in peace.

(49) While he was yet speaking, there comes one from the ruler of the synagogue's house, saying to him: Thy daughter is dead; trouble not the Teacher. (50) But Jesus hearing it, answered him: Fear not; only believe, and she shall be restored.

(51) And entering into the house, he suffered no one to go in with him, save Peter and James and John, and the father of the maiden, and the mother. (52) And all were weeping and bewailing her. And he said: Weep not; she is not dead, but is sleeping. (53) And they laughed him to scorn, knowing that she was dead. (54) And he, taking hold of her by the hand, called, saying: Maiden, arise. (55) And her spirit returned, and she immediately arose; and he commanded that food should be given her. (56) And her parents were astonished. But he charged them to tell no one what was done.

<u>**Compare:**</u>
Matthew 9:18-26
Mark 5:21-43

<u>**Notes**</u>

1. The 'return' evidently refers to the other side of the Sea of Galilee.
2. Physicians were often cruel by our standards, healing by bleeding and by 'mystical arts.'

<u>**Questions for Reflection**</u>

1. Does Jesus see a risk for either Jarius or Himself in this episode? Why do you think so?

2. How does Jesus seem to experience the chaos of the pressing crowds?

> When I am quiet and aware of Your presence, Father in heaven, it's wonderful. I ask for Your wisdom to help me discern how to respond to the needs of my community. I also ask that You use me for Your glory by following the lead of Your Son, Jesus, in whose name I pray. Amen.

Instructions for the Twelve: Luke 9:1-6

AND having called the twelve together, he gave them power and authority over all the demons, and to cure diseases. (2) And he sent them to preach the kingdom of God, and to heal the sick. (3) And he said to them: Take nothing for the journey, neither staff, nor bag, nor bread, nor money, nor have two coats apiece. (4) And into whatever house ye enter, there abide, and thence depart. (5) And whoever will not receive you, when ye go out from that city, shake off even the dust from your feet for a testimony against them.

(6) And going forth, they went through the villages, publishing the good news, and healing everywhere.

Compare:
Matthew 9:35, 10:1, 9-11, 14
Mark 6:7-13
Luke 10:4-11

Notes
1. This stands in stark contrast to Luke 22:35-38 because when Jesus sends out his inner circle this first time, He is still popular. In chapter 22 there is major risk being associated with Him.
2. Note the strict discipline required, for these inexperienced workers, to keep them focused on the task at hand.

Questions for Reflection
1. How does Jesus display confidence in them as He sends them out?

2. Why is it important for Luke's Gentile readers to see these passages?

Herod's Questions: Luke 9:7-9

(7) And Herod the tetrarch heard of all the things that were done. And he was perplexed, because it was said by some: John has risen from the dead; (8) and by some: Elijah has appeared; and by others: One of the old prophets has risen again. (9) And Herod said: John I beheaded; but who is this, of whom I hear such things? And he desired to see him.

Compare:
Matthew 14:1-2
Mark 6:14-16

Notes
1. This was undoubtedly Herod Antipas, son of Herod the Great.
2. Notice the double connection made for Herod to both Jesus' cousin John and Elijah. In the superstitious Greco-Roman world, both reincarnations and spontaneous resurrections were believed to occur.

Questions for Reflection

1. Why do you think Luke inserts this into his stories about Jesus?

2. Does this anecdote tell us anything further about Herod?

Feeding of Five Thousand: Luke 9:10-17

(10) And the apostles, returning, related to him all that they did. And taking them with him, he retired privately to a city called Bethsaida. (11) And the multitudes, when they knew it, followed him. And receiving them, he spoke to them concerning the kingdom of God, and healed those who had need of healing.

(12) And the day began to decline. And the twelve came, and said to him: Dismiss the multitude, that they may go into the villages around, and the fields, and lodge, and find food; for here we are in a desert place. (13) And he said to them: Do ye give them to eat. And they said: We have not more than five loaves and two fishes; except we should go and buy food for all this people. (14) For they were about five thousand men. And he said to his disciples: Make them lie down in companies of fifty. (15) And they did so, and made them all lie down. (16) And taking the five loaves and the two fishes, he looked up to heaven and blessed them, and broke, and gave to the disciples to set before the multitude. (17) And they ate, and were all filled. And there were taken up of fragments that remained to them twelve baskets.

Compare:
Matthew 14:13-21
Mark 6:30-44
John 6:1-14

Notes

1. This miracle or sign is recounted in all four gospels.
2. The testimonies of both Mark and John are noticeably longer, demonstrating differences in testimony for particular audiences.

Questions for Reflection

1. In light of Luke's testimony, how do you think Luke wants his Gentile audience to respond?

2. How do you, as a Gentile, respond to the words and actions of Jesus in this story?

The Confession of Peter: Luke 9:18-22

(18) And it came to pass, as he was alone praying, that his disciples were with him; and he asked them, saying: Who do the multitudes say that I am? (19) They answering said: John the Immerser; and others, Elijah; and others, that one of the old prophets has risen again. (20) And he said to them: But who do ye say that I am? Peter answering said: The Christ of God. (21) And strictly charging them, he commanded them to say this to no one; (22) saying: The Son of man must suffer many things, and be rejected on the part of the elders and chief priests and scribes, and be killed, and rise on the third day.

Compare:
Matthew 16:13-23
Mark 8:27-33

Notes
1. While we note with satisfaction Peter's confession of faith, His apparent rejection in the testimony of others is worth noting also.
2. Jesus' acceptance of the contrast between Peter's confession and the testimony of others seems to be implied.

Questions for Reflection
1. Do you believe Jesus was encouraged by Peter's confession? Why?

2. Do you think it was hard for Peter to do this in light of being the first? Why?

The Cost of Discipleship: Luke 9:23-27

(23) And he said to all: If any one will come after me, let him deny himself, and take up his cross daily, and follow me. (24) For whoever will save his life shall lose it; and whoever may lose his life for my sake, the same shall save it (25) For what is a man profited, when he has gained the whole world, and lost or forfeited himself? (26) For whoever is ashamed of me and of my words, of him will the Son of man be ashamed, when he shall come in his glory, and in that of the Father and of the holy angels. (27) And I say to you of a truth, there are some of those standing here, who shall not taste of death, till they see the kingdom of God.

Compare:
Matthew 16:24-28
Mark 8:34-9:1

Questions for Reflection
1. If you were there, listening to Jesus say this to His disciples, what tone or mood might you hear in His voice?

2. Are you concerned that the same kinds of risks are beginning to surface more obviously in our world today? Why?

Jesus is Transfigured: Luke 9:28-36

(28) And it came to pass, about eight days after these sayings, that he took with him Peter and John and James, and went up into the mountain to pray. (29) And it came to pass, while he was praying, that the appearance of his countenance became changed, and his raiment white and glistening. (30) And, behold, two men were talking with him, who were Moses and Elijah; (31) who appeared in glory, and spoke of his departure, which he was about to fulfill in Jerusalem.

(32) But Peter and they who were with him were heavy with sleep; and awaking, they saw his glory, and the two men that stood with him. (33) And it came to pass, that, as they were departing from him, Peter said to Jesus: Master, it is good for us to be here; and let us make three tents, one for thee, and one for Moses, and one for Elijah; not knowing what he said. (34) While he said this, there came a cloud, and overshadowed them; and they feared as they entered into the cloud. (35) And there came a voice out of the cloud, saying: This is my chosen Son; hear ye him.

(36) And when the voice had come, Jesus was found alone. And they kept silent, and told no one in those days any of the things which they had seen.

Compare:
Matthew 17:1-8
Mark 9:2-8

Notes
1. Their typical time of prayer and meditation grows into an entirely different kind of experience.
2. Evidently the dialogue Jesus has about his impending death is all but lost on His sleepy disciples.

Questions for Reflection
1. What does Luke want his Gentile audience to know about Jesus here?

2. Do you believe that there was a difference in Jesus internally after this experience? Why?

A Child Possessed or with Epilepsy: Luke 9:37-45

(37) And it came to pass, on the next day, when they had come down from the mountain, that a great multitude met him. (38) And, behold, a man from the multitude cried, saying: Teacher, I beseech thee, look upon my son; for he is my only child. (39) And, behold, a spirit takes him, and he suddenly cries out; and it tears him with foaming, and hardly departs from him, bruising him. (40) And I entreated thy disciples to cast him out; and they could not.

(41) And Jesus answering said: O faithless and perverse generation, how long shall I be with you, and bear with you? Bring hither thy son. (42) And while he was yet coming, the demon threw him down, and tore him. And Jesus rebuked the unclean spirit, and healed the child, and gave him back to his father. (43) And all

were amazed at the mighty power of God.

But while all were wondering at all things which Jesus did, he said to his disciples: (44) Do ye let these words sink into your ears, for the Son of man will be delivered into the hands of men. (45) But they understood not this saying, and it was hidden from them, that they perceived it not; and they feared to ask him concerning that saying.

<u>Compare:</u>
Matthew 17:14-21
Mark 9:14-29

<u>Notes</u>
1. It is inferred that the previous experience on the mountain took place at night.
2. Jesus' question about the 'perverse generation' appears to be a rhetorical one, reflecting his previous experience.

<u>Questions for Reflection</u>
1. Do you think Jesus felt He had failed to teach his followers adequately because they failed to heal the boy, or was His exclamation based on something else?

2. What do you suppose might be Jesus' other emotions as he continues his ministry after the transfiguration?

<u>The Signs of Greatness: Luke 9:46-50</u>
(46) And there arose in them the thought[9:46], which of them was greatest. (47) And Jesus, perceiving the thought of their heart, took a child and placed it by him, (48) and said to them: Whoever shall receive this child in my name, receives me; and whoever shall receive me, receives him who sent me; for he that is least among you all, the same is great.

(49) And John answering said: Master, we saw one casting out demons in thy name; and we forbade him, because he follows not with us. (50) And Jesus said to him: Forbid him not; for he that is not against us is for us.

<u>Compare:</u>
Matthew 18:1-5
Mark 9:33-41

<u>Notes</u>
1. Jesus' use of a child as a teaching tool uses both exaggeration and an unusual perspective to make His point.
2. The mention of another exorcist seems to imply that they associate greatness with that kind of power.

<u>**Questions for Reflection**</u>
1. What are the qualities of a child that Jesus values here?

2. Who are the important ones in the deeds of power, in light of Jesus' comment about the other exorcist?

<u>Hostility in Samaria: Luke 9:51-56</u>

(51) And it came to pass, when the days were being completed that he should be received up, he steadfastly set his face to go to Jerusalem. (52) And he sent messengers before his face; and they went and entered into a village of the Samaritans, to make ready for him. (53) And they did not receive him, because his face was directed toward Jerusalem. (54) And his disciples, James and John, seeing it, said: Lord, wilt thou that we command fire to come down from heaven, and consume them, as also Elijah did? (55) And he turned, and rebuked them, and said: Ye know not[9:55] of what spirit ye are. (56) And they went to another village.

<u>Compare:</u>
John 4:9

<u>Note</u>
> The hostility was not to Jesus specifically, but to all Jews, particularly those headed towards Jerusalem. Samaritans worshiped on a mountain in their own region.

<u>Questions for Reflection</u>
1. Would you be angry if you had gone into that village to get supplies and got that reception? Why?

2. Why was Jesus not angry?

<u>Calling to Discipleship: Luke 9:57-62</u>

57) And as they were going in the way, a certain one said to him: I will follow thee whithersoever thou goest. (58) And Jesus said to him: The foxes have holes, and the birds of the air have nests; but the Son of man has not where to lay his head.

(59) And he said to another: Follow me. But he said: Lord permit me first to go and bury my father. (60) And he said to him: Let the dead bury their own dead; but do thou go and announce the kingdom of God.

(61) And another also said; I will follow thee, Lord; but first permit me to bid farewell to those in my house. (62) And Jesus said to him: No one, having put his hand to the plow, and looking back, is fit for the kingdom of God.

<u>Compare:</u>
Matthew 8:19-22

<u>Questions for Reflection</u>

1. If you suddenly felt the call to follow Jesus 100% of the time, what would be your roadblocks?

2. Do you believe that Jesus understands how you feel when He places His call upon your life?

> I am Yours, Lord, all that I am and have. Please show me more effective ways to fulfill Your mission You have given me to my community around me. Thank You for delivering me from the evils that so often plague where I live. I don't deserve Your blessings and patience, as I continue to be a sinner. I love You, Father, and I honor, praise You and pray through Your Son, Jesus. Amen.

Missionary Outreach: Luke 10:1-20

AFTER these things the Lord appointed also seventy others, and sent them two and two before his face, into every city and place, whither he himself was about to come. (2) And he said to them: The harvest indeed is great, but the laborers are few. Pray therefore the Lord of the harvest, that he will send forth laborers into his harvest. (3) Go your ways; behold, I send you forth as lambs among wolves. (4) Carry neither purse, nor bag, nor sandals; and salute no one by the way. (5) And into whatever house ye enter, first say: Peace be to this house. (6) And if a son of peace be there, your peace shall rest upon it; and if not, it shall return to you. (7) And in that house remain, eating and drinking such things as they give[10:7]; for the laborer is worthy of his hire. Go not from house to house. (8) And into whatever city ye enter and they receive you, eat what is set before you; (9) and heal the sick that are therein, and say to them: The kingdom of God has come nigh unto you. (10) But into whatever city ye enter and they receive you not, go out into the streets of the same, and say: (11) Even the dust of your city that cleaves to our feet, we wipe off to you[10:11]; yet know this, that the kingdom of God has come nigh. (12) I say to you, that it will be more tolerable in that day for Sodom, than for that city.

(13) Woe to thee, Chorazin! Woe to thee, Bethsaida! For if the miracles had been done in Tyre and Sidon, which were done in you, they would long ago have repented, sitting in sackcloth and ashes. (14) But it will be more tolerable for Tyre and Sidon in the judgment, than for you. (15) And thou, Capernaum, that art exalted to heaven, shalt be brought down to the underworld.

(16) He that hears you, hears me; and he that rejects you, rejects me; and he that rejects me, rejects him who sent me.

(17) And the seventy returned with joy, saying: Lord, even the demons are subjected to us in thy name. (18) And he said to them: I beheld Satan fall as lightning from heaven. (19) Behold, I have given you power to tread on serpents and scorpions, and over all the power of the enemy; and nothing shall hurt you. (20) But yet, rejoice not in this, that the spirits are subjected to you; but rejoice, that your names are written in heaven.

Compare:
Matthew 9:37-38, 10:7-16

Notes
1. A few of the manuscripts indicate that Jesus sent out 72 instead of 70, but this is a minor detail.
2. The instructions here are basically identical to those given to the twelve in the earlier passage.

Questions for Reflection
1. The same powers to heal are given to the seventy as to the twelve. How does that speak to you as a person many generations hence?

2. What would it take to convince you that Jesus had bestowed the spiritual gift of healing upon you?

Jesus' Prayer: Luke 10:21-22

(21) In that hour he rejoiced in spirit, and said: I thank thee, O Father, Lord of heaven and earth, that thou didst hide these things from the wise and discerning, and reveal them to babes; yea, O Father, that so it seemed good in thy sight. (22) All things were delivered to me by my Father; and no one knows who the Son is but the Father, and who the Father is but the Son, and he to whom the Son is pleased to reveal him.

<u>Compare:</u>
Matthew 11:25-27

<u>Questions for Reflection</u>

1. How is this prayer different from the others you associate with Jesus?

2. What are your thoughts about this particular blessing that Jesus offers?

<u>Two Questions Answered: Luke 10:23-37</u>

(23) And turning to the disciples, he said privately: Happy are the eyes that behold what ye are beholding. (24) For I say to you, that many prophets and kings desired to see what ye are beholding, and saw not, and to hear what ye are hearing, and heard not.

(25) And, behold, a certain lawyer stood up, tempting him, saying: Teacher, what shall I do to inherit eternal life? (26) He said to him: What is written in the law? How readest thou? (27) And he answering said: Thou shalt love the Lord thy God with all thy heart, and with all thy soul, and with all thy strength, and with all thy mind; and thy neighbor as thyself. (28) And he said to him: Thou answeredst rightly. This do, and thou shalt live. (29) But he, desiring to justify himself, said to Jesus: Who then is my neighbor?

(30) And Jesus answering said: A certain man was going down from Jerusalem to Jericho, and fell among robbers, who stripped him of his raiment, and wounded him, and departed, leaving him half dead. (31) And by chance a certain priest was going down that way; and seeing him, he passed by on the other side. (32) And in like manner also a Levite, arriving at the place, came and saw, and passed by on the other side.

(33) And a certain Samaritan, as he was journeying, came where he was, and seeing him had compassion; (34) and coming to him, bound up his wounds, pouring in oil and wine; and setting him on his own beast, he brought him to an inn, and took care of him. (35) And on the morrow when he departed, he took out two denaries[10:35] and gave to the host, and said: Take care of him; and whatever thou spendest more, when I come again, I will repay thee.

(36) Which now of these three, thinkest thou, was neighbor to him that fell among the robbers? (37) And he said: He that had mercy on him. And Jesus said to him: Go, and do thou likewise.

<u>Compare:</u>
Matthew 22-23-40
Mark 12:28-31

<u>Notes</u>

1. The scribe (religious lawyer) had responsibility for writing interpretations of the Torah in response to everyday experiences.
2. The parable is designed to simply illustrate the gracious compassion of God.

Questions for Reflection

1. With Jesus asking us to be willing to take major risks in pursuit of discipleship, how do you feel about that aspect of the call upon your life?

2. What do you believe that Jesus understands your fears as well as your hopes as you try to respond to His call?

Reception in Bethany: Luke 10:38-42

(38) And it came to pass, as they were going, that he entered into a certain village; and a certain woman named Martha received him into her house. (39) And she had a sister called Mary, who also sat at the feet of Jesus, and heard his word. (40) But Martha was encumbered with much serving; and she came to him, and said: Lord, dost thou not care that my sister left me to serve alone? Bid her therefore that she help me. (41) And Jesus answering said to her: Martha, Martha, thou art anxious and troubled about many things. (42) But one thing is needful; and Mary chose the good part, which shall not be taken away from her.

Questions for Reflection

1. Which person do you feel like most often, Mary or Martha? Why?

2. Jesus responds to both women compassionately but differently. How were the responses different?

3. How does this speak to your own walk with faith in Jesus?

> Loving God, thank You for another chance to walk with Jesus today. Teach me to live as well as pray in the power of Jesus' name. I surrender all that I am and have to You in that same power of Jesus' name. Amen.

Teachings About Prayer: Luke 11:1-13

AND it came to pass that, as he was in a certain place praying, when he ceased, one of his disciples said to him: Lord, teach us to pray, as also John taught his disciples. (2) And he said to them: When ye pray, say; Father, hallowed be thy name. Thy kingdom come. (3) Give us day by day our daily bread[11:3]. (4) And forgive us our sins; for we ourselves forgive every one indebted to us. And bring us not into temptation.

(5) And he said to them: Who of you shall have a friend, and shall go to him at midnight, and say to him: (6) Friend, lend me three loaves; for a friend of mine is come to me from a journey, and I have nothing to set before him; (7) and he from within shall answer and say, Trouble me not; the door is already shut, and my children with me are in bed; I can not rise and give thee? (8) I say to you, though he will not rise and give him because he is his friend, yet because of his importunity he will rise and give him as many as he needs. (9) I also say to you: Ask, and it shall be given you; seek, and ye shall find; knock, and it shall be opened to you. (10) For every one that asks receives; and he that seeks finds; and to him that knocks it shall be opened.

(11) And what father is there among you, of whom if his son ask bread, he will give him a stone; or a fish, will instead of a fish give him a serpent? (12) Or if he shall ask an egg, will he give him a scorpion? (13) If ye then, being evil, know how to give good gifts to your children, how much more will your heavenly Father give the Holy Spirit to those who ask him?

Compare:

Matthew 6:9-13

Note

➢ The parable centers on asking for what one needs, and the gift of the Holy Spirit is the response. Jesus seems to be saying that all sincere prayers are answered in the sense of the presence and power of the Spirit.

Questions for Reflection

1. How satisfied are you with your prayer life?

2. When you pray, do you try to see things from Jesus' perspective? How so?

Revelations About Power: Luke 11:14-28

(14) And he was casting out a demon, and it was dumb. And it came to pass, when the demon was gone out, that the dumb man spoke; and the multitudes wondered. (15) But some of them said: He casts out the demons through Beelzebul, the prince of the demons. (16) And others, tempting, sought of him a sign from heaven. (17) But he, knowing their thoughts, said to them: Every kingdom divided against itself is brought to desolation, and a house divided against a house falls[11:17]. (18) And if Satan also is divided against himself, how shall his kingdom stand? because ye say that I cast out the demons through Beelzebul. (19) And if I through Beelzebul cast out the demons, through whom do your sons cast them out? Therefore they shall be your judges. (20) But if with the finger of God I cast out the demons, then is the kingdom of God come near to you.

(21) When a strong man armed keeps his palace, his goods are in peace. (22) But when a stronger than he shall come upon him and overcome him, he takes away his whole armor, wherein he trusted, and divides his spoils. (23) He that is not with me is against me; and he that gathers not with me scatters abroad.

(24) When the unclean spirit is gone out from the man, he goes through dry places, seeking rest; and not finding it, he says, I will return into my house whence I came out. (25) And coming, he finds it swept and set in order. (26) Then he goes, and takes with him seven other spirits more wicked than himself, and they enter in and dwell there; and the last state of that man becomes worse than the first.

(27) And it came to pass, as he was saying these things, that a certain woman lifting up her voice from the multitude, said to him: Happy the womb that bore thee, and breasts which thou didst suck! (28) And he said: Yea, rather, Happy they who hear the word of God, and keep it!

Compare:
Matthew 12:22-30
Mark 3:22-27

Notes
1. In psychiatric terms, the casting out of demons can be likened to relief from schizophrenia and/or psychosis.
2. When someone is healed of disease, whether physical or mental, that person's resistance is initially down and is therefore vulnerable to further disease until strength is achieved.
3. Jesus sees disciplined obedience to God as armor against evil.

Questions for Reflection
1. If your spiritual life has sufficient discipline, what do you do to accomplish it?

2. Do you turn to Jesus when you feel that your life was out of control? How?

Looking for Information: Luke 11:29-32

(29) And the multitudes gathering more and more, he began to say: This generation is an evil generation. It seeks a sign; and no sign shall be given it, but the sign of Jonah. (30) For as Jonah became a sign to the Ninevites, so shall also the Son of man be to this generation.

(31) A queen of the south will rise up in the judgment with the men of this generation, and will condemn them; because she came from the utmost parts of the earth to hear the wisdom of Solomon; and, behold, a greater than Solomon is here. (32) Men of Nineveh will rise in the judgment with this generation, and will condemn it; because they repented at the preaching of Jonah; and behold, a greater than Jonah is here.

Compare:
Matthew 12:6, 39

Note
➢ In today's culture, a direct parallel can be drawn to interest in astrology and psychics.

Questions for Reflection

1. Why might someone consider consulting an astrologer or psychic instead of praying?

2. When you're not seeing an answer to your prayers, how do you respond?

The Parable of Light: Luke 11:33-36

(33) No one, having lighted a lamp, puts it in a secret place, or under the bushel, but on the lamp-stand, that they who come in may see the light. (34) The lamp of the body is thine eye. When thine eye is single, thy whole body also is light; but when it is evil, thy body also is dark. (35) Take heed therefore, lest the light that is in thee is darkness[11:35]. (36) If therefore thy whole body is light, having no part dark, it shall be all light as when the lamp, with its bright shining, gives thee light.

Compare:

Matthew 5:15, 6:22-23

Note

➢ In the ancient world, light was often a metaphor for knowledge and/or wisdom.

Question for Reflection

➢ How does this parable speak to your faith?

A Critique of Legalists: Luke 11:37-54

(37) And as he was speaking, a Pharisee asked him to dine with him and he went in, and reclined at table. (38) And the Pharisee, seeing it, wondered that he did not first immerse himself before dinner. (39) And the Lord said to him: Now ye Pharisees cleanse the outside of the cup and the platter; but your inward part is full of rapacity and wickedness. (40) Fools! Did not he, who made the outside, make the inside also? (41) But give that which ye have in alms[11:41]; and, behold, all things are clean to you.

(42) But woe to you, Pharisees! because ye pay tithe of mint and rue and every herb, and pass by judgment and the love of God. These oughtye to have done, and not leave those undone.

(43) Woe to you, Pharisees! because ye love the first seat in the synagogues, and the greetings in the markets. (44) Woe to you! because ye are as tombs that appear not, and men walking over them know it not.

(45) And a certain one of the lawyers answering says to him: Teacher, in saying these things thou reproachest us also. (46) And he said: Woe to you lawyers also! because ye load men with burdens grievous to be borne, and ye yourselves touch not the burdens with one of your fingers.

(47) Woe to you! because ye build the sepulchres of the prophets, and your fathers killed them. (48) So then ye bear witness to and approve the deeds of your fathers; because they indeed killed them, and ye build their sepulchres[11:48]. (49) Therefore also said the wisdom of God: I will send them prophets and apostles, and some of them they will slay and persecute; (50) that the blood of all the prophets, which was shed from the foundation of the world, may be required of this generation, (51) from the blood of Abel unto the blood of

Zachariah, who perished between the altar and the temple. Verily I say to you, it shall be required of this generation.

(52) Woe to you lawyers! because ye took away the key of knowledge; ye entered not in yourselves, and those who were entering in ye hindered.

(53) And as he said these things to them, the scribes and the Pharisees began to urge him vehemently, and to provoke him to speak of many things; (54) lying in wait for him, seeking to catch something out of his mouth, that they might accuse him.

<u>Compare:</u>
Matthew 23:1-36

Notes

1. 'Wash before dinner' in the original Greek is literally 'baptize before dinner' and refers to ceremonial washing rather than a real concern for physical cleanliness.

2. Some scholars believe that 'The Wisdom of God' refers to an ancient book long since lost. Many if not most think it likely that it refers to Jesus' own interpretation of scriptures.

3. The scribes, as teachers and interpreters of Jewish law, evidently see themselves as functioning apart from the law to the same degree that the U.S. Congress often exempts itself from the laws it writes. They seem to have little interest in how they came to have such authority.

<u>Questions for Reflection</u>

1. Are you more interested in doing what you perceive is right or in pleasing God? Why?

2. Are you more interested in feeling good about yourself or in having a good relationship with Jesus?

> O God, You have searched me and know me. You even know my thoughts. For those who feel isolated, anxious, and helpless, Lord, provide them every necessary support, and be glorified in their lives and mine. Let my prayers be humble offerings in Jesus' name. Amen.

Jesus' Emotional Support: Luke 12:1-12

IN the mean time, the multitude having gathered together in tens of thousands, so that they trod one upon another, he began first to say to his disciples: Beware of the leaven of the Pharisees, which is hypocrisy. (2) For there is nothing covered, that shall not be revealed, nor hidden, that shall not be known. (3) Wherefore, whatever ye said in the darkness, shall be heard in the light; and what ye spoke in the ear in closets, shall be proclaimed on the house-tops.

(4) And I say to you, my friends, be not afraid of those who kill the body, and after that have no more that they can do. (5) But I will warn you whom ye shall fear; fear him, who after he has killed has power to cast into hell; yea, I say to you, fear him. (6) Are not five sparrows sold for two pence? And not one of them is forgotten before God. (7) But even the hairs of your head are all numbered. Fear not; ye are of more value than many sparrows.

(8) And I say to you: Every one that shall acknowledge me before men, him will the Son of man also acknowledge before the angels of God; (9) but he that denied me before men shall be denied before the angels of God. (10) And every one that shall speak a word against the Son of man, it will be forgiven him; but to him that blasphemes against the Holy Spirit, it shall not be forgiven.

(11) And when they bring you to the synagogues, and magistrates, and authorities, take not thought how or what ye shall answer, or what ye shall say. (12) For the Holy Spirit will teach you in that very hour what ye ought to say.

Compare:

Matthew 10:26-33

Notes

1. Jesus encourages not so much by telling His disciples they have done well, but by putting His disciples? struggles in perspective so that they can see just how well things are going.
2. Jesus calms His disciples' fears by offering reminders of who is really in charge rather than simply saying not to be afraid.

Questions for Reflection

1. Are you comforted by Jesus? assurances here? Why?

2. How sure are you that He really understands your struggles?

A Parable of Foolishness: Luke 12:13-21

(13) And a certain one of the multitude said to him: Teacher, speak to my brother, that he divide the inheritance with me. (14) And he said to him: Man, who made me a judge or a divider over you? (15) And he said to them: Take heed, and beware of all covetousness; because a man's life consists not in the abundance of his possessions.

(16) And he spoke a parable to them, saying: The ground of a certain rich man brought forth plentifully. (17) And he thought within himself, saying: What shall I do, because I have not where to store my fruits? (18) And he said: This will I do; I will pull down my barns, and will build greater; and there I will store all my fruits and my goods. (19) And I will say to my soul: Soul, thou hast many goods laid up for many years; take thine

ease, eat, drink, be merry. (20) But God said to him: Fool! this night thy soul shall be required of thee; and whose shall those things be, which thou didst provide? (21) So is he that lays up treasure for himself, and is not rich toward God.

Notes

1. This parable is without parallel in the other gospels.
2. According to Jewish law, the oldest son inherits double what his sibling brothers receive. Daughters did not inherit from their father's estate unless they had no brothers.

Questions for Reflection

1. Why do you suppose Luke passes on this parable to his Gentile readers, when the other gospel writers did not?

2. When you, as a Gentile, read this parable, what is Jesus teaching you about yourself?

Worry and Anxiety: Luke 12:22-34

(22) And he said to his disciples: Therefore I say to you, take not thought for the life, what ye shall eat, nor for the body, what ye shall put on. (23) The life is more than food, and the body than raiment. (24) Consider the ravens, that they sow not nor reap; which have neither storehouse nor barn; and God feeds them. How much better are ye than the birds! (25) And which of you by taking thought can add a cubit to his stature[12:25]? (26) If therefore ye can not do even that which is least, why take ye thought for the rest?

(27) Consider the lilies, how they grow; they toil not, nor spin; and I say to you, that even Solomon, in all his glory was not arrayed like one of these. (28) And if God so clothes the grass, which to-day is in the field, and to-morrow is cast into the oven, how much more you, ye of little faith? (29) And ye, seek not what ye shall eat, or what ye shall drink, and be not of a doubtful mind. (30) For all these things do the nations of the world seek after; and your Father knows that ye have need of these. (31) But seek his kingdom, and these things shall be added to you.

(32) Fear not, little flock; for it is your Father's good pleasure to give you the kingdom. (33) Sell what ye have, and give alms; provide yourselves purses that wax not old, a treasure unfailing in the heavens, where a thief approaches not, nor moth corrupts. (34) For where your treasure is, there will your heart be also.

Compare:

Matthew 6:25-33

Note

➤ Once again, Jesus encourages by offering His perspective along with the assurance of real authority in God.

Questions for Reflection

1. How is your faith affected by the fact that Jesus wants you to never worry?

2. When you pray, how do you share any of your anxiety with Him?

Being Observant: Luke 12:35-48

(35) Let your loins be girded about, and your lamps burning; (36) and ye like men waiting for their lord, when he shall return from the wedding; that, when he comes and knocks, they may open to him immediately. (37) Happy those servants, whom their lord when he comes shall find watching! Verily I say to you, that he will gird himself, and make them recline at table, and will come forth and serve them. (38) And if he shall come in the second watch, or in the third watch, and find it so, happy are those servants. (39) And this know, that if the master of the house had known at what hour the thief is coming, he would have watched, and not have suffered his house to be broken through. (40) Be ye also ready; for at an hour when ye think not, the Son of man comes.

(41) And Peter said to him: Lord, speakest thou this parable to us, or also to all? (42) And the Lord said: Who then is the faithful, the wise steward, whom his lord will set over his household, to give the portion of food in due season? (43) Happy that servant, whom his lord when he comes shall find so doing! (44) Of a truth I say to you, that he will make him ruler over all his goods.

(45) But if that servant say in his heart: My lord delays his coming; and shall begin to beat the menservants and maidservants, and to eat and drink, and to be drunken; (46) the lord of that servant will come in a day when he looks not for it, and in an hour when he is not aware, and will cut him asunder, and appoint his portion with the faithless.

(47) And that servant, who knew his lord's will, and prepared not, nor did according to his will, shall be beaten with many stripes; (48) but he that knew not, and did things worthy of stripes, shall be beaten with few. For to whomsoever much was given, of him much will be required; and to whom they committed much, of him they will require the more.

Compare:
Matthew 24:43-51

Questions for Reflection

1. What are some things you do to help you be patient while you wait?

2. When you wait for God to bring something about, are you also waiting upon God, serving Him?

Teachings on Judgment: Luke 12:49-59

(49) I came to send fire upon the earth; and what will I, if it is already kindled[12:49]? (50) But I have an immersion to undergo; and how am I straitened till it be accomplished! (51) Suppose ye that I came to give peace in the earth? I tell you, nay; but only division. (52) For from this time forth, five in one house will be divided, three against two, and two against three. (53) They will be divided, father against son, and son against father; mother against the daughter, and daughter against the mother; mother-in-law against her daughter-in-law, and daughter-in-law against the mother-in-law.

(54) And he said also to the multitudes: When ye see the cloud rising from the west, straightway ye say: A shower is coming and so it comes to pass. (55) And when ye see a south wind blowing, ye say: There will be

heat; and it comes to pass. (56) Hypocrites! Ye know how to judge of the face of the earth and the sky; but how is it that ye know not how to judge of this time? (57) And why even of yourselves do ye not judge what is right? (58) For when thou art going with thine adversary to the magistrate, on the way give diligence that thou mayest be delivered from him; lest he drag thee to the judge, and the judge deliver thee to the exactor, and the exactor cast thee into prison. (59) I say to thee, thou shalt not depart thence, till thou hast paid the very last mite.

Notes

1. Pieces of this passage are paralleled in the other gospels, but this is Luke's particular slant for his Gentile audience.
2. Winds from the west are higher in humidity because they came off of the Mediterranean Sea. Winds from the east are dry, coming in from over vast areas of desert.

Questions for Reflection

1. How often do you think about world events in terms of God's judgment?

2. How is your faith encouraged by Jesus wanting us to be aware of God's participation in our entire world?

> Deliver me, Lord God, for the world around me seems out of control. I know You are in command, and I thank You for hearing me and answering my prayers. I kneel before You and worship, for You are the creator and redeemer of all. In the name of my Lord Jesus, I pray. Amen.

Jesus' Emotional Support: Luke 12:1-12

IN the mean time, the multitude having gathered together in tens of thousands, so that they trod one upon another, he began first to say to his disciples: Beware of the leaven of the Pharisees, which is hypocrisy. (2) For there is nothing covered, that shall not be revealed, nor hidden, that shall not be known. (3) Wherefore, whatever ye said in the darkness, shall be heard in the light; and what ye spoke in the ear in closets, shall be proclaimed on the house-tops.

(4) And I say to you, my friends, be not afraid of those who kill the body, and after that have no more that they can do. (5) But I will warn you whom ye shall fear; fear him, who after he has killed has power to cast into hell; yea, I say to you, fear him. (6) Are not five sparrows sold for two pence? And not one of them is forgotten before God. (7) But even the hairs of your head are all numbered. Fear not; ye are of more value than many sparrows.

(8) And I say to you: Every one that shall acknowledge me before men, him will the Son of man also acknowledge before the angels of God; (9) but he that denied me before men shall be denied before the angels of God. (10) And every one that shall speak a word against the Son of man, it will be forgiven him; but to him that blasphemes against the Holy Spirit, it shall not be forgiven.

(11) And when they bring you to the synagogues, and magistrates, and authorities, take not thought how or what ye shall answer, or what ye shall say. (12) For the Holy Spirit will teach you in that very hour what ye ought to say.

Compare:
Matthew 10:26-33

Notes

1. Jesus encourages not so much by telling His disciples they have done well, but by putting His disciples? struggles in perspective so that they can see just how well things are going.
2. Jesus calms His disciples' fears by offering reminders of who is really in charge rather than simply saying not to be afraid.

Questions for Reflection

1. Are you comforted by Jesus? assurances here? Why?

2. How sure are you that He really understands your struggles?

A Parable of Foolishness: Luke 12:13-21

(13) And a certain one of the multitude said to him: Teacher, speak to my brother, that he divide the inheritance with me. (14) And he said to him: Man, who made me a judge or a divider over you? (15) And he said to them: Take heed, and beware of all covetousness; because a man's life consists not in the abundance of his possessions.

(16) And he spoke a parable to them, saying: The ground of a certain rich man brought forth plentifully. (17) And he thought within himself, saying: What shall I do, because I have not where to store my fruits? (18) And he said: This will I do; I will pull down my barns, and will build greater; and there I will store all my fruits and my goods. (19) And I will say to my soul: Soul, thou hast many goods laid up for many years; take thine ease, eat, drink, be merry. (20) But God said to him: Fool! this night thy soul shall be required of thee; and whose

shall those things be, which thou didst provide? (21) So is he that lays up treasure for himself, and is not rich toward God.

Notes

1. This parable is without parallel in the other gospels.
2. According to Jewish law, the oldest son inherits double what his sibling brothers receive. Daughters did not inherit from their father's estate unless they had no brothers.

Questions for Reflection

1. Why do you suppose Luke passes on this parable to his Gentile readers, when the other gospel writers did not?

2. When you, as a Gentile, read this parable, what is Jesus teaching you about yourself?

Worry and Anxiety: Luke 12:22-34

(22) And he said to his disciples: Therefore I say to you, take not thought for the life, what ye shall eat, nor for the body, what ye shall put on. (23) The life is more than food, and the body than raiment. (24) Consider the ravens, that they sow not nor reap; which have neither storehouse nor barn; and God feeds them. How much better are ye than the birds! (25) And which of you by taking thought can add a cubit to his stature[12:25]? (26) If therefore ye can not do even that which is least, why take ye thought for the rest? (27) Consider the lilies, how they grow; they toil not, nor spin; and I say to you, that even Solomon, in all his glory was not arrayed like one of these. (28) And if God so clothes the grass, which to-day is in the field, and to-morrow is cast into the oven, how much more you, ye of little faith? (29) And ye, seek not what ye shall eat, or what ye shall drink, and be not of a doubtful mind. (30) For all these things do the nations of the world seek after; and your Father knows that ye have need of these. (31) But seek his kingdom, and these things shall be added to you.

(32) Fear not, little flock; for it is your Father's good pleasure to give you the kingdom. (33) Sell what ye have, and give alms; provide yourselves purses that wax not old, a treasure unfailing in the heavens, where a thief approaches not, nor moth corrupts. (34) For where your treasure is, there will your heart be also.

Compare:

Matthew 6:25-33

Note

➤ Once again, Jesus encourages by offering His perspective along with the assurance of real authority in God.

Questions for Reflection

1. How is your faith affected by the fact that Jesus wants you to never worry?

2. When you pray, how do you share any of your anxiety with Him?

Being Observant: Luke 12:35-48

(35) Let your loins be girded about, and your lamps burning; (36) and ye like men waiting for their lord, when he shall return from the wedding; that, when he comes and knocks, they may open to him immediately. (37) Happy those servants, whom their lord when he comes shall find watching! Verily I say to you, that he will gird himself, and make them recline at table, and will come forth and serve them. (38) And if he shall come in the second watch, or in the third watch, and find it so, happy are those servants. (39) And this know, that if the master of the house had known at what hour the thief is coming, he would have watched, and not have suffered his house to be broken through. (40) Be ye also ready; for at an hour when ye think not, the Son of man comes.

(41) And Peter said to him: Lord, speakest thou this parable to us, or also to all? (42) And the Lord said: Who then is the faithful, the wise steward, whom his lord will set over his household, to give the portion of food in due season? (43) Happy that servant, whom his lord when he comes shall find so doing! (44) Of a truth I say to you, that he will make him ruler over all his goods.

(45) But if that servant say in his heart: My lord delays his coming; and shall begin to beat the men-servants and maidservants, and to eat and drink, and to be drunken; (46) the lord of that servant will come in a day when he looks not for it, and in an hour when he is not aware, and will cut him asunder, and appoint his portion with the faithless.

(47) And that servant, who knew his lord's will, and prepared not, nor did according to his will, shall be beaten with many stripes; (48) but he that knew not, and did things worthy of stripes, shall be beaten with few. For to whomsoever much was given, of him much will be required; and to whom they committed much, of him they will require the more.

Compare:
Matthew 24:43-51

Questions for Reflection

1. Do you constantly watch while you wait, paying attention?

2. What are some things you do to help you be patient while you wait?

3. When you wait for God to bring something about, are you also waiting upon God, serving Him?

Teachings on Judgment: Luke 12:49-59

(49) I came to send fire upon the earth; and what will I, if it is already kindled[12:49]? (50) But I have an immersion to undergo; and how am I straitened till it be accomplished! (51) Suppose ye that I came to give peace in the earth? I tell you, nay; but only division. (52) For from this time forth, five in one house will be divided, three against two, and two against three. (53) They will be divided, father against son, and son against father;

mother against the daughter, and daughter against the mother; mother-in-law against her daughter-in-law, and daughter-in-law against the mother-in-law.

(54) And he said also to the multitudes: When ye see the cloud rising from the west, straightway ye say: A shower is coming and so it comes to pass. (55) And when ye see a south wind blowing, ye say: There will be heat; and it comes to pass. (56) Hypocrites! Ye know how to judge of the face of the earth and the sky; but how is it that ye know not how to judge of this time? (57) And why even of yourselves do ye not judge what is right? (58) For when thou art going with thine adversary to the magistrate, on the way give diligence that thou mayest be delivered from him; lest he drag thee to the judge, and the judge deliver thee to the exactor, and the exactor cast thee into prison. (59) I say to thee, thou shalt not depart thence, till thou hast paid the very last mite.

<u>Notes</u>

1. Pieces of this passage are paralleled in the other gospels, but this is Luke's particular slant for his Gentile audience.
2. Winds from the west are higher in humidity because they came off of the Mediterranean Sea. Winds from the east are dry, coming in from over vast areas of desert.

<u>Questions for Reflection</u>

1. How often do you think about world events in terms of God's judgment?

2. How is your faith encouraged by Jesus wanting us to be aware of God's participation in our entire world?

Deliver me, Lord God, for the world around me seems out of control. I know You are in command, and I thank You for hearing me and answering my prayers. I kneel before You and worship, for You are the creator and redeemer of all. In the name of my Lord Jesus, I pray. Amen.

A Call to Repentance: Luke 13:1-9

THERE were present at that season some who brought him word concerning the Galilaeans, whose blood Pilate mingled with their sacrifices. (2) And answering he said to them: Suppose ye that these Galilaeans were sinners above all the Galilaeans, because they have suffered such things? (3) I tell you, nay; but, except ye repent, ye shall all in like manner perish. (4) Or those eighteen, on whom the tower in Siloam fell, and slew them, suppose ye that they were sinners above all the men who dwell in Jerusalem? (5) I tell you, nay; but, except ye repent, ye shall all in like manner perish.

(6) He spoke also this parable: A certain man had a fig-tree planted in his vineyard; and he came seeking fruit thereon, and found none. (7) And he said to the vine-dresser: Behold, three years I come seeking fruit on this fig-tree, and find none. Cut it down; why does it also encumber[13:7] the ground? (8) And he answering says to him: Lord, let it alone this year also, till I shall dig about it, and cast in manure. (9) And if it bear fruit--; and if not, hereafter thou shalt cut it down.

Notes

1. This passage is unique for Luke and his Gentile audience.
2. Pilate had ordered people killed in the Temple while they were making sacrifices.
3. Jesus does not make a clear distinction here between natural disasters and moral evil.

Questions for Reflection

1. How often do you think of yourself as needing to repent?

2. How are specific confessions regularly part of your prayer life helping you grow your faith?

An Unrequested Healing: Luke 13:10-17

(10) And he was teaching in one of the synagogues on the sabbath. (11) And, behold, there was a woman who had a spirit of infirmity eighteen years, and was bowed together, and wholly unable to raise herself up. (12) And Jesus seeing her, called her to him, and said to her: Woman, thou art loosed from thine infirmity. (13) And he laid his hands on her; and immediately she was made straight, and glorified God. (14) And the ruler of the synagogue answering (being indignant because Jesus healed on the sabbath) , said to the multitude: There are six days in which it is proper to work; in them therefore come and be healed, and not on the sabbath. (15) And the Lord answered him, and said: Hypocrites! Does not each of you on the sabbath loose his ox or ass from the manger, and lead him away to water him? (16) And ought not this woman, being a daughter of Abraham, whom Satan bound, lo, eighteen years, to be loosed from this bond on the sabbath? (17) And as he said these things, all his adversaries were ashamed; and all the multitude rejoiced for all the glorious things that were done by him.

Notes

1. Jesus attributes both physical and psychological disorders to Satan. Satan's perceived role in evil gradually has been transformed through the centuries.

2. Jesus? healings on the Sabbath were a major source of consternation for the Temple authorities.

<u>**Questions for Reflection**</u>

1. Can you credit Jesus and/or God to particular healings in your life for which you did not pray? Are there any examples?

2. How often do you perceive Jesus as actively involved in your deliverance from evil even when you do not request it?

<u>**Parables of the Kingdom: Luke 13:18-21**</u>

(18) He said therefore: To what is the kingdom of God like? And to what s0hall I liken it? (19) It is like to a grain of mustard, which a man took, and cast into his garden; and it grew, and became a great tree, and the birds of the air lodged in its branches.

(20) And again he said: To what shall I liken the kingdom of God? (21) It is like to leaven, which a woman took and hid in three measures of meal, till the whole was leavened.

<u>**Compare:**</u>
Matthew 13:31-33
Mark 4:30-32

<u>**Notes**</u>

1. Mustard seeds are exceedingly small. Yeast was maintained in dough that had previously risen but had not been baked.
2. Jews understood the importance of paying close attention to details, but Gentiles need to be reminded as well.

<u>**Questions for Reflection**</u>

1. What disciplines are part of your spiritual life?

2. What do you try to do for maintaining a good relationship with Jesus in all aspects of your life?

<u>**Parable of Final Judgment: Luke 13:22-30**</u>

(22) And he went through cities and villages, teaching, and journeying toward Jerusalem.

(23) And a certain one said to him: Lord, are there few that are saved? (24) And he said to them: Strive to enter in through the strait gate; for many, I say to you, will seek to enter in, and will not be able. (25) When once the master of the house has risen and shut the door, and ye begin to stand without, and to knock at the door, saying, Lord, open to us, and he answering shall say to you, I know you not whence ye are; (26) then will ye begin to say, We ate and drank in thy presence, and thou didst teach in our streets. (27) And he will say, I tell you, I know not whence ye are; depart from me, all workers of unrighteousness. (28) There will be the weeping,

and the gnashing of teeth, when ye shall see Abraham, and Isaac, and Jacob, and all the prophets, in the kingdom of God, and yourselves thrust out. (29) And they will come from east and west, and from north and south, and will recline at table in the kingdom of God. (30) And, behold, there are last who will be first, and there are first who will be last.

Notes

1. Parts of this passage are paralleled in the other three gospels.
2. The host in the parable is clearly Jesus.

Questions for Reflection

1. Are you sometimes looking forward to seeing Jesus on the Day of Judgment?

2. Do you sometimes share specific thoughts about your looking forward to meeting Jesus face to face?

A Message for Herod: Luke 13:31-33

(31) On that day there came certain Pharisees, saying to him: Depart, and go hence; for Herod desires to kill thee. (32) And he said to them: Go, tell that fox, Behold, I cast out demons and perform cures to-day and to-morrow, and the third day I am perfected. (33) But yet, I must go to-day, and to-morrow, and the day following; because it may not be that a prophet perish out of Jerusalem.

Note

➢ Herod's domain was Galilee and Perea. This is undoubtedly Herod Antipas.

Questions for Reflection

1. If you were Herod, would you take this warning seriously?

2. What do you think the Pharisees were thinking here, since they usually were not supportive of Jesus?

Tears for Jerusalem: Luke 13:34-35

(34) Jerusalem! Jerusalem! that kills the prophets, and stones those sent to her; how often would I have gathered thy children together, as a hen her brood under her wings, and ye would not! (35) Behold, your house is left to you desolate. And I say to you: Ye shall not see me, until the time come when ye shall say, Blessed is he that comes in the name of the Lord.

<u>**Compare:**</u>
Matthew 23:37-39

<u>**Questions for Reflection**</u>

1. Describe your impression of Jesus' passion on behalf of Jerusalem.

2. Do you think Luke expects his Gentile audience to share that passion? Why?

3. Do you share that passion? Why?

> All-knowing and glorious God, there's no corner so dark You do not see, and there's no whisper so soft You cannot hear, I often worry about my health and the health of those I love, so I submit to Your healing and redemption. It is in the name of Jesus that I pray. Amen.

Another Healing on a Sabbath: Luke 14:1-6

AND it came to pass, as he went into the house of one of the chief of the Pharisees to eat bread on the sabbath, that they watched him. (2) And, behold, there was a certain man before him who had the dropsy. (3) And Jesus answering spoke to the lawyers and Pharisees, saying: Is it lawful to heal on the sabbath, or not? And they were silent. (4) And taking hold of him, he healed him, and let him go. (5) And to them he said: Who is there of you, whose ox or ass[14:5] shall fall into a pit, and he will not straightway draw him up on the sabbath day? (6) And they could not answer him again to these things.

Compare:

Matthew 12:9-14
Mark 3:1-6
Luke 6:6-11, 13:10-17

Note

➢ Dropsy is an old designation for edema or fluid retention.

Questions for Reflection

1. If you have known someone who had fluid retention and prayed for its healing, how did you pray for them?

2. What do you think is more important for Luke's audience, the healing itself or the attitude of the Pharisees?

Teaching About Humility: Luke 14:7-14

(7) And he spoke a parable to those who were bidden, when he marked how they chose out the first places; saying to them: (8) When thou art bidden by any one to a wedding, recline not in the first place at table, lest one more honorable than thou may have been bidden by him; (9) and he that bade thee and him shall come and say to thee, Give place to this man; and then thou shalt begin with shame to take the lowest place. (10) But when thou art bidden, go and recline in the lowest place; that when he that bade thee comes, he may say to thee, Friend, go up higher. Then shalt thou have honor in the presence of those who recline at table with thee. (11) For every one that exalts himself shall be humbled; and he that humbles himself shall be exalted.

(12) And he said also to him who bade him: When thou makest a dinner or a supper, call not thy friends, nor thy brothers, nor thy kinsmen, nor rich neighbors; lest they also bid thee again, and a recompense be made thee. (13) But when thou makest a feast, call the poor, the maimed, the lame, the blind. (14) And happy shalt thou be, because they can not recompense thee; for thou shalt be recompensed at the resurrection of the righteous.

Notes

1. We need to remember that humility does not mean thinking less of ourselves, but rather thinking of ourselves less.
2. Jesus offers a fresh perspective on the relationship between 'worldly' gain and spiritual growth.

Questions for Reflection

1. Have you ever denied yourself something in order to grow spiritually, as some do during Lent or Advent?

2. Have you considered nurturing your relationship with Christ by humbling yourself at various opportunities?

The Parable of the Great Banquet: Luke 14:15-24

(15) And a certain one of those who reclined at table with him, hearing these things, said to him: Happy is he, who shall eat bread in the kingdom of God! (16) And he said to him: A certain man made a great

supper, and bade many. (17) And he sent his servant, at the hour of the supper, to say to those who were bidden: Come, for all things are now ready. (18) And they all, with one mind, began to excuse themselves. The first said to him: I bought a piece of ground, and I must needs go out and see it; I pray thee let me be excused. (19) And another said: I bought five yoke of oxen, and I am going to make trial of them; I pray thee let me be excused. (20) And another said: I married a wife; and therefore I can not come.

(21) And the servant came, and reported these things to his lord. Then the master of the house, being angry, said to his servant: Go out quickly into the streets and lanes of the city, and bring in hither the poor, and maimed, and lame, and blind. (22) And the servant said: Lord, it is done as thou didst command, and yet there is room. (23) And the Lord said to the servant: Go out into the highways and hedges, and compel them[14:23] to come in, that my house may be filled; (24) for I say to you, that none of those men who were bidden shall taste of my supper.

Compare:

Matthew 22:1-10

Notes

1. Special occasion banquets in those days were seen as the ideal settings of celebration.
2. Coveting the sharing in God's kingdom, according to the parable, may prevent a person from entering.

Questions for Reflection

1. Have you thought about being with Jesus in eternal celebration?

2. What does the parable teach about being ready to go with Jesus?

More Costs of Discipleship: Luke 14:25-35

(25) And great multitudes were going with him; and turning, he said to them: (26) If any one comes to me, and hates not his father, and mother, and wife, and children, and brothers, and sisters, and even his own life besides, he can not be my disciple. (27) And whoever does not bear his cross, and come after me, can not be my disciple. (28) For who of you, intending to build a tower, does not first sit down, and count the cost, whether he has sufficient to finish it? (29) Lest haply, when he has laid a foundation, and is not able to finish, all that behold begin to mock him, (30) saying: This man began to build, and was not able to finish. (31) Or what king, going to make war against another king, does not first sit down and consult, whether he is able, with ten thousand, to meet him who comes against him with twenty thousand? (32) Else, while he is yet a great way off, he sends an embassy, and desires conditions of peace.

(33) So then, whoever of you forsakes not all that he has can not be my disciple. (34) Salt therefore is good; but if even the salt has become tasteless, wherewith shall it be seasoned? (35) It is fit neither for the land, nor for the dunghill; they cast it out. He that has ears to hear, let him hear.

Notes

1. Salt was mingled with rocks quarried from the Dead Sea area. Salt was kept in a bag to soak in a pot with foods to add flavor. Salt would 'lose its flavor' when all the salt in the rocks had dissolved.

2. Jesus uses the exaggeration of hating as a tool for teaching us about perspective.

Questions for Reflection

1. Does Jesus' call upon your life seem radical? Why?

2. How does the cost of discipleship concern you?

> When I impose my own will over Yours, forgive me merciful Father in heaven. I adore You because You are my great provider and so much more. Lord, I thank You because You are bigger than all my problems, and You are my shield. Help me find lives that are lost and lead them to salvation in Jesus. In His Holy name I offer my prayer. Amen.

Parables of The Lost Sheep: Luke 15:1-7

AND there were drawing near to him all the publicans and the sinners to hear him. (2) And the Pharisees and the scribes murmured, saying: This man receives sinners, and eats with them.

(3) And he spoke this parable to them, saying: (4) What man of you, having a hundred sheep, and having lost one of them, does not leave the ninety and nine in the wilderness, and go after that which is lost, until he finds it? (5) And having found it, he lays it on his shoulders, rejoicing. (6) And coming home, he calls together his friends and neighbors, saying to them: Rejoice with me; because I found my sheep which was lost. (7) I say to you, that so there will be joy in heaven over one sinner that repents, more than over ninety and nine just persons, who have no need of repentance.

Compare:
Matthew 18:12-14

Notes
1. The main point is God's concern for those who cannot find God.
2. There is no concern for the 99 left behind since everyone knew that a shepherd would leave such a task in the hands of another shepherd, perhaps a slave.

Questions for Reflection
1. Have you ever been lost in the literal sense? How did you recognize the fact that you were lost?

2. Have you ever felt that there was some kind of barrier between you and God? Please describe.

Parable of The Lost Coin: Luke 15:8-10

(8) Or what woman having ten pieces of silver, if she lose one piece, does not light a lamp, and sweep the house, and seek carefully till she finds it? (9) And having found it, she calls her friends and neighbors together, saying: Rejoice with me; because I found the piece which I lost. (10) So, I say to you, there is joy in the presence of the angels of God over one sinner that repents.

Notes
1. This parable is unique to Luke's gospel.
2. The addition of this parable in the sequence emphasizes both human helplessness and God's empathy.

Questions for Reflection
1. Have you ever lost something that was precious to you, causing you to search high and low?

2. Why do you suppose Luke included this parable for His Gentile audience?

Parable of The Loving Father: Luke 15:11-32

(11) And he said: A certain man had two sons. (12) And the younger of them said to his father: Father, give me the portion of the property that falls to me. And he divided to them his living. (13) And not many days after, the younger son gathered all together, and went abroad into a far country, and there wasted his substance in riotous living. (14) And when he had spent all, there arose a grievous famine in that country; and he began to be in want. (15) And he went and joined himself to one of the citizens of that country; and he sent him into his fields to feed swine. (16) And he would fain have filled his belly with the husks which the swine ate; and no one gave to him. (17) And coming to himself, he said: How many hired servants of my father have bread enough and to spare, and I perish here with hunger! (18) I will arise and go to my father, and will say to him: Father, I sinned against heaven, and before thee. (19) I am no longer worthy to be called thy son; make me as one of thy hired servants.

(20) And he arose, and came to his father. But when he was yet a great way off, his father saw him and had compassion, and ran and fell on his neck, and kissed him. (21) And the son said to him: Father, I sinned against heaven, and before thee; I am no longer worthy to be called thy son. (22) But the father said to his servants: Bring forth a robe, the best, and put it on him; and put a ring on his hand, and sandals on his feet; (23) and bring the fatted calf, and kill it; and let us eat and be merry. (24) Because this my son was dead and is alive again, was lost and is found. And they began to be merry.

(25) Now his elder son was in the field. And as he came, and drew near to the house, he heard music and dancing. (26) And calling to him one of the servants, he inquired what these things meant. (27) And he said to him: Thy brother is come; and thy father killed the fatted calf, because he received him back, safe and sound. (28) And he was angry, and would not go in; and his father came out, and entreated him. (29) And he answering said to his father: Lo, so many years do I serve thee, and never transgressed thy command; and to me thou never gavest a kid, that I might make merry with my friends. (30) But when this thy son came, who devoured thy living with harlots, thou didst kill for him the fatted calf. (31) And he said to him: Child, thou art ever with me, and all that I have is thine. (32) It was meet that we should make merry, and be glad; because this thy brother was dead and is alive again; and was lost, and is found.

Notes

1. This parable is unique to Luke.
2. The wallowing with pigs would be the ultimate indignity for a devout Jew, and not particularly pleasant for Gentiles either.
3. The parable emphasizes God's willingness to receive with joy the return of a rebel.
4. A robe was a luxury of a family member; the shoes emphasize the rebel's not being a slave; and the ring affirms the son's right to hold authority within the family.

Questions for Reflection

1. Have you ever known a teenaged rebel who turned out terrific as an adult?

2. Was there a period in your life when you felt estranged from God? Describe.

> I yield to Your divine authority, O God. I am thankful I am so abundantly blessed. I certainly don't deserve all that You provide me out of Your abundant love. Help me to seek those who need Jesus and disciple them as my faith grows. I praise You and glorify You in the name of Your Son Jesus, and pray in His name. Amen.

The Shrewd Steward: Luke 16:1-13

AND he said also to the disciples: There was a certain rich man, who had a steward; and the same was accused to him as wasting his goods. (2) And having called him, he said to him: What is this that I hear of thee? Give account of thy stewardship; for thou canst be no longer steward. (3) And the steward said within himself: What shall I do? For my master takes away from me the stewardship. I am not able to dig; to beg I am ashamed. (4) I am resolved what to do, that, when I am put out of the stewardship, they may receive me into their houses. (5) And having called to him each one of his master's debtors, he said to the first: How much owest thou to my master? (6) And he said: A hundred measures of oil. And he said to him: Take thy bill, and sit down quickly, and write fifty. (7) Then he said to another: And how much owest thou? And he said: A hundred measures of wheat. And he said to him: Take thy bill, and write fourscore. (8) And the master commended the unjust steward, because he had done wisely; because the sons of this world are, in their generation, wiser than the sons of light. (9) And I say to you: Make to yourselves friends of the mammon of unrighteousness; that, when it fails, they may receive you into the everlasting habitations. (10) He that is faithful in that which is least is faithful also in much; and he that is unjust in the least is unjust also in much. (11) If therefore ye were not faithful in the unrighteous mammon, who will entrust to you the true riches? (12) And if ye were not faithful in that which is another's, who will give to you your own? (13) No servant can serve two masters; for either he will hate the one, and love the other, or he will hold to one, and despise the other. Ye can not serve God and Mammon.

Notes

1. This parable is unique to Luke.
2. The thrust of the parable, in verses 8-9, is that the steward took advantage of opportunities in the present to secure his future. Believers are encouraged to be equally shrewd about this life and life eternal.
3. The phrase, children of light, is used elsewhere to indicate those who are spiritually enlightened.

Questions for Reflection

1. Have you thought about taking advantage of opportunities in this life so as to 'lay up treasures in heaven'?

2. Do you believe that Jesus is emphasizing earthly works rather than faith in Him, or in addition to that faith?

The Role of the Law: Luke 16:14-18

(14) And the Pharisees also; who were covetous, heard all these things; and they derided him. (15) And he said to them: Ye are they who justify themselves before men; but God knows your hearts; for that which is highly esteemed among men is abomination before God.

(16) The law and the prophets were until John; from that time the good news of the kingdom of God is published, and every man presses into it. (17) And it is easier that heaven and earth should pass away, than that one tittle of the law should fail.

(18) Every one who puts away his wife, and marries another, commits adultery; and he who marries her when put away from a husband commits adultery.

Compare:

Matthew 19:16-30, 5:17-18, 5:31-32
Mark 10:11-12

Notes

1. The phrase, what is prized, seems to refer to those things that are regarded as belonging to God.

2. Both John and Jesus proclaimed the Kingdom of God as being here and now, not something in the future.

3. Sometimes men 'put away' their wives [the literal meaning in this passage] into protected seclusion rather than get a divorce, which might cause family problems, financial problems, or both. They would then take on another wife.

Questions for Reflection

1. What are the things you give the highest value?

2. Do you pray as though everything belongs to God? Why?

3. If a Christian gets a divorce, do you think that person should also ask God for release from the marriage vows?

The Story of Lazarus: Luke 16:19-31

(19) There was a certain rich man, who was clothed in purple and fine linen, and fared sumptuously every day. (20) And there was a certain beggar named Lazarus, who was laid at his gate, full of sores, (21) and desiring to be fed with the crumbs that fell from the rich man's table. Moreover the dogs came and licked his sores. (22) And it came to pass, that the beggar died; and he was borne away by the angels into Abraham's bosom. The rich man also died, and was buried; (23) and in the underworld, lifting up his eyes, being in torments, he sees Abraham afar off, and Lazarus in his bosom. (24) And he cried and said: Father Abraham, have mercy on me, and send Lazarus, that he may dip the tip of his finger in water, and cool my tongue; for I am tormented in this flame. (25) But Abraham said: Child, remember that in thy lifetime thou receivedst thy good things in full, and Lazarus in like manner his evil things; but now here, he is comforted and thou art tormented. (26) And besides all this, between us and you a great gulf is fixed; that they who would pass from hence to you may not be able, nor those from thence pass over to us. (27) And he said: I pray thee therefore, father, that thou wouldst send him to my father's house. (28) For I have five brothers; that he may testify to them, that they may not also come into this place of torment. (29) Abraham says to him: They have Moses and the prophets let them hear them. (30) And he said: Nay, father Abraham; but if one should go to them from the dead, they will repent. (31) And he said to him: If they hear not Moses and the prophets, neither will they be persuaded, though one should rise from the dead.

Notes

1. Because it is not known whether this story refers to a real contemporary individual, it is not necessarily labeled a parable.

2. The point is that the message of the Hebrew Scriptures should be a sufficient call to repentance. Jesus infers that even His future resurrection will not be sufficient for some.

<u>Questions for Reflection</u>

1. How do you feel when you drive past a beggar on the street?

2. If you help a beggar who does not really need help, whose problem is it?

> Gracious Heavenly Father, You have always provided for my needs. When I encountered someone in need, I have responded. If you want me to do more, please lead me and empower me. In Jesus' name I offer my prayer. Amen.

The Sources of Sin: Luke 17:1-10

AND he said to his disciples: It is impossible that causes of offense should not come; but woe to him through whom they come! (2) It were better for him that a mill stone were placed about his neck, and he were thrown into the sea, than that he should cause one of these little ones to offend.

(3) Take heed to yourselves. If thy brother sin, rebuke him; and if he repent, forgive him. (4) And if he sin against thee seven times in the day, and seven times turn to thee saying, I repent, thou shalt forgive him.

(5) And the apostles said to the Lord: Increase our faith. (6) And the Lord said: If ye had faith as a grain of mustard, ye would say to this sycamine-tree, Be thou plucked up by the root, and planted in the sea; and it would have obeyed you.

(7) And who of you, having a servant plowing, or feeding cattle, will say to him immediately, when he has come in from the field, Come and recline at table; (8) and will not rather say to him, Make ready wherewith I may sup, and gird thyself and serve me, till I have eaten and drunken, and afterward thou shalt eat and drink? (9) Does he thank that servant, because he did the things that were commanded? I think not. (10) So also ye, when ye shall have done all the things that were commanded you, say, We are unprofitable servants; we have done that which was our duty to do.

Notes

1. We are not sinners because we sin; rather, we sin because we are sinners.
2. The meaning of sin is often equated with missing the mark and with stumbling.
3. The source of Sin is often seen as a matter of approach or attitude. Many have said that pride or thinking of ourselves as being in charge and taking the credit, is the root of all evil.

Questions for Reflection

1. Have you ever flown on a plane and pressed the 'call' button to get a flight attendant? Have you thought about that person's role as your [voluntary and paid] servant?

2. Have you ever raised a prayer with the same attitude as pressing one of those call buttons?

Healing Lepers: Luke 17:11-19

(11) And it came to pass, as he was going to Jerusalem, that he went through the midst of Samaria and Galilee. (12) And as he was entering into a certain village, there met him ten leprous men, who stood afar off. (13) And they lifted up their voice, saying: Jesus, Master, have mercy on us. (14) And seeing it, he said to them: Go, show yourselves to the priests. And it came to pass that, as they went, they were cleansed. (15) And one of them, seeing that he was healed, turned back, with a loud voice glorifying God, (16) and fell down on his face at his feet, giving thanks to him; and he was a Samaritan. (17) And Jesus answering said: Were not the ten cleansed? And where are the nine? (18) Were none found returning to give glory to God, except this stranger? (19) And he said to him: Arise, and go; thy faith has made thee whole.

Compare

Leviticus 13:1-23

Notes

1. Jesus does not perform healings here, either by word or deed.
2. Jesus heals the Samaritan along with the Jews without making a distinction.

Questions for Reflection

1. Since all were healed, by coming to Jesus in faith, why do you suppose Jesus thought it important to affirm the Samaritan's faith?

2. Do you know people who fail to praise God when they are healed?

The Kingdom of God: Luke 17:20-37

(20) And being asked by the Pharisees, when the kingdom of God would come, he answered them and said: The kingdom of God comes not with observation; (21) nor shall they say, Lo here! or, Lo there! for, behold, the kingdom of God is within you[17:21].

(22) And he said to the disciples: Days will come, when ye will desire to see one of the days of the Son of man, and ye will not see it. (23) And they will say to you, See here; or, See there; go not away, and follow not. (24) For as the lightning, that lightens out of the one part under heaven, shines unto the other part under heaven, so will the Son of man be in his day. (25) But first he must suffer many things, and be rejected on the part of this generation.

(26) And as it was in the days of Noah, so will it be also in the days of the Son of man. (27) They ate, they drank, they married, they were given in marriage, until the day that Noah entered into the ark, and the flood came and destroyed all. (28) In like manner also as it was in the days of Lot; they ate, they drank, they bought, they sold, they planted, they builded; (29) but the same day that Lot went out from Sodom, it rained fire and brimstone from heaven, and destroyed all. (30) After the same manner will it be, in the day when the Son of man is revealed.

(31) In that day, he who shall be on the house-top, and his goods in the house, let him not come down to take them away; and he that is in the field, let him likewise not turn back. (32) Remember Lot's wife. (33) Whoever shall seek to save his life shall lose it; and whoever may lose his life shall preserve it.

(34) I say to you, in that night there will be two men in one bed; one will be taken, and the other will be left. (35) Two women will be grinding together; one will be taken, and the other left. (37) And they answering say to him: Where, Lord? And he said to them: Where the body is, there also will the eagles be gathered together.

Compare:

Matthew 24

Notes

1. Those raising the questions probably were thinking of the material benefits of the coming of the Kingdom of God.
2. Jesus' answer to the final question [37] is indirect, but it gives them more information than was requested.

<u>Questions for Reflection</u>

1. If you knew that Judgment Day was tomorrow, would you act any differently today? Why?

2. If you saw the signs of judgment appearing in the sky, what would your reaction be?

> Father God of all good, I'm tempted to worry about what this day may hold. Thank You for the vision to see where You're leading me. Whether this is just another day of serving You or my very last day, help me to make the most of every opportunity. I pray in Jesus' name. Amen.

The Unrighteous Judge: Luke 18:1-8

AND he spoke also a parable to them, to the end that they ought always to pray, and not to faint; (2) saying: There was in a certain city a certain judge, who feared not God, nor regarded man. (3) And there was a widow in that city; and she came to him, saying: Avenge me of my adversary. (4) And he would not for a while; but afterward he said within himself: Though I fear not God, nor regard man, (5) yet because this widow troubles me, I will avenge her, lest continually coming she weary me.

(6) And the Lord said: Hear what the unjust judge says. (7) And will not God avenge his chosen, who cry to him day and night, though he is long suffering in respect to them? (8) I say to you, that he will avenge them speedily. But yet, when the Son of man comes, will he find faith on the earth?

Notes

1. This parable is unique to Luke for his Gentile audience.
2. Unlike most parables, Jesus states the point of His parable very clearly, perhaps because the situation is so unlike everyday life.
3. The persistent prayer of which He speaks requires solid faith.

Questions for Reflection

1. It's called importunate prayer. Have you ever prayed for something with this kind of persistence? With what result?

2. What is the difference between persistence based on our wanting our way, and persistence based on our belief in God's willingness to answer our prayer?

Parable of Two Sinners: Luke 18:9-14

(9) And he spoke this parable to some who trust in themselves that they are righteous, and despise others. (10) Two men went up into the temple to pray; one a Pharisee, and the other a publican. (11) The Pharisee stood, and prayed thus with himself: God, I thank thee, that I am not as other men, extortioners, unjust, adulterers, or even as this publican. (12) I fast twice in the week; I give tithes of all that I possess[18:12]. (13) And the publican, standing afar off, would not even lift up his eyes to heaven, but smote upon his breast, saying: God be merciful to me, the sinner. (14) I say to you, this man went down to his house justified, rather than the other. For every one that exalts himself shall be humbled; and he that humbles himself shall be exalted.

Notes

1. This parable is unique to Luke.
2. The term righteous technically means having the quality of fulfilling a relationship. In this case, it means fulfilling one's relationship with God. The Pharisee thinks in terms of fulfilling his relationship with the law.
3. Fasting twice a week usually meant Mondays and Thursdays.

<u>Questions for Reflection</u>

1. Have you ever been righteous with one friend while being unrighteous before another?

2. Is the tax collector's humble surrender a sign of strength, weakness, or both?

<u>The Blessing of Children: Luke 18:15-17</u>

(15) And they brought to him also infants, that he might touch them; and the disciples seeing it rebuked them. (16) But Jesus calling them to him, said: Suffer the little children to come to me, and forbid them not; for to such belongs the kingdom of God. (17) Verily I say to you, whoever shall not receive the kingdom of God as a little child, shall not enter therein.

<u>Compare:</u>
Matthew 19:13-15
Mark 10:13-16

<u>Notes</u>

1. Jesus' point is that God's creation belongs to those with an attitude of simple trust in God.
2. Jesus seems to imply that the term, good, implies perfection.

<u>Questions for Reflection</u>

1. What was the effect on the parents in bringing their children to be blessed?

2. Why were the disciples upset at first?

<u>Righteous Wealth: Luke 18:18-30</u>

(18) And a certain ruler asked him, saying: Good Teacher, what shall I do to inherit eternal life? (19) And Jesus said to him: Why dost thou call me good? None is good save one, God. (20) Thou knowest the commandments: Do not commit adultery, Do not kill, Do not steal, Do not bear false witness, Honor thy father and thy mother. (21) And he said: All these I kept from my youth. (22) And Jesus hearing it said to him: Yet lackest thou one thing; sell all that thou hast, and distribute to the poor, and thou shalt have treasure in heaven; and come, follow me. (23) And hearing this, he became very sorrowful; for he was exceedingly rich. (24) And Jesus seeing him became very sorrowful, said: How hardly shall they that have riches enter into the kingdom of God! (25) For it is easier for a camel to go through the eye of a needle, than for a rich man to enter into the kingdom of God. (26) And they who heard it said: And who can be saved? (27) And he said: The things that are impossible with men are possible with God.

(28) And Peter said: Lo, we forsook all, and followed thee. (29) And he said to them: Verily I say to you, there is no one that forsook house, or parents, or brothers, or wife, or children, for the sake of the kingdom of God, (30) who shall not receive manifold more in this present time, and in the world to come life everlasting.

<u>**Compare:**</u>
Matthew 19:16-30
Mark 10:17-31

<u>**Note**</u>
> ➤ The order of the commandments, while not following the order found in the Hebrew scriptures, does follow the order found in the Septuagint, the Greek translation in circulation after the Jews returned from Babylon. Literate Gentiles would have been more likely familiar with that translation.

<u>**Questions for Reflection**</u>
1. If you know any Christians of deep faith who are wealthy, what are your thoughts when reading this?

2. If you were rich, do you think you would struggle with this passage?

<u>**Another Prediction: Luke 18:31-34**</u>

(31) And taking with him the twelve, he said to them: Behold, we are going up to Jerusalem, and all the things written by the prophets for the Son of man shall be accomplished. (32) For he will be delivered to the Gentiles, and will be mocked, and insulted, and spit upon, (33) and they will scourge him, and put him to death; and on the third day he will rise again. (34) And they understood none of these things; and this saying was hidden from them, and they knew not the things that were said.

<u>**Compare:**</u>
Matthew 20:17-19
Mark 10:32-34
Luke 9:44-45

<u>**Healing a Blind Man: Luke 18:35-43**</u>

(35) And it came to pass, that as he came near to Jericho, a certain blind man was sitting by the wayside, begging. (36) And hearing a multitude passing by, he inquired what this was. (37) And they told him, that Jesus of Nazareth is passing by. (38) And he called aloud, saying: Jesus, Son of David, have mercy on me. (39) And they who went before rebuked him, that he should hold his peace. But he cried much the more: Son of David, have mercy on me. (40) And Jesus stood still, and commanded him to be brought to him. And when he was come near, he asked him, (41) saying: What wilt thou that I shall do to thee? And he said: Lord, that I may receive sight. (42) And Jesus said to him: Receive sight; thy faith has made thee whole. (43) And immediately he received sight, and followed him, glorifying God. And all the people, seeing it, gave praise to God.

<u>**Compare:**</u>
Matthew 20:29-34
Mark 10:46-52

<u>Note</u>

➤ In this version, Bartimaeus [Mark's version] is heard to address Jesus only as Son of David and is not himself named.

<u>Questions for Reflection</u>

1. What did he have to know in order for him to call out as he did?

2. Why did Jesus ask him what he wanted?

> Your divine faithfulness is why I love to give my loyalty to You, O God. Sometimes my past seems to haunt me, so I need the forgiveness of my great physician, Jesus, my Savior. I love putting my trust in You and Your divine timing through Jesus, while in His name I pray. Amen.

Another Encounter in Jericho: Luke 19:1-10

AND having entered in, he was passing through Jericho. (2) And behold, there was a man named Zaccheus, and he was a chief publican; and this man was rich. (3) And he sought to see Jesus, who he was; and he could not on account of the multitude, because he was small in stature. (4) And running before, he climbed up into a sycamore-tree to see him; because by that way he was to pass through. (5) And Jesus, when he came

to the place, looked up and saw him, and said to him: Zaccheus, make haste and come down; for to-day I must abide at thy house. (6) And he made haste, and came down, and received him joyfully. (7) And seeing it, they all murmured, saying that he went in to be a guest with a sinner.

(8) And Zaccheus stood up, and said to the Lord: Behold, Lord, the half of my goods I give to the poor; and if I took aught from any one by false accusation, I restore fourfold. (9) And Jesus said to him: This day is salvation come to this house, inasmuch as he also is a son of Abraham. (10) For the Son of man came to seek and to save that which was lost.

Notes

1. Jericho is a major intersection of trade routes even today. Several civilizations have built communities at this location.

2. As a tax collector, Zacheus was not actually paid by the emperor. He was charged with collecting a minimum amount of money in taxes. Any additional money he collected was his to keep. Rome did not care if a tax collector was fair or not. It only wanted results. While tax collectors were accepted as necessary, they were usually resented for being part of the Roman power structure, even if they were fair.

Questions for Reflection

1. If someone were a tax collector and a member of the church, what would your relationship be like?

2. How, if any, is your attitude different towards paying taxes to the government and giving to the church?

Parable of the Stewards: Luke 19:11-27

(11) And as they were hearing these things, he added and spoke a parable, because he was nigh to Jerusalem, and because they thought that the kingdom of God would immediately appear. (12) He said therefore: A certain nobleman went into a far country to receive for himself a kingdom, and to return. (13) And having called his ten servants, he gave them ten pounds, and said to them: Traffic, till I come.

(14) But his citizens hated him, and sent an embassy after him, saying: We will not have this man to reign over us.

(15) And it came to pass, when he had returned, having received the kingdom, that he commanded these servants to be called to him, to whom he gave the money, that he might know what each gained by trading. (16) And the first came, saying: Lord, thy pound gained ten pounds. (17) And he said to him: Well done, good servant; because thou wast faithful in a very little, have thou authority over ten cities.

(18) And the second came, saying: Lord, thy pound made five pounds. (19) And he said also to this man: And be thou over five cities. (20) And another came, saying: Lord, behold thy pound, which I kept laid up in a napkin. (21) For I feared thee, because thou art an austere man; thou takest up what thou layedst not down, and reapest what thou didst not sow. (22) And he says to him: Out of thy mouth will I judge thee, wicked servant.

Thou knewest that I was an austere man, taking up what I laid not down, and reaping what I did not sow? (23) Why then didst thou not put my money into the bank? and I, at my coming, should have required it with interest. (24) And he said to those standing by: Take from him the pound, and give it to him that has the ten pounds. (25) And they said to him: Lord, he has ten pounds. (26) For I say to you, that to every one that has shall be given; and from him that has not, even what he has shall be taken away.

(27) But those my enemies, who would not that I should reign over them, bring hither, and slay them before me.

<u>Compare:</u>
Matthew 25:14-30 [similar but different]

<u>Notes</u>
1. Although there are ten slaves mentioned at the beginning, and three are at the core of the story, the parable's focus is on stewardship in general.
2. The parable must be seen as a whole. It is not the return on investments that counts. Though there was a vast difference in the returns of the two investors mentioned, both were praised equally. The hostile attitude of the poor stewards brings the anger, not the failure to invest.

<u>Questions for Reflection</u>
1. If you invest money you have received, can you think of it as investing it on behalf of the Lord who provided the ability to invest?

2. How do we invest ourselves in Christ's church?

<u>'Palm' Sunday: Luke 19:28-44</u>
(28) And having spoken these things, he went before, going up to Jerusalem. (29) And it came to pass, as he drew near to Bethphage and Bethany, at the mount called Olivet, that he sent forth two of his disciples, (30) saying: Go into the opposite village, in which as ye are entering ye will find a colt tied, whereon no man ever sat; loose and bring him. (31) And if any one ask you, why do ye loose him? Thus shall ye say to him: Because the Lord has need of him. (32) And they that were sent forth departed, and found even as he said to them. (33) And as they were loosing the colt, its owners said to them: Why loose ye the colt? (34) And they said: The Lord has need of him. (35) And they brought him to Jesus; and having cast their garments upon the colt, they set Jesus thereon. (36) And as he went, they spread their garments in the way. (37) And as he was drawing near, just at the descent of the mount of the Olives, the whole multitude of the disciples began to rejoice, and praise God with a loud voice for all the miracles which they saw; (38) saying: Blessed be the King who comes in the name of the Lord! Peace in heaven, and glory in the highest!

(39) And some of the Pharisees from the multitude said to him: Teacher, rebuke thy disciples. (40) And answering he said to them: I tell you that if these shall hold their peace, the stones will cry out.

(41) And when he came near, as he saw the city, he wept over it, (42) saying: If even thou hadst known, at least in this thy day, the things that belong to thy peace! But now they are hidden from thine eyes. (43) For days will come upon thee, that thine enemies will cast up a mound about thee, and compass thee round, and shut thee in on every side, (44) and will level thee with the ground, and thy children within thee, and will not leave in thee one stone upon another; because thou knewest not the time of thy visitation.

<u>Compare:</u>
Matthew 21:1-9
Mark 11:1-10
John 12:12-18

<u>Notes</u>

1. Jesus' path was along a ridge in the Kidron Valley, between the Mount of Olives and Jerusalem.

2. The children [44] of which Jesus speaks are undoubtedly the inhabitants of Jerusalem.

3. His choice of animal denoted humility, part of the 'scandal? which kept many Jews from believing in Him. A conquering messiah, in traditional values, would ride in on a horse.

<u>Questions for Reflection</u>

1. Why do you suppose that Jesus held off those who would proclaim Him king until this point, and why would he now make this grand entrance?

2. If He had succumbed to the temptation of entering on a horse, do you think it would have made any difference?

<u>Unrighteous Capitalism: Luke 19:45-48</u>

(45) And entering into the temple, he began to cast out those who sold; (46) saying to them: It is written, And my house shall be a house of prayer; but ye made it a den of robbers.

(47) And he was teaching daily in the temple; and the chief priests and the scribes and the chief of the people were seeking to destroy him, (48) and could not find what they might do; for all the people hung, listening, upon him.

<u>Compare:</u>
Matthew 21:12-13
Mark 11:15-19
John 2:13-17

<u>Notes</u>

1. John's gospel portrays this event as happening during the first year of His earthly ministry rather than now. Jesus may have done this more than once.

2. Since Jews came from outside of Israel as well as from within, the changing of currency was necessary. Evidently such commerce had moved from outside the Temple gates to the 'Court of the Gentiles' perhaps even further into the Temple.

Questions for Reflection

1. Have you ever seen people performing business transactions in a church worship area during a time of worship?

2. Have you ever been angry when you observed an activity during worship that you thought was inappropriate?

> I submit to Your divine authority, O God. I need you to guide me towards my future. I'm grateful that You have delivered me from so much evil and thankful that I am abundantly blessed. I am not worthy of all the blessings You give me through Your abundant love. I praise and glorify You, for I live and pray in the name of Your Son Jesus. Amen.

Jesus' Origin of Authority: Luke 20:1-8

AND it came to pass, on one of the days, as he was teaching the people in the temple, and publishing the good news, that the chief priests and the scribes came to him with the elders, (2) and spoke to him, saying: Tell us, by what authority doest thou these things? Or who is he that gave thee this authority? (3) And he answering said to them: I also will ask you one thing; and tell it me. (4) John's immersion, was it from heaven, or from men? (5) And they reasoned with themselves, saying: If we say, From heaven, he will say, Why, then did ye not believe him? (6) But if we say, From men, all the people will stone us; for they are persuaded that John was a prophet. (7) And they answered, that they knew not whence it was. (8) And Jesus said to them: Neither do I say to you, by what authority I do these things.

Compare:

Matthew 21:23-27
Mark 11:27-33
John 2:18-22

Notes

1. Since there were no resident prophets in Jerusalem, ultimate religious authority rested in Hebrew Scriptures, similar to our use of the U.S. Constitution.

2. Authority came from anointing. A king could lay hands on people, anointing them with his authority, making them his ambassadors. A father could anoint his son with authority to carry out business transactions. The question concerning the authority of John the Baptist was therefore entirely appropriate.

Questions for Reflection

1. On what occasion(s) was Jesus anointed with authority?

2. How does a church leader gain recognized authority today?

The Rebellious Farmers: Luke 20:9-19

(9) And he began to speak to the people this parable: A man planted a vineyard, and let it out to husbandmen, and went abroad for a long time. (10) And at the season he sent a servant to the husbandmen, that they should give him of the fruit of the vineyard; but the husbandmen beat him, and sent him away empty. (11) And again he sent another servant; and him also, having beaten and treated him shamefully, they sent away empty. (12) And again he sent a third; and they wounded him also, and cast him out.

(13) And the lord of the vineyard said: What shall I do? I will send my beloved son; perhaps, seeing him, they will reverence him. (14) But when the husbandmen saw him, they reasoned among themselves, saying: This is the heir; come, let us kill him, that the inheritance may become ours. (15) So they cast him out of the vineyard, and killed him. What therefore will the lord of the vineyard do to them? (16) He will come and destroy these husbandmen, and will give the vineyard to others. And hearing it, they said: Far be it! (17) And he, looking on them, said: What then is this that is written,

The stone which the builders disallowed, The same is become the head of the corner.

(18) Every one that falls upon that stone shall be broken; but on whomsoever it shall fall, it will grind

him to powder.

(19) And the scribes and the chief priests sought to lay hands on him in that hour; and they feared the people; for they knew that he spoke this parable against them.

<u>Compare:</u>
Matthew 21:33-46
Mark 12:1-12

<u>Notes</u>

1. Tenant farming was a common phenomenon in Jesus? day. Most people could not afford land of their own, so they rented the land and paid the rent with crops.
2. Vineyards, unlike today, were as common as farms that grew other crops, because wine was the primary drink on all occasions.

<u>Questions for Reflection</u>

1. Do you know of anyone who abuses his or her rental privileges?

2. Do you think the Temple leaders really understood what He was saying about them?

<u>The Righteous Taxpayer: Luke 20:20-26</u>

(20) And watching him[20:20], they sent forth spies, feigning themselves to be just men, that they might take hold of his words, in order to deliver him up to the magistracy, and to the authority of the governor. (21) And they asked him, saying: Teacher, we know that thou sayest and teachest rightly, and regardest not the person of any, but teachest the way of God truly. (22) Is it lawful that we should give tribute to Caesar, or not? (23) And perceiving their craftiness, he said to them: (24) Show me a denary[20:24]. Whose image and inscription has it? And answering they said: Caesar's. (25) And he said to them: Render therefore to Caesar the things that are Caesar's, and to God the things that are God's. (26) And they could not take hold of his words before the people; and they marveled at his answer, and held their peace.

<u>Compare:</u>
Matthew 22:15-22
Mark 12:13-17

<u>Notes</u>

1. The Greek text [20] implies that they were pretending to be concerned about legal correctness or righteousness.
2. While this logic seems painfully obvious in today's culture, in the culture of Jesus, His response was creatively brilliant.

<u>**Questions for Reflection**</u>

1. In the context of Christian witness, what do you think belongs to God?

2. Is what belongs to God different from an offering or a gift? How so?

<u>**Responsibility in Life: Luke 20:27-40**</u>

(27) And some of the Sadducees, who deny that there is a resurrection, coming to him, asked him, (28) saying: Teacher, Moses wrote to us, if a man's brother die, having a wife, and he die childless, that his brother should take his wife, and raise up seed to his brother.

(29) There were therefore seven brothers; and the first took a wife, and died childless; (30) and the second and the third took her; (31) and in like manner also the seven left no children, and died. (32) At last the woman also died. (33) In the resurrection, therefore, of which of them is she wife? For the seven had her for a wife.

(34) And Jesus answering said to them: The sons of this world marry, and are given in marriage. (35) But they who are accounted worthy to obtain that world, and the resurrection from the dead, neither marry, nor are given in marriage; (36) for neither can they die any more; for they are equal to the angels, and are sons of God, being sons of the resurrection.

(37) Now that the dead are raised, even Moses showed, at The Bush, when he calls the Lord the God of Abraham, and the God of Isaac, and the God of Jacob. (38) For he is not a God of the dead, but of the living; for to him all live.

(39) And some of the scribes answering said: Teacher, thou saidst well. (40) For they no longer dared to ask him any question.

<u>**Compare:**</u>
Matthew 22:23-33
Mark 12:18-27

<u>**Notes**</u>

1. Luke makes the point to his Gentile audience with a different perspective. The point is that relationships and existence are very different in this life and the next.

2. Levirate marriage was conceived to protect women when they became widowed. If the woman was of childbearing age, the closest relative of her late husband took over the marital responsibilities. Any child born would be descended from her late husband and not from the brother.

3. The Temple authorities thought they could cause Jesus to make a mistake by weaving together two different and complicated issues. Instead, Jesus seizes the opportunity to teach some far greater truths about God and about all of creation.

<u>**Questions for Reflection**</u>

1. What advantages are there for the man in levirate marriage?

2. What advantages are there for the woman in levirate marriage?

3. What do you learn about the overall creation of God from this teaching? Do you have a clearer idea about Jesus' viewpoint? Is he being fully human and fully divine?

Perspective as Son of David: Luke 20:41-44

(41) And he said to them: How say they that the Christ is son of David? (42) And David himself says in the book of Psalms:

The LORD said to my Lord, Sit on my right hand, (43) Till I make thine enemies thy footstool.

(44) David therefore calls him Lord, and how is he his son?

Compare:

Matthew 22:41-46
Mark 12:35-37

Notes

1. The quotation [42] is from Psalm 110:1.
2. The conflict is cultural: It is impossible for a father to call his son 'Lord.'

Questions for Reflection

1. What does Jesus' being called 'son of David? mean to you?

2. Does this passage give a deeper meaning to the phrase, 'King of Kings'?

Pride and Humility in Perspective: Luke 20:45-47

(45) And in the hearing of all the multitude, he said to his disciples: (46) Beware of the scribes, who desire to go about in long robes, and love greetings in the markets, and the first seats in the synagogues, and the first places at feasts; (47) who devour widows' houses, and for a pretense make long prayers. These shall receive greater condemnation.

Notes

1. Many theologians hold pride in being the root of all evil and the source of all sin.
2. Healthy pride comes from knowing the source of your gifts and experience.

<u>Questions for Reflection</u>

1. What is a good way to keep one's pride under control?

2. Has anyone ever described you as proud?

Forgive my selfish pride, Lord God in heaven, for I like to think I can depend upon myself and not You. Nothing is too difficult for You, our amazingly gracious God. All that I am, I surrender to Your divine care in Jesus' name. Amen.

An Offering from a Widow: Luke 21:1-4

AND looking up, he saw the rich men casting their gifts into the treasury. (2) And he saw also a certain poor widow casting in thither two mites. (3) And he said: Of a truth I say to you, that this poor widow cast in more than all. (4) For all these, out of their abundance, cast into the offerings; but she, out of her want, cast in all the living that she had.

Compare:

Mark 12:41-44

Notes

1. The treasury was a large container shaped like an inverted horn to discourage theft. It also refers to a room in the Temple.
2. The copper coin [lepton] had virtually no actual material value, but for purposes of offerings and gifts it had great religious significance.

Questions for Reflection

1. Are you aware that statistically, the more affluent a person is the smaller the portion they are likely to give to charity? Why do you suppose this is true?

2. Do you believe that you are giving sacrificially to the church?

Prediction of Destruction and the End of the Age: Luke 21:5-38

(5) And as some were saying of the temple, that it has been adorned with beautiful stones and offerings, he said: (6) As for these things which ye behold, days will come in which there shall not be left one stone upon another, that shall not be thrown down. (7) And they asked him, saying: Teacher, when therefore will these things be, and what will be the sign when these things are about to come to pass?

(8) And he said: Take heed that ye be not led astray. For many will come in my name, saying: I am he, and the time is at hand. Go not after them. (9) And when ye shall hear of wars and commotions, be not terrified; for these things must first come to pass; but the end is not immediately.

(10) Then said he to them: Nation will rise against nation, and kingdom against kingdom; (11) and there will be great earthquakes, and in divers places famines and pestilences; and there will be great portents and signs from heaven. (12) And before all these, they will lay their hands on you, and persecute you, delivering you up into synagogues and prisons, being brought before kings and rulers for my name's sake. (13) And it shall turn out to you for a testimony.

(14) Settle it therefore in your hearts, not to meditate before what ye shall answer. (15) For I will give you a mouth and wisdom, which all your adversaries shall not be able to gainsay or withstand. (16) And ye will be delivered up both by parents, and brothers, and kindred, and friends; and some of you they will cause to be put to death. (17) And ye will be hated by all for my name's sake. (18) And there shall not a hair of your head perish. (19) In your patience possess your souls.

(20) And when ye shall see Jerusalem encompassed by armies, then know that its desolation is at hand. (21) Then let those in Judaea flee into the mountains; and let those in the midst of it depart out; and let those in the fields not enter into it. (22) Because these are the days of vengeance, that all the things which are written

may be fulfilled.

(23) Woe to those who are with child, and to those who give suck, in those days! For there shall be great distress upon the land, and wrath to this people. (24) And they shall fall by the edge of the sword, and shall be led away captive into all the nations; and Jerusalem shall be trodden down by the Gentiles, until the times of the Gentiles shall be fulfilled.

(25) And there shall be signs in the sun, and moon, and stars; and on the earth distress of nations, in perplexity for the roaring of the sea and waves; (26) men's hearts failing them for fear, and for looking for those things that are coming on the world; for the powers of heaven shall be shaken. (27) And then shall they see the Son of man coming in a cloud, with power and great glory. (28) And when these things begin to come to pass, then look up, and lift up your heads; for your redemption is drawing nigh.

(29) And he spoke to them a parable: Behold the fig-tree, and all the trees. (30) When they already shoot forth, seeing it ye know of yourselves that the summer is already near. (31) So also ye, when ye see these things coming to pass, know that the kingdom of God is near. (32) Verily I say to you, this generation shall not pass away, till all shall have come to pass. (33) Heaven and earth shall pass away; but my words shall not pass away.

(34) And take heed to yourselves, lest at any time your hearts be overcharged with surfeiting, and drunkenness, and cares of this life, and that day come upon you unawares. (35) For as a snare shall it come on all that dwell on the face of the whole earth. (36) And watch, in every time praying that ye may be accounted worthy to escape all these things that shall come to pass, and to stand before the Son of man.

(37) And in the daytime he was teaching in the temple; and at night he went out, and abode in the mount that is called Olivet. (38) And all the people came early in the morning to him in the temple, to hear him.

Compare:
Matthew 24:1-36
Mark 13:1-37

Notes

1. The first destruction of the Temple brought about the end of the age of the Kings of Israel. The association is thus made between repeated destruction of the Temple and the end of the current age.
2. Judas Maccabeus in 66 CE led a rebellion, and Rome responded in 67 CE with the destruction of all of Jerusalem.

Questions for Reflection

1. What would you visualize to be the mark of the end of the American era?

2. If you saw judgment day approaching, would you live any differently than you do now?

> Gracious God, I worship and love You. Please forgive me for taking your trial for my sins for granted. Despite my own trials, I can still praise You because You are the reason why I have joy. In Jesus' name, I pray. Amen.

The Last Supper: Luke 22:1-38

NOW the feast of unleavened bread was drawing near, which is called the Passover; (2) and the chief priests and the scribes were seeking how they might kill him; for they feared the people.

(3) And Satan entered into Judas called Iscariot, being of the number of the twelve. (4) And he went away, and consulted with the chief priests and captains, how he might deliver him up to them. (5) And they were glad, and covenanted to give him money. (6) And he promised, and sought opportunity to deliver him up to them in the absence of the multitude.

(7) And the day of unleavened bread came, when the Passover must be killed. (8) And he sent away Peter and John, saying: Go, and prepare us the Passover, that we may eat it. (9) And they said to him: Where wilt thou that we prepare? (10) And he said to them: Behold, when ye have entered into the city, there will meet you a man bearing a pitcher of water; follow him into the house where he enters in. (11) And ye shall say to the master of the house: The Teacher says to thee, Where is the guest chamber, where I may eat the Passover with my disciples? (12) And he will show you a large upper room furnished; there make ready. (13) And they went away, and found as he had said to them. And they made ready the Passover.

(14) And when the hour came, he reclined at table, and the apostles with him. (15) And he said to them: I earnestly desired to eat this Passover with you before I suffer. (16) For I say to you, I shall eat of it no more, until it be fulfilled in the kingdom of God. (17) And having received a cup, he gave thanks and said: Take this, and divide it among yourselves. (18) For I say to you, I will not drink of the fruit of the vine, until the kingdom of God shall come.

(19) And taking a loaf, he gave thanks, and broke it, and gave to them, saying: This is my body which is given for you; this do in remembrance of me. (20) And the cup in like manner after supper, saying: This cup is the new covenant in my blood, which is shed for you.

(21) But, behold, the hand of him that betrays me is with me on the table. (22) For the Son of man indeed goes, as it was determined; but woe to that man by whom he is betrayed! (23) And they began to inquire among themselves, who then it might be that should do this thing?

(24) And there arose also a contention among them, which of them should be accounted the greatest. (25) And he said to them: The kings of the Gentiles exercise lordship over them; and they who exercise authority over them are called benefactors. (26) But ye are not so; but let the greatest among you become as the younger, and he that is chief as he that serves. (27) For which is greater, he that reclines at table, or he that serves? Is not he that reclines at table? But I am in the midst of you as he that serves. (28) Ye are they who have continued with me in my temptations; (29) and I appoint to you a kingdom, as my Father appointed to me, (30) that ye may eat and drink at my table in my kingdom; and ye shall sit on thrones, judging the twelve tribes of Israel.

(31) And the Lord said: Simon, Simon, behold, Satan asked for you, to sift as the wheat. (32) But I prayed for thee, that thy faith fail not; and thou, when thou hast turned, strengthen thy brethren.

(33) And he said to him: Lord, I am ready to go with thee, both to prison and to death. (34) And he said: I say to thee, Peter, a cock will not crow this day, till thou shalt thrice deny that thou knowest me.

(35) And he said to them: When I sent you without purse, and bag, and sandals, lacked ye anything? And they said: Nothing. (36) Therefore said he to them: But now, he that has a purse let him take it, and likewise a bag; and he that has not, let him sell his garment and buy a sword. (37) For I say to you, that yet this which is written must be accomplished in me: And he was reckoned among transgressors; for the things concerning me

have an end.

(38) And they said: Lord, behold, here are two swords. And he said: It is enough!

<u>Compare:</u>
Matthew 26:17-35
Mark 14:12-31

<u>Notes</u>
1. Seeing a man carrying a jar of water would be unusual and therefore noteworthy because it was normally deemed to be a woman's work in that culture.
2. Who made the arrangements is not clear, but by doing this in advance there was less chance of attracting attention to Jesus and his inner circle. Normally the meal would begin after sundown.
3. Trying to identify the householder would be pointless. Unless the householder was one of the inner circle, there would be no relevance. Countless homeowners rented out space during Passover for such gatherings.
4. For those in the Roman Catholic, Eastern Orthodox, and Episcopal traditions, the 'keys to the kingdom' statement [28-30] is central to their understanding of their heritage.
5. This sending forth [35-38] is unique to Luke, and it is radically different from the previous instance because it is no longer popular to be a follower of Jesus.

<u>Questions for Reflection</u>
1. Have you ever participated in a Passover meal? Would doing so make your celebration of Easter more meaningful?

2. There were four cups in a traditional Passover meal: Praise, Penitence, Redemption, and Elijah. Since they sang a hymn after partaking of the cup, it was the third cup [redemption]. What does that mean for your faith?

3. As you read this version of what happened in the upper room, what are some of the things that Luke includes that you believe are important to Gentiles?

4. Do you believe that you have the keys to the kingdom?

5. In light of verses 35-38, how should Christians be equipped today?

<u>In the Garden: Luke 22:39-53</u>

(39) And going out, he went as he was wont to the mount of the Olives; and his disciples also followed him. (40) And when he was at the place, he said to them: Pray that ye enter not into temptation. (41) And he withdrew from them about a stone's throw; and kneeling down, he prayed, (42) saying: Father, if thou art willing to remove this cup from me! Yet, not my will but thine be done.

(43) And there appeared to him an angel from heaven, strengthening him. (44) And being in an agony he prayed more earnestly; and his sweat became as it were great drops of blood falling down to the ground. (45) And rising up from prayer, and coming to the disciples, he found them sleeping, from sorrow. (46) And he said to them: Why sleep ye? Arise and pray, that ye enter not into temptation.

(47) While he was yet speaking, behold a multitude, and he that was called Judas, one of the twelve, went before them and drew near to Jesus to kiss him. (48) But Jesus said to him: Judas, betrayest thou the Son of man with a kiss? (49) And they who were about him, seeing what would follow, said to him: Lord, shall we smite with the sword? (50) And a certain one of them smote the servant of the high priest, and took off his right ear. (51) And Jesus answering said: Suffer thus far. And he touched his ear, and healed him.

(52) And Jesus said to the chief priests and captains of the temple and elders, who were come to him: Have ye come out as against a robber, with swords and staves? (53) When I was daily with you in the temple, ye stretched not forth your hands against me. But this is your hour, and the power of darkness.

<u>Compare:</u>
Matthew 26:36-46
Mark 14:32-42

<u>Notes</u>
1. When Jesus refers to the cup, it is a Jewish metaphor for that portion which is allotted by God.
2. The sweating of blood is not in all early manuscripts of Luke and is unique to this gospel. It is a tradition that dates from the first century. Some physicians have pointed out that it is physiologically possible for high tension to cause capillaries of the skin to burst, though it is very rare.
3. Luke is unique in pointing out the role of Jewish leaders at the time of His arrest.

<u>Questions for Reflection</u>
1. Do you believe that the disciples knew at this point what was about to happen? Why?

2. Why do you suppose Luke includes the story of the slave's ear with such detail?

<u>The Religious Trial: Luke 22:54-71</u>

(54) And they took him, and led him away, and brought him into the house of the high priest. And Peter followed afar off.

(55) And they having kindled a fire in the midst of the court, and sat down together, Peter sat down among them. (56) And a certain maid seeing him as he sat by the fire, and looking intently upon him, said: This man also was with him. (57) And he denied him, saying: Woman, I do not know him.

(58) And after a little while, another seeing him said: Thou also art of them. And Peter said: Man, I am not.

(59) And about the space of one hour after, another confidently affirmed, saying: Of a truth this one also

was with him; for he is a Galilaean. (60) And Peter said: Man, I know not what thou sayest. And immediately, while he was yet speaking, a cock crowed.

(61) And the Lord turning looked upon Peter. And Peter remembered the word of the Lord, how he said to him: Before a cock crows this day, thou wilt deny me thrice. (62) And Peter went out, and wept bitterly.

(63) And the men who held Jesus mocked him, beating him; (64) and having blindfolded him they asked him, saying: Prophesy, who is it that smote thee? (65) And many other things they said, reviling him.

(66) And when it was day, the elders of the people[22:66], and the chief priests and scribes, came together; and they brought him up into their council, saying: (67) If thou art the Christ, tell us. And he said to them: If I tell you, ye will not believe. (68) And if I ask, ye will not answer. (69) But henceforth shall the Son of man sit on the right hand of the power of God. (70) And they all said: Art thou then the Son of God? And he said to them: Ye say it; for I am. (71) And they said: Why need we any further witness? For we ourselves heard it from his own mouth.

Compare:
John 18:12-27

Notes

1. This confrontation took place at the High Priest's house because the activity was inappropriate for the Temple at Passover.
2. The role of high priest was supposedly determined by the prophetic casting of lots at the beginning of the year.
3. It was important to have logical charges to bring against Jesus in order to justify their actions. Charges required two witnesses to be valid.

Questions for Reflection

1. In the midst of the storm being generated by the religious leaders, does Jesus seem calm? Why?

2. Was Peter truly focused upon what was happening to Jesus?

3. Was Peter truly afraid, or was he simply putting the girl off?

Lord God, some people take communion. It is received by some. As I worship Him, I want to be open to what Jesus offers me. May we have the ears to hear whatever Jesus reveals to us as I share the bread and cup with my sisters and brothers in Christ. In His name I pray. Amen.

Jesus Before Pilate the First Time: Luke 23:1-5

AND the whole multitude of them arose, and led him unto Pilate. (2) And they began to accuse him, saying: We found this man perverting our nation, and forbidding to give tribute to Caesar, saying that he himself is Christ, a king. (3) And Pilate asked him, saying: Art thou the King of the Jews? And he answering said to him: Thou sayest it. (4) And Pilate said to the chief priests and the multitudes: I find no fault in this man. (5) And they were the more violent, saying: He stirs up the people, teaching throughout all Judaea, beginning from Galilee, unto this place.

Compare:

Matthew 27:1-2, 11-14
Mark 15:1-5
John 18:28-40

Notes

1. The charges presented to Pilate are worded to sound like treason, but he is not fooled. He refuses to mix religion and politics. His primary task was to keep the populace reasonably calm and orderly. Any threat of a riot would trigger his responsibilities as Roman procurator.
2. Although life was cheap, Pilate was typical of Romans in his superstitious attitude towards life. Jesus, as a religious figure got the attention of his superstitions.

Questions for Reflection

1. What seems to be Jesus' attitude towards Pilate?

2. Does Pilate fulfill his responsibilities as Procurator in the way in which he handles Jesus' case?

3. How would you describe Pilate in terms of his capabilities, his temperament, and his fairness?

Herod and Pilate Become Friends: Luke 23:6-12

(6) When Pilate heard of Galilee, he asked if the man is a Galilaean. (7) And learning that he belonged to Herod's jurisdiction, he sent him up to Herod, who also was himself in Jerusalem at that time.

(8) And Herod, when he saw Jesus, rejoiced greatly; for he had desired for a long time to see him, because he had heard concerning him; and he hoped to see some sign wrought by him. (9) And he questioned him in many words; but he answered him nothing. (10) And the chief priests and scribes stood, vehemently accusing him. (11) And Herod with his men of war set him at naught, and mocked him, and arraying him in a gorgeous robe sent him back to Pilate. (12) And Pilate and Herod on that day became friends with each other; for before they were at enmity between themselves.

<u>**Notes**</u>

1. Luke is unique in reporting this part of the story to his Gentile audience.
2. Herod would seem to have jurisdiction because Jesus grew up in Nazareth, a part of Galilee.

<u>**Questions for Reflection**</u>

1. What is Herod's real interest in Jesus?

2. What seems to be Jesus' attitude towards Herod?

3. Why do you think Luke want us to know this part of the story?

<u>Jesus Before Pilate Again: Luke 23:13-25</u>

(13) And Pilate, having called together the chief priests and the rulers and the people, (14) said to them: Ye brought to me this man, as one perverting the people; and, behold, I, having examined him before you, found no fault in this man, touching those things whereof ye accuse him. (15) No, nor yet Herod; for I sent you up to him; and behold, nothing worthy of death has been done by him. (16) I will therefore chastise, and release him. (17) [23:17] (18) And they cried out all at once, saying: Away with this man, and release to us Barabbas! (19) (who for a certain sedition made in the city, and for murder, was cast into prison.)

(20) Again, therefore, Pilate spoke to them, desiring to release Jesus. (21) But they cried, saying: Crucify, crucify him. (22) And a third time he said to them: What evil then has this man done? I found no cause of death in him. I will therefore chastise, and release him. (23) And they were urgent with loud voices, requiring that he should be crucified. And their voices and those of the chief priests prevailed. (24) And Pilate gave sentence, that what they required should be done. (25) And he released him who for sedition and murder was cast into prison, whom they required; but Jesus he delivered up to their will.

<u>**Note**</u>

➢ Having Jesus flogged was a cruel act of mercy. The result was that Jesus would go into shock, the pain of the crucifixion would be lessened, and death would come sooner.

<u>**Questions for Reflection**</u>

1. Has Pilate exhausted all possibilities for finding a way to release Jesus?

2. Was Jesus sensitive at this point to Pilate's needs and concerns?

The Atonement on the Cross: Luke 23:26-56

(26) And as they led him away, they laid hold of one Simon a Cyrenian, coming from the country, and on him they laid the cross, that he might bear it after Jesus. (27) And there followed him a great company of the people, and of women who also bewailed and lamented him. (28) But Jesus turning to them said: Daughters of Jerusalem, weep not for me, but weep for yourselves, and for your children. (29) For, behold, days are coming in which they shall say: Happy the barren, and wombs that never bore, and breasts that never gave suck. (30) Then shall they begin to say to the mountains: Fall on us; and to the hills: Cover us. (31) For if they do these things in the green tree, what shall be done in the dry?

(32) And there were also two others, malefactors, led with him to be put to death. (33) And when they had gone away to the place which is called A Skull, there they crucified him, and the malefactors, one on the right hand, and the other on the left. (34) And Jesus said: Father, forgive them; for they know not what they do. And they divided his garments, casting lots.

(35) And the people stood beholding. And the rulers also scoffed, saying: Others he saved; let him save himself, if he is the Christ, the chosen of God. (36) And the soldiers also coming to him mocked him, offering him vinegar, (37) and saying: If thou art the King of the Jews, save thyself. (38) And there was an inscription written over him: THIS IS THE KING OF THE JEWS.

(39) And one of the malefactors who were hanged railed at him, saying: If thou art the Christ, save thyself and us. (40) But the other answering rebuked him, saying: Dost thou not even fear God, seeing thou art in the same condemnation? (41) And we indeed justly; for we are receiving the due reward of our deeds; but this man did nothing amiss. (42) And he said to Jesus: Remember me, when thou comest in thy kingdom. (43) And Jesus said to him: Verily I say to thee, to-day thou shalt be with me in paradise.

(44) And it was about the sixth hour; and darkness came over the whole land until the ninth hour. (45) And the sun was darkened; and the vail of the temple was rent in the midst. (46) And Jesus, crying with a loud voice, said: Father, into thy hands I commit my spirit. And having said this, he expired.

(47) And the centurion, seeing what was done, glorified God, saying: Verily, this man was righteous! (48) And all the multitudes who had come together to that sight, having beheld the things that were done, returned, beating their breasts. (49) And all his acquaintance were standing afar off, and women who had followed him from Galilee, beholding these things.

(50) And, behold, a man named Joseph, a counselor, a good and just man, (51) (he had not consented to their counsel and deed) , from Arimathaea a city of the Jews, who was waiting for the kingdom of God, (52) this man went to Pilate, and asked for the body of Jesus. (53) And taking it down, he wrapped it in linen, and laid it in a sepulchre that was hewn in the rock, where no one was yet laid. (54) And it was the day of preparation, and the sabbath drew on. (55) And the women also, who had come with him out of Galilee, followed after, and viewed the sepulchre, and how his body was laid. (56) And returning, they prepared spices and ointments; and on the sabbath they rested, according to the commandment.

Compare:

Matthew 27:27-44
Mark 15:16-47
John 19:16-42

Notes

1. The proverb about green wood [31] probably means, 'If this happens to an innocent man, what about the guilty'?
2. The robber's request [42] is probably based upon the charges leveled against Jesus.
3. Paradise [43] for most Jews was the dwelling place one had after death while awaiting resurrection.
4. What happened to the sun [42] is unclear.
5. Beating one's breast [48] is a Jewish expression of profound grief.

6. To a Jew, the Sabbath begins at sundown. For Luke's Gentile audience verse 54 emphasizes this.

7. Joseph's act is one of profound courage as well as empathy.

<u>Questions for Reflection</u>

1. On the cross, do you see Jesus as 'a man of sorrows'?

2. Do you see a real connection between Jesus' death on the cross and your own sins?

Knowing that You have forgiven me through Jesus' death on the cross, my heavenly Father, makes it easier to forgive others. I give my heart to You, as it is His sacrifice that unites me with His church. Grant that I may clearly see the path You've prepared for me, for Your way is always better. I am insignificant without You, but with You, everything is possible, and I pray in the name of Jesus. Amen.

<u>**History's Pivotal Event: Luke 24:1-12**</u>

NOW on the first day of the week, very early in the morning, they came to the sepulchre, bringing the spices which they prepared. (2) And they found the stone rolled away from the sepulchre. (3) And entering in, they found not the body of the Lord Jesus. (4) And it came to pass, that as they were much perplexed concerning this, behold two men stood by them in shining garments. (5) And they being afraid and bowing their faces to the earth, they said to them: Why seek ye the living among the dead? (6) He is not here, but is risen. Remember how he spoke to you when he was yet in Galilee, (7) saying: The Son of man must be delivered into the hands of sinful men, and be crucified, and on the third day rise again. (8) And they remembered his words. (9) And returning from the sepulchre, they reported all these things to the eleven, and to all the rest. (10) And it was Mary the Magdalene, and Joanna, and Mary the mother of James, and the other women with them, who said these things to the apostles. (11) And their words seemed to them as idle talk, and they believed them not.

(12) But Peter rose up, and ran to the sepulchre; and stooping down, he beholds the linen cloths lying by themselves; and he departed to his home, wondering at that which was come to pass.

<u>**Compare:**</u>
Matthew 28:1-10
Mark 16:1-8
John 20:1, 11-18

<u>**Notes**</u>
1. Verse 12 may not be part of the original manuscript of Luke and may be influenced by John's account.
2. Verse 6 apparently alludes to the larger circle of followers, rather than merely those gathered at the tomb.

<u>**Questions for Reflection**</u>
1. What seems to be Luke's attitude towards the women in this passage?

2. What information is not here (or elsewhere) regarding the first Easter that you wish was here?

<u>**Encounter on a Country Road: Luke 24:13-35**</u>

(13) And, behold, two of them were going on that same day to a village called Emmaus, distant sixty furlongs from Jerusalem. (14) And they were conversing together concerning all these things that had taken place. (15) And it came to pass, that while they were conversing and reasoning, Jesus himself drew near, and went with them. (16) But their eyes were holden that they should not know him.

(17) And he said to them: What communications are these, that ye have one with another, as ye walk, and are sad? (18) And one, whose name was Cleopas, answering said to him: Dost thou alone sojourn in Jerusalem and not know the things that have come to pass there in these days? (19) And he said to them: What things? And they said to him: The things concerning Jesus of Nazareth, who was a prophet mighty in deed and word before God and all the people; (20) and how the chief priests and our rulers delivered him up to be condemned to death, and crucified him. (21) But we were hoping that it was he who was to redeem Israel. But indeed, beside all this, to-day is the third day since these things were done. (22) Yea, and certain women also of our company made us astonished, who were early at the sepulchre; (23) and not finding his body, came saying, that they had also seen a vision of angels, who say that he is alive. (24) And some of those who were with us went away to the sepulchre, and found it even so as the women said; but him they saw not.

(25) Then he said to them: O foolish, and slow of heart to believe all that the prophets have spoken! (26)

Was it not necessary, that the Christ should suffer these things, and enter into his glory? (27) And beginning from Moses, and all the prophets, he explained to them in all the Scriptures the things concerning himself.

(28) And they drew near to the village, whither they were going; and he made as though he would go further. (29) But they constrained him, saying: Abide with us; for it is toward evening, and the day has declined. And he went in to abide with them.

(30) And it came to pass, that as he was reclining at table with them, he took bread, and blessed it, and breaking, gave to them. (31) And their eyes were opened, and they knew him; and he vanished out of their sight. (32) And they said one to another: Did not our heart burn within us, while he talked to us in the way, and while he opened to us the Scriptures?

(33) And rising up in the same hour, they returned to Jerusalem; and they found the eleven and those who were with them gathered together, (34) saying: The Lord is risen indeed, and he appeared to Simon. (35) And they related what things were done in the way, and how he became known by them in the breaking of bread.

Notes

1. Except for an oblique reference to this in Mark 16:12, which probably was not part of the original Mark manuscript, this passage is unique to Luke.
2. The conversation seems to center on the difference between differing perspectives on Jesus' identity.
3. Jewish scriptures are traditionally divided into three sections: the law, the prophets, and the writings.

Questions for Reflection

1. What are some possible explanation

2. s as to why they did not recognize Jesus at first?

3. Why do you think Luke see this conversation as important to his Gentile audience?

Sending Out Ambassadors: Luke 24:36-53

(36) And while they were speaking these things, he himself stood in the midst of them, and says to them: Peace be to you. (37) But they were terrified and affrighted, and supposed that they beheld a spirit. (38) And he said to them: Why are ye troubled? And wherefore do thoughts arise in your hearts? (39) See my hands and my feet, that it is I myself. Handle me, and see; for a spirit has not flesh and bones, as ye see me have. (40) And having said this, he showed them his hands and his feet. (41) And while they yet believed not for joy, and wondered, he said to them: Have ye here anything to eat? (42) And they gave him a piece of a broiled fish, and of a honeycomb. (43) And he took, and ate it before them. (44) And he said to them: These are my words which I spoke to you, while I was yet with you, that all things must be fulfilled, which are written in the law of Moses, and the prophets, and psalms, concerning me. (45) Then he opened their understanding, that they might understand the Scriptures. (46) And he said to them: Thus it is written, that the Christ should suffer, and should rise from the dead on the third day; (47) and that repentance and remission of sins should be preached in his name among all the nations, beginning at Jerusalem. (48) Ye are witnesses of these things.

(49) And, behold, I send forth the promise of my Father upon you. But do ye tarry in the city, until ye are endued with power from on high.

(50) And he led them out as far as to Bethany; and lifting up his hands, he blessed them. (51) And it came to pass, while he blessed them, that he parted from them, and was borne up into heaven. (52) And they, having worshiped him, returned to Jerusalem with great joy; (53) and were continually in the temple, praising and blessing God.

Compare:
John 20:19-23

Notes
1. It is important for the Christian community that Jesus is indeed not dead, and this passage supplies evidence.
2. One of the oldest heresies of the church was that Jesus? resurrection was merely of His spiritual body, and not a resurrection of His physical body. This passage, along with John's, goes to great lengths to refute that heresy.
3. Testimony of seeing the actual wounds serves to emphasize the idea that Jesus really did die.
4. This briefer account of Christ's ascension into heaven is redoubled in the first chapter of Acts, which is the 'second volume? by the same author.

Questions for Reflection
1. Why is it important for Luke's Gentile audience to know the Jewish scriptures affirming His identity at this point?

2. Why do you suppose He wanted them to wait in Jerusalem until they were anointed by the power of the Holy Spirit?

3. As Jesus reviews the message that these 'ambassadors' are to take to the nations, why is it important to your faith that you know this information well?

4. If you were waiting with the disciples in Jerusalem, what would be on your mind as you were waiting?

I humbly ask You to hear my prayer, divine loving God. Please keep my eyes open to where You're leading me. I know I always need Your forgiveness and grace. I'm in awe of You, and praise and worship You. Thank You for delivering another tomorrow, another chance, I pray in the name of the risen Savior and Lord, Jesus Christ. Amen.

The Acts of the Apostles

Experiences with the Risen Christ in the First Volume: Acts 1:1-5

THE former narration I made, O Theophilus, concerning all things that Jesus began both to do and to teach, (2) until the day when he was taken up, after he had given commandment, through the Holy Spirit, to the apostles whom he chose; (3) to whom also he showed himself living, after he had suffered, by many infallible proofs, during forty days appearing to them, and speaking the things concerning the kingdom of God.

(4) And, being assembled together with them, he commanded them not to depart from Jerusalem, but to wait for the promise of the Father, which ye heard from me; (5) for John indeed immersed in water; but ye shall be immersed in the Holy Spirit, not many days hence.

Compare:

Matthew 28:16-20
Mark 16:9-20
Luke 24:13-53
John 21
Also: 1 Corinthians 15:1-8

Notes

1. The author establishes that this is the second volume of a two-volume set, the first volume being the Gospel of Luke.
2. The name, Theophilus, means "lover of God." Since punctuation was not part of the original Greek text, it is possible that it is not a proper name, but that the book is addressed to anyone with that description.
3. In the original Greek, the term translated staying {4} could also be translated eating.
4. The idea of baptism by the Holy Spirit {5} was articulated by John the Baptist, but that same idea was also found in the Dead Sea Scrolls.
5. The scriptures listed for comparison offer examples of the convincing proofs {3}.

Questions for Reflection

1. Why do you think it may be important that the coming of the Holy Spirit is a "promise of the Father?"

2. Why do you suppose the writer wants to continue his testimony beyond the ascension of Jesus, when the other gospel writers do not?

Jesus Ascends into Heaven: Acts 1:6-11

(6) They therefore, having come together[1:6], asked him, saying: Lord, wilt thou at this time restore again the kingdom to Israel? (7) And he said to them: It is not yours to know times or seasons, which the Father appointed by his own authority[1:7]. (8) But ye shall receive power, when the Holy Spirit is come upon you; and ye shall be my witnesses both in Jerusalem, and in all Judaea, and Samaria, and unto the utmost part of the earth.

(9) And having spoken these things, while they beheld he was borne up, and a cloud received him out of their sight. (10) And while they were looking intently into heaven as he went, behold, two men stood by them in white apparel; (11) who also said: Men of Galilee, why stand ye looking into heaven? This Jesus, who was taken

up from you into heaven, shall so come in like manner as ye saw him going into heaven.

<u>Compare:</u>
Luke 24:50-51

<u>Notes</u>

1. Since Jesus is historically tied to King David, it was assumed that the Messiah would restore David's kingdom.
2. Whereas the term apostle had previously meant simply messenger or ambassador, here Jesus transforms the term to also mean a witness to His resurrection. Verses 21-22 will affirm this.

<u>Question for Reflection</u>

➢ Why is it important for the author to record Jesus' ascension into heaven?

<u>Renewal of the Twelve: Acts 1:12-26</u>

(12) Then they returned to Jerusalem from the mount called Olivet, which is near Jerusalem, a sabbath day's journey. (13) And when they came in, they went up into the upper room, where were abiding both Peter, and James, and John, and Andrew, Philip and Thomas, Bartholomew and Matthew, James the son of Alpheus, and Simon Zelotes, and Judas the brother of James. (14) These all continued with one accord in prayer, with women, and Mary the mother of Jesus, and his brothers.

(15) And in those days Peter stood up in the midst of the brethren, and said (the number of names together was about a hundred and twenty) : (16) Men, brethren, it was necessary that the scripture should be fulfilled, which the Holy Spirit by the mouth of David spoke before concerning Judas, who became guide to those who took Jesus. (17) Because he was numbered with us, and obtained the office of this ministry.--(18) Now this man purchased a field with the wages of iniquity; and falling headlong, he burst asunder in the midst, and all his bowels gushed out. (19) And it became known to all who dwell at Jerusalem; so that that field was called, in their own tongue, Aceldama, that is, Field of blood.--(20) For it is written in the book of Psalms:

Let his habitation be made desolate,

And let no one dwell therein.

And:

Let another take his office.

(21) Therefore, of these men, who accompanied us all the time that the Lord Jesus went in and out among us, (22) beginning from John's immersion, unto the day when he was taken up from us, must one be made a witness with us of his resurrection.

(23) And they appointed two, Joseph called Barsabas, who was surnamed Justus, and Matthias. (24) And they prayed, saying: Thou, Lord, who knowest the hearts of all, show which of these two thou didst choose, (25) that he may take part in this ministry and apostleship, from which Judas by transgression fell away, that he might go to his own place. (26) And they gave their lots[1:26]; and the lot fell upon Matthias; and he was numbered with the eleven apostles.

<u>Notes</u>

1. Casting lots was considered a legitimate way to determine God's will.
2. There seems to be a desire to restore the number in the inner circle to number of tribes of Israel.
3. The list of the eleven, although in a different order, is the same as that of Luke 6:14-16.

4. The term for Judas' suicide literally means to fall flat, but the original meaning may be lost in that Matthew 27:5 says that Judas hanged himself -- another kind of falling.

<u>Questions for Reflection</u>

1. What are some reasons the inner circle might feel the need to replace Judas?

2. What justification did they have to set up the initial requirements for a replacement?

3. Is it significant to you that they cast lots [like flipping a coin] to replace Judas?

> Gracious Father, the youngest apostle of Jesus, John, says You are love, and I love You. Your divine love flows steadily and dependably as You forgive your sheep. Help me to be kind and loving towards those outside my local church and help us lead them to Jesus. May you use me in Your way as I follow the footsteps of Your Son, Jesus. I pray in His name. Amen.

The Baptism of the Holy Spirit: Acts 2:1-13

AND when the day of Pentecost was fully come, they were all with one accord in one place. (2) And suddenly there came a sound out of heaven as of a rushing mighty wind, and it filled all the house where they were sitting. (3) And there appeared to them tongues as of fire, distributed among them; and it sat upon each of them. (4) And they were all filled with the Holy Spirit, and began to speak with other tongues, as the Spirit gave them utterance.

(5) Now there were dwelling in Jerusalem, Jews, devout men, from every nation under heaven. (6) And this being noised abroad[2:6], the multitude came together, and were confounded, because every man heard them speak in his own language. (7) And all were amazed, and wondered, saying one to another Behold, are not all these who speak Galilaeans? (8) And how do we hear, every man in our own tongue, wherein we were born, (9) Parthians and Medes and Elamites, and those who inhabit Mesopotamia, Judaea and Cappadocia, Pontus and Asia, (10) Phrygia and Pamphylia, Egypt and the parts of Libya about Cyrene, and strangers of Rome, both Jews and proselytes, (11) Cretes and Arabians, hear them speak in our tongues the wonderful works of God? (12) And all were amazed, and were in doubt, saying one to another: What may this mean? (13) But others mocking said: They are filled with sweet wine.

Compare:

Leviticus 23:15-21

Notes

1. Jewish tradition holds that the law [Torah] was given by Moses to the Israelites on the 50th day after Passover. Hence, the celebration of Pentecost
2. In John the Baptist's wilderness message he said that the Holy Spirit would come with fire.
3. The reference to other languages is the Greek term glossolalia. It refers to unintelligible speech. Luke might be making a comparison between this and the Tower of Babel in Genesis.

Questions for Reflection

1. Have you ever heard someone speaking in tongues as part of worship? If so, what did you think?

2. Do you think having the gift of tongues is a useful gift? How so?

3. Do you have another gift that you believe is empowered by the Holy Spirit that is at work within you? Please describe it and explain why you believe it is spirit-empowered.

Peter's Sermon: Acts 2:14-36

(14) But Peter, standing up with the eleven, lifted up his voice, and said to them: Men of Judaea, and all that dwell in Jerusalem, be this known to you, and hearken to my words. (15) For these are not drunken, as ye suppose, for it is the third hour of the day. (16) But this is what was spoken through the prophet Joel:

(17) And it shall be in the last days, saith God,

That I will pour out of my Spirit upon all flesh;

And your sons and your daughters shall prophesy,

And your young men shall see visions,

And your old men shall dream dreams;

(18) And even on my servants and on my handmaids,

I will pour out of my Spirit in those days,

And they shall prophesy.

(19) And I will show wonders in heaven above,

And signs in the earth beneath,

Blood, and fire, and vapor of smoke.

(20) The sun shall be turned into darkness,

And the moon into blood,

Before the great and notable day of the Lord shall come.

(21) And it shall be, that every one who shall call on the name of the Lord shall be saved.

(22) Men of Israel, hear these words! Jesus the Nazarene, a man accredited to you from God by miracles, and wonders, and signs, which God wrought by him in the midst of you, as ye yourselves know; (23) this man, delivered up according to the established counsel and foreknowledge of God, ye slew, crucifying him by the hand of lawless ones; (24) whom God raised up, having loosed the pains of death; because it was not possible that he should be held by it. (25) For David says concerning him:

I saw the Lord always before me;

Because he is on my right hand, that I should not be moved.

(26) For this my heart rejoiced, and my tongue exulted;

Moreover also my flesh shall rest in hope;

(27) Because thou wilt not abandon my soul to the underworld,

Nor wilt thou suffer thy Holy One to see corruption.

(28) Thou didst make known to me the ways of life;

Thou wilt make me full of joy with thy presence.

(29) Men, brethren, I may speak freely to you of the patriarch David, that he both died and was buried, and his sepulchre is among us unto this day. (30) Being a prophet, therefore, and knowing that God swore to him, with an oath, that of the fruit of his loins one should sit on his throne, (31) he, foreseeing, spoke of the resurrection of the Christ, that neither was his soul abandoned to the underworld, nor did his flesh see corruption.

(32) This Jesus God raised up, whereof we all are witnesses. (33) Being therefore exalted to the right hand of God, and having received from the Father the promise of the Holy Spirit, he poured forth this, which ye now see and hear. (34) For David did not ascend into heaven; but he says himself:

The Lord said to my Lord,

Sit on my right hand,

(35) Until I make thy foes thy footstool.

(36) Therefore let all the house of Israel know assuredly, that God made him, this Jesus whom ye crucified, both Lord and Christ.

Notes

1. Like other historians of his era, Luke includes speeches to establish the importance of the characters in his narrative.

2. Peter continues to be a primary spokesman for the witnesses to the resurrection.

3. The phrase 'In the last days' Peter adds to his quotation of Joel 2:28-32.

4. Notice that the crucifixion of Jesus by Jews and Gentiles is portrayed as part of an overall plan.

5. That Jesus was 'exalted' refers to the ascension.

6. In quoting the Psalms (34-35) , early Christian preaching saw such passages as referring to Jesus as well as to David.

Questions for Reflection

1. In what ways does Peter sound convincing to you?

2. Other than being shorter, how is this sermon different from the ones you have typically heard in your community of faith?

The Call to Repentance: Acts 2:37-41

(37) And hearing this, they were pierced to the heart, and said to Peter and the rest of the apostles: Men, brethren, what shall we do? (38) And Peter said to them: Repent, and be each of you immersed, upon the name of Jesus Christ, unto remission of sins, and ye shall receive the gift of the Holy Spirit. (39) For the promise is to you, and to your children, and to all those afar off, as many as the Lord our God shall have called.

(40) And with many other words did he bear witness and exhort, saying: Save yourselves from this perverse generation.

(41) They therefore, having received[2:41] his word, were immersed and on that day there were added about three thousand souls.

Notes

1. Verses 37-41 form a call to repentance. First century preaching was designed to lead the listener to ask, 'What must I do to be saved'? In most of the preaching since Martin Luther, the preachers have answered the question without being asked.

2. Here, the gift of the Holy Spirit follows baptism, but there is variety elsewhere.

3. Verse 39 quotes Isaiah 57:19 and Joel 2:32.

4. The phrase, 'all who are far away' indicates that from the beginning he understood the universal nature of the church.

5. Three thousand people being added to the church's numbers illustrates the power of the Holy Spirit in Peter's sermon.

Questions for Reflection

1. What are some reasons you think Peter's sermon was so powerful?

2. Do you think this type of sermon reaches the hearts of people today?

3. In your community of faith, is a call to repentance often heard, either in routine worship or in other gatherings? Do you think this is important? If so, why?

Community Life: Acts 2:42-47

(42) And they were constantly attending on the teaching of the apostles, and the distribution, and the breaking of bread, and prayers. (43) And fear came upon every soul; and many wonders and signs were wrought through the apostles. (44) And all that believed were together, and had all things common; (45) and sold their possessions and goods, and divided them among all, as any one had need. (46) And daily attending with one accord in the temple, and breaking bread from house to house, they partook of food with gladness and singleness of heart, (47) praising God, and having favor with all the people. And the Lord added to the church daily those who are saved.

Notes

1. The breaking of bread meant both a common meal and the Lord's supper. It was common to all gatherings for worship.
2. When signs and wonders were performed it was both a fulfillment of the prophet Joel and a fulfillment of the work of Jesus.
3. At this point the growing number of followers are all devout Jews who remain close to the Temple.

Questions for Reflection

1. Is it important to you how often do you want to share in the Lord's supper with other believers? Why?

2. Have you witnessed signs and wonders being performed? If so, give examples.

> Out of Your divine love, heavenly Father, You have made my voice, so now I sing Your praises in public worship. For wasting Your gifts, and forgetting Your divine love and gifts of ministry, have mercy on me. I pray faithful leaders will emerge to do needed ministries with the gifts you have provided. I offer my heart as I pray in Jesus' name. Amen.

Peter Heals at the Temple: Acts 3:1-10

AND Peter and John were going up together into the temple at the hour of prayer, being the ninth hour. (2) And a certain man lame from his mother's womb was carried along, whom they laid daily at the gate of the temple, the one called Beautiful, to ask alms of those entering into the temple; (3) who, seeing Peter and John about to go into the temple, asked alms. (4) And Peter, looking intently upon him, with John, said: Look upon us. (5) And he gave heed to them, expecting to receive something from them. (6) And Peter said: Silver and gold have I none; but what I have, that I give thee. In the name of Jesus Christ, the Nazarene, rise up and walk. (7) And seizing him by the right hand, he raised him up. And immediately his feet and ankles received strength; (8) and leaping forth, he stood, and walked, and entered with them into the temple, walking, and leaping, and praising God. (9) And all the people saw him walking and praising God; (10) and they recognized him, that this was he who sat for alms at the beautiful gate of the temple; and they were filled with wonder and amazement at that which had happened to him.

Notes

1. The apostles seem to center their activity in the Temple so as to follow through on the work of Jesus. Note that so far John is still in the area and appears with Peter.
2. The Beautiful Gate was probably the gate made of Corinthian bronze on the east side of the Temple.
3. Reference to the name of Jesus and its use is an important concept of the Book of Acts, as will be seen later.
4. Afternoon sacrifices were offered at three in the afternoon.

Questions for Reflection

1. When you're talking with someone who needs healing, do you offer to pray with them then and there

2. When you hear about someone who needs healing, do you want to be a healer? Why? Do you pray?

3. Do beggars often get what they want? Do they get what they need?

Peter Offers an Explanation: Acts 3:11-26

(11) And as he held fast to Peter and John, all the people ran together to them in the porch that is called Solomon's, greatly wondering. (12) And Peter, seeing it, answered to the people: Men of Israel, why wonder ye at this? Or why look ye so intently on us, as though by our own power or godliness we had made this man to walk? (13) The God of Abraham, and of Isaac, and of Jacob, the God of our fathers, glorified his servant Jesus; whom ye delivered up, and denied him in the presence of Pilate, when he decided to release him. (14) But ye denied the Holy and Just, and demanded that a murderer should be granted to you. (15) But the Author of life ye killed; whom God raised from the dead, whereof we are witnesses[3:15]. (16) And his name, upon the faith in his name, made this man strong, whom ye see and know; and the faith, which is through Him, gave him this perfect soundness in the presence of you all.

(17) And now, brethren, I know that ye acted in ignorance, as also your rulers. (18) But thus God fulfilled what he before announced by the mouth of all his prophets, that the Christ should suffer. (19) Repent therefore, and turn, that your sins may be blotted out, in order that the times of refreshing may come from the presence of

the Lord; (20) and that he may send forth Jesus Christ, before appointed for you; (21) whom the heavens, indeed, must receive, until the times of the restoration of all things, which God spoke of by the mouth of all his holy prophets from the beginning. (22) Moses said: A Prophet will the Lord your God raise up to you of your brethren, like unto me; him shall ye hear in all things whatever he shall say to you. (23) And it shall be that every soul, that will not hear that Prophet, shall be utterly destroyed from among the people. (24) And also all the prophets from Samuel, both he and they who followed, as many as spoke, also foretold these days.

(25) Ye are sons of the prophets, and of the covenant which God made with our fathers, saying to Abraham: And in thy seed shall all the nations of the earth be blessed. (26) Unto you first, God, having raised up his servant Jesus, sent him to bless you, in turning away every one of you from your iniquities.

Notes

1. Solomon's Portico is located by the Roman historian Josephus as being on the east side of the Temple.
2. The murderer referred to is Barabbas.
3. The word translated 'author' can also mean pioneer, founder, or leader.
4. Notice the reference to Jesus' name again.

Questions for Reflection

1. What do you think Peter meant when he said they acted in ignorance?

2. When Peter says that that Jesus was sent 'first' to them, what did he mean?

> I need your grace to help me forgive myself for past mistakes. It is wonderful to be divinely loved by You, Lord. Thank you for giving me more chances. I offer all that I am through my prayer support for those in my community of faith in the power of Jesus' name. Amen.

Arrested and Released: Acts 4:1-22

AND while they were speaking to the people, the priests, and the captain of the temple, and the Sadducees, came upon them, (2) being indignant because they taught the people, and announced in Jesus the resurrection from the dead. (3) And they laid hands on them, and put them in prison unto the morrow; for it was now evening.

(4) But many of those who heard the word believed; and the number of the men became about five thousand.

(5) And it came to pass on the morrow, that their rulers, and elders, and scribes, (6) and Annas the high priest, and Caiaphas, and John, and Alexander, and as many as were of the kindred of the high priest, were gathered together unto Jerusalem. (7) And having set them in the midst, they asked: By what power, or by what name, did ye do this?

(8) Then Peter, filled with the Holy Spirit, said to them: Rulers of the people, and elders of Israel; (9) if we are this day examined in respect to a good deed done to an impotent man, by what means this person has been made whole; (10) be it known to you all, and to all the people of Israel, that by the name of Jesus Christ the Nazarene, whom ye crucified, whom God raised from the dead, by him does this man stand here before you whole. (11) He is the stone that was set at naught by you the builders, which is become the head of the corner. (12) And there is salvation in no other; for neither is there any other name under heaven, that is given among men, in which we must be saved.

(13) And seeing the boldness of Peter and John, and perceiving that they were unlearned and obscure men, they wondered; and they recognized them, that they were with Jesus. (14) And beholding the man who had been healed standing with them, they had nothing to say against it. (15) But having commanded them to go aside out of the council, they conferred among themselves, (16) saying: What shall we do to these men? For that a notorious miracle has been done by them is manifest to all that dwell in Jerusalem, and we are not able to deny it. (17) But that it spread no further among the people, let us strictly threaten them, that they speak henceforth to no man in this name. (18) And having called them, they commanded them not to speak at all, nor teach, in the name of Jesus.

(19) But Peter and John answering said to them: Whether it is right in the sight of God to hearken to you rather than to God, judge ye. (20) For we can not but speak the things which we saw and heard.

(21) And they, having further threatened them, let them go, finding no way to punish them, on account of the people, because all glorified God for that which was done; (22) for the man was above forty years old, on whom this sign of the healing had been wrought.

Notes

1. The captain of the Temple was the officer in charge of the Temple police.
2. The Sadducees were composed of both priestly and lay nobility who did not believe in the resurrection of the dead.
3. The mention of the five thousand illustrates the rapid growth of the church after the first Easter. This theme is often mentioned in conjunction with opposition to the Christian community.
4. The phrase, 'no other name' is the answer to the question that prompts the sermon.
5. The boldness of uneducated and typical people is a constant theme in Acts.

Questions for Reflection

1. How often have you had to defend your faith? What did you say?

2.   Do you sense power in the name of Jesus today? If so, describe it.

3.   How bold are you in expressing your faith?

Community Prayer: Acts 4:23-31

(23) And being dismissed, they went to their own company, and reported all that the chief priests and elders said to them. (24) And they, hearing it, lifted up their voice to God with one accord, and said: Lord, thou art he who made heaven, and earth, and the sea, and all things in them; (25) who by the mouth of thy servant David said:

Why did the heathen rage,

And the peoples imagine vain things?

(26) The kings of the earth stood near,

And the rulers assembled together,

Against the Lord, and against his Christ.

(27) For in truth there assembled in this city, against thy holy servant Jesus, whom thou didst anoint, both Herod, and Pontius Pilate, with the Gentiles, and the peoples of Israel, (28) to do whatever thy hand and thy counsel before determined to be done. (29) And now, Lord, behold their threatenings; and grant to thy servants, that with all boldness they may speak thy word, (30) by stretching forth thy hand for healing, and that signs and wonders may be wrought through the name of thy holy servant Jesus. (31) And when they had prayed, the place was shaken where they were assembled; and they were all filled with the Holy Spirit, and they spoke the word of God with boldness.

Notes

1.   The quotations are of Psalms 146:6 and 2:1-2.
2.   The plea, 'look at their threats,' is a request to shield them from harm.

Questions for Reflection

1.   Have you ever felt something physical after a prayer so that you knew your prayer had been heard?

2.   If the earth moved under your feet after a prayer, how would you react?

> Gracious God, You hold the future through Jesus, my Savior. Help me strain out the truth from the waterfall of words coming from the media. Thank You for hearing all my prayers and answering out of Your kindness and mercy. Your Son shed his blood to wash away my many sins, saving me. My Father, I am Yours, and I always want to serve You Your way. I pray through Jesus, amen.

Community Sharing: Acts 4:32-5:11

(32) And the multitude of those who believed were of one heart and of one soul; and not one said that aught of the things which he possessed was his own, but they had all things common. (33) And with great power the apostles gave the testimony to the resurrection of the Lord Jesus; and great grace was upon them all. (34) For there was no one among them that lacked; for as many as were possessors of lands or houses sold them, and brought the prices of the things sold, (35) and laid them at the feet of the apostles; and distribution was made to each one, according as he had need.

(36) And Joseph, who by the apostles was surnamed Barnabas (which is interpreted, Son of consolation) , a Levite, born in Cyprus, (37) having land sold it, and brought the money, and laid it at the feet of the apostles.

Acts 5.

BUT a certain man named Ananias, with Sapphira his wife, sold a possession, (2) and kept back part of the price, his wife also being aware of it, and brought a certain part, and laid it at the feet of the apostles. (3) But Peter said: Ananias, why did Satan fill thy heart, that thou shouldst lie to the Holy Spirit, and keep back part of the price of the land? (4) While it remained, was it not thine own? And after it was sold, was it not in thine own power? Why didst thou conceive this thing in thy heart? Thou didst not lie to men, but to God. (5) And Ananias hearing these words fell down, and expired; and great fear came on all that heard these things. (6) And the young men arose, wrapt him up, and carried him out[5:6], and buried him.

(7) And it was about the space of three hours after, when his wife, not knowing what was done, came in. (8) And Peter answered her: Tell me, whether ye sold the land for so much? And she said: Yes, for so much. (9) And Peter said to her: Why is it that ye agreed together to tempt the Spirit of the Lord? Behold, the feet of those who buried thy husband are at the door, and shall carry thee out. (10) And immediately she fell at his feet, and expired; and coming in, the young men found her dead, and carried her forth, and buried her by her husband.

(11) And great fear came upon all the church, and upon all that heard these things.

Notes

1. The communal sharing of all their goods was an ideal of the early church.
2. Barnabas later becomes Paul's missionary companion. The name means 'son of encouragement.?
3. In Acts the church is a representative of the Holy Spirit, which in turn is in opposition to evil.
4. The deception of Ananias and Sapphira becomes a sin when they portray their donation as representing everything they had.

<u>**Questions for Reflection**</u>

1. Do you think that today's churches would be stronger if they shared more of their earthly possessions with one another?

2. How are you both a giver and receiver of encouragement?

3. Is there hypocrisy in today's church that is as evil as that of Ananias and Sapphira?

<u>**Miracles: Acts 5:12-16**</u>

(12) And by the hands of the apostles were many signs and wonders wrought among the people; and they were all with one accord in Solomon's porch. (13) But of the rest no one dared to join himself to them; but the people honored them; (14) (and still more were believers added to the Lord, multitudes both of men and women) ; (15) so that along the streets they brought forth the sick, and laid them on beds and pallets, that, as Peter was passing, the shadow at least might overshadow some one of them. (16) And the multitude also of the cities around came together to Jerusalem, bringing sick persons, and those who were vexed by unclean spirits; and they were all healed.

<u>**Notes**</u>

1. For the first time, Christians are now seen by the public as a well-defined group.
2. Peter is acknowledged even by non-Christians as the leader.

<u>**Questions for Reflection**</u>

1. Do you think that non-believers see you as part of the Christian community? Why would they?

2. Do those within the Christian community recognize the depth of your faith? Why do they?

<u>**Another Arrest: Acts 5:17-42**</u>

(17) But the high priest rose up, and all that were with him, which is the sect of the Sadducees, and were filled with indignation, (18) and laid their hands on the apostles, and put them in the public prison.

(19) But an angel of the Lord by night opened the prison doors; and having brought them forth, he said: (20) Go, stand and speak in the temple to the people all the words of this life. (21) And hearing it, they went into the temple at early dawn, and taught.

And the high priest came, and they that were with him, and called the council together, and all the eldership of the children of Israel, and sent to the prison to have them brought. (22) But the officers, when they came, found them not in the prison; and returning, they reported, (23) saying: The prison indeed we found shut with all security, and the keepers standing without before the doors; but when we opened them, we found no one within.

(24) And when the priest and the captain of the temple and the chief priests heard these things, they were at a loss concerning them, to what this might grow. (25) But one came and told them, saying: Behold, the men whom ye put in the prison are in the temple, standing and teaching the people. (26) Then went the captain with the officers, and brought them, not with violence (for they feared the people) , that they might not be stoned. (27) And having brought them, they set them before the council. And the high priest asked them, (28) saying: Did we not strictly command you not to teach in this name? And, behold, ye have filled Jerusalem with your teaching, and intend to bring this man's blood upon us.

(29) And Peter answering, and the apostles, said: We ought to obey God rather than men. (30) The God of our fathers raised up Jesus, whom ye slew, hanging him on a tree. (31) Him, as a prince and a Savior, did God exalt to his right hand, to give repentance to Israel, and remission of sins. (32) And we are his witnesses of these things, and the Holy Spirit also, which God gave to those who obey him.

(33) And they, hearing it, were convulsed with rage, and took counsel to slay them. (34) But there stood up one in the council, a Pharisee, named Gamaliel, a teacher of the law, honored by all the people, and commanded to put the men forth a little while; (35) and said to them: Men of Israel, take heed to yourselves, what ye are about to do in respect to these men. (36) For before these days arose Theudas, boasting himself to be somebody; to whom a number of men, about four hundred, joined themselves; who was slain, and all, as many as obeyed him, were scattered and brought to naught. (37) After this man arose Judas the Galilaean, in the days of the registering, and drew away much people after him; he also perished, and all, as many as obeyed him, were dispersed. (38) And now I say to you, refrain from these men, and let them alone; for if this counsel or this work be of men, it will come to naught; (39) but if it is of God ye can not overthrow them; lest haply ye be found also fighting against God.

(40) And to him they assented; and having called the apostles, they scourged them, and commanded them not to speak in the name of Jesus, and let them go.

(41) They therefore went rejoicing from the presence of the council, because for that name they were counted worthy to suffer shame. (42) And every day, in the temple, and from house to house, they ceased not to teach, and to publish the glad tidings of Jesus the Christ.

Notes

1. Obeying God rather than people is presented to the council.
2. The reference to the 'tree' or cross is seen in Deuteronomy 21:22-23.
3. Verse 31 is a one-sentence summary of the theology of the Book of Acts.
4. Gamaliel, the elder/leader pharisee, is later identified as the Apostle Paul's teacher.
5. According to Josephus, the Roman historian, Theudas raised his revolt some years after this speech. The statement seems to be a comment made by Luke in the speech. Quotation marks were not part of the manuscript.
6. Judas the Galilean was a revolutionary leader who opposed new taxes during the time of Quirinius, who was Ceasar at the time of Christ's birth.

Questions for Reflection

1. When someone makes a statement about what God is up to regarding the future, do you think about the 'prophet's' qualifications?

2. How often are you aware of prophecies being fulfilled?

Lord God, you usually speak to me in silence and seldom use thunder or physical gestures. I want to pay attention when you speak to me in your way for your glory. Please help me to know your ways. In the power of Jesus' name, I pray. Amen.

Choosing Seven: Acts 6:1-7

AND in these days, when the number of the disciples was multiplied, there arose a murmuring of the Grecian Jews against the Hebrews, because their widows were neglected in the daily ministration. (2) And the twelve called the multitude of the disciples to them, and said: It is not proper that we should leave the word of God, and serve tables. (3) Therefore, brethren, look ye out among you seven men of good repute, full of the Holy Spirit and of wisdom, whom we will appoint over this business. (4) But we will give ourselves to prayer, and to the ministry of the word.

(5) And the saying pleased the whole multitude. And they chose Stephen, a man full of faith and of the Holy Spirit, and Philip, and Prochorus, and Nicanor, and Timon, and Parmenas, and Nicolas a proselyte of Antioch, (6) whom they set before the apostles; and having prayed, they laid their hands on them.

(7) And the word of God increased; and the number of the disciples multiplied in Jerusalem greatly; and a great company of the priests were obedient to the faith.

Notes

1. Tradition says that these are the first deacons, but there is no sense of ecclesiastical office here.
2. Outside of the gospel accounts, the group of twelve are only referred to here in Acts.
3. All the names here are Greek.
4. The term proselyte here refers to converts to Judaism. At this point, the Christian community sees itself as an extension of Judaism.
5. The laying on of hands is a ritual of consecration and historically implied the transfer of nephesh, the life force seen as part of all living things.

Questions for Reflection

1. Do you see yourself as one of God's servants? Why?

2. What are some things you do where you are conscious of serving God as you do them?

The Arrest of Stephen: Acts 6:8-7:1

(8) And Stephen, full of grace and of power, did great wonders and signs among the people. (9) And there arose certain ones of the synagogue so called of the Freedmen[6:9], and Cyrenians, and Alexandrians, and of those from Cilicia and Asia, disputing with Stephen. (10) And they were not able to resist the wisdom and the spirit with which he spoke. (11) Then they suborned men, who said: We have heard him speak blasphemous words against Moses, and against God.

(12) And they stirred up the people, and the elders, and the scribes; and coming upon him, they seized him, and brought him to the council, (13) and set up false witnesses, Who said: This man ceases not to speak words against this holy place, and the law. (14) For we have heard him say, that this Jesus the Nazarene will destroy this place, and will change the customs which Moses delivered to us. (15) And all that sat in the council, looking intently upon him, saw his face as the face of an angel.

Acts 7

AND the high priest said: Are then these things so?

<u>Notes</u>

1. Stephen performs miracles just as the Apostles do.
2. 'Freedmen' is found in an inscription found in Jerusalem that some think refers to this synagogue. The term refers to former slaves, both Jews and proselytes.
3. Cyrenians are from Cyrene in northern Africa. Celicia, the Apostle Paul's home province, was the southeastern portion of Asia Minor. Here 'Asia' refers to Rome's western province in Asia Minor.
4. The change in customs is found in Mark 14:55-57.

<u>Question for Reflection</u>

➤ If you were being questioned about your faith by people who had the authority to execute you, would you be bold in the way in which you respond?

Stephen's Speech and Lynching: Acts 7:2-8:1a

(2) And he said: Brethren, and fathers, hearken. The God of glory appeared to our father Abraham, when he was in Mesopotamia, before he dwelt in Haran, (3) and said to him: Go forth from thy country, and from thy kindred, and come into the land which I shall show thee. (4) Then he went forth from the land of the Chaldaeans, and dwelt in Haran; and from thence, after his father was dead, he caused him to remove into this land, wherein ye now dwell. (5) And he gave him no inheritance in it, not even a foot-breadth; and he promised to give it to him for a possession, and to his seed after him, when he had no child. (6) And God spoke after this manner, that his seed shall be a sojourner in a strange land, and they will bring them into bondage, and afflict them four hundred years. (7) And the nation to whom they shall be in bondage I will judge, said God; and after that they shall come forth, and shall serve me in this place. (8) And he gave him the covenant of circumcision; and thus he begot Isaac, and circumcised him the eighth day, and Isaac, Jacob, and Jacob the twelve patriarchs. (9) And the patriarchs, moved with envy, sold Joseph into Egypt. And God was with him, (10) and delivered him out of all his afflictions, and gave himfavor and wisdom in the sight of Pharaoh king of Egypt; and he made him governor over Egypt and all his house.

(11) And there came a famine over all the land of Egypt and Canaan, and a great affliction; and our fathers found no sustenance. (12) But Jacob, hearing that there was grain in Egypt, first sent out our fathers. (13) And at the second time, Joseph was recognized by his brothers; and the race of Joseph was made known to Pharaoh. (14) Then Joseph sent, and called for Jacob his father, and all his kindred, threescore and fifteen souls. (15) And Jacob went down into Egypt, and died, he and our fathers, (16) and were removed to Shechem, and laid in the tomb that Abraham bought for a sum of money of the sons of Hamor, the father of Shechem.

(17) But as the time of the promise drew near, which God declared to Abraham, the people grew and multiplied in Egypt, (18) until another king arose who knew not Joseph. (19) He, dealing subtly with our race, afflicted our fathers, so that they should cast out their infants, that they might not be preserved alive. (20) In which time Moses was born, and was exceeding fair[7:20], who was nourished three months in his father's house. (21) And when he was cast out, Pharaoh's daughter took him up, and nourished him for herself as a son.

(22) And Moses was instructed in all the wisdom of the Egyptians, and was mighty in words and in deeds. (23) And when he was forty years old, it came into his heart to visit his brethren the sons of Israel. (24) And seeing one of them suffer wrong, he defended him, and avenged the one oppressed by smiting the Egyptian. (25) For he supposed his brethren would understand, that God by his hand would deliver them; but they understood not. (26) And on the following day he showed himself to them as they were contending, and urged them to peace, saying: Ye are brethren; why wrong ye one another? (27) But he who was wronging his neighbor thrust him away, saying: Who made thee a ruler and a judge over us? (28) Wilt thou kill me, as thou didst kill the Egyptian yesterday? (29) And Moses fled at this saying, and became a sojourner in the land of Midian, where he begot two sons. (30) And when forty years were completed, there appeared to him in the wilderness of the mount Sinai an angel in a flame of fire, in a bush. (31) And Moses, seeing it, wondered at the sight; and as he drew near to behold it, the voice of the Lord came to him, saving: (32) I am the God of thy fathers, the God of Abraham, and the God of Isaac, and the God of Jacob. And Moses trembled, and durst not behold. (33) And the Lord said to him: Loose the sandals from thy feet; for the place where thou standest is holy ground. (34) Truly, I saw the affliction of my people in Egypt, and I heard their groaning, and came down to deliver them. And now come, I will send thee into Egypt. (35) This Moses whom they denied, saying: Who made thee a ruler and a judge? him did God send as a ruler and a redeemer by the hand[7:35] of the angel who appeared to him in the bush. (36) He brought them out, working wonders and signs in the land of Egypt, and in the Red sea, and in the wilderness forty years.

(37) This is the Moses who said to the children of Israel: A Prophet will God raise up to you of your brethren, like unto. (38) This is he who was in the congregation in the wilderness with the angel who spoke to him in the mount Sinai, and with our fathers; who received the living oracles to give to us; (39) to whom our fathers would not be obedient, but thrust him from them, and in their hearts turned back again into Egypt, (40) saying to Aaron: Make us gods who shall go before us; for as for this Moses, who brought us out of the land of Egypt, we know not what is become of him.

(41) And they made a calf in those days, and offered sacrifice to the idol, and rejoiced in the works of their own hands. (42) And God turned away, and gave them up to worship the host of heaven; as it is written in

the book of the prophets:

> Did ye offer to me slain beasts and sacrifices,

> Forty years in the wilderness, O house of Israel?

> (43) And ye took up the tabernacle of Moloch,

> And the star of the god Remphan,

> The figures which ye made to worship them;

> And I will carry you away beyond Babylon.

(44) Our fathers had the tabernacle of the testimony in the wilderness, as he who spoke to Moses commanded, that he should make it according to the pattern that he had seen; (45) which also our fathers received, and brought in with Joshua into the possession of the heathen, whom God drove out before our fathers, unto the days of David; (46) who found favor before God, and asked that he might find a habitation for the God of Jacob. (47) But Solomon built a house for him. (48) Yet the Most High dwells not in temples made with hands; as says the prophet:

> (49) Heaven is my throne,

> And the earth is my footstool.

> What house will ye build for me, saith the Lord;

> Or what is my place of rest?

> (50) Did not my hand make all these things?

(51) Stiff-necked, and uncircumcised in heart and ears! Ye always resist the Holy Spirit; as your fathers did, so do ye. (52) Which of the prophets did not your fathers persecute? And they slew those who announced beforehand concerning the coming of the Just One; of whom ye have now become the betrayers and murderers; (53) who received the law as the ordinances of angels, and kept it not.

(54) Hearing these things, they were enraged in their hearts, and gnashed their teeth against him. (55) But, being full of the Holy Spirit, he looked intently into heaven, and saw the glory of God, and Jesus standing on the right hand of God, and said: (56) Behold, I see the heavens opened, and the Son of man standing on the right hand of God. (57) And crying out with a loud voice, they stopped their ears, and rushed upon him with one accord; (58) and having cast him out of the city, they stoned him. And the witnesses laid off their garments at the feet of a young man named Saul, (59) and stoned Stephen, calling and saying: Lord Jesus, receive my spirit. (60) And kneeling down, he cried with a loud voice: Lord, lay not this sin to their charge. And saying this, he fell asleep.

Acts 8

AND Saul was consenting to his death.

Notes

1. Stephen's speech contains about thirty references to the Septuagint, the Greek translation of Jewish scripture.
2. The book of the twelve minor prophets, Hosea through Malachi, was seen as a unit by Jewish scholars.
3. 'Made with human hands' was a phrase associated with idolatry in the Hebrew Bible.
4. Stephen seems to be the victim of a lynching, but since there were witnesses who were legally required to cast the first stone, the implication is that of a legal execution.

Questions for Reflection

1. Can you effectively quote scriptures to defend your faith like Stephen did?

2.   Are you willing to die for your beliefs if necessary? Why?

Divine Heavenly Father, when I thirst for You, I find Your Living Water, Jesus, and I praise You for His presence. I need Your salvation in Jesus' blood that was shed for me. Help me to be kind like Jesus amid difficult people. They challenge me to live out my faith and declare what I believe honestly. I am Yours through Jesus and pray in the power of His name. Amen.

The Good News Spreads: Acts 8:1b-8

And on that day there arose a great persecution against the church which was at Jerusalem; and all were scattered abroad throughout the regions of Judaea and Samaria, except the apostles. (2) And devout men carried Stephen to his burial, and made great lamentation over him. (3) But Saul laid waste the church, entering house after house, and dragging both men and women, committed them to prison.

(4) They, therefore, that were scattered, went abroad, preaching the word. (5) And Philip went down to the city[8:5] of Samaria, and preached to them the Christ. (6) And the multitudes with one accord gave heed to the things said by Ph ilip, when they heard, and saw the signs which he wrought. (7) For out of many who had unclean spirits they went forth, crying with loud voice; and many that were palsied, and that were lame, were healed. (8) And there was great joy in that city.

Notes

1. At this point the good news now begins reaching into non-Jewish parts of the world.
2. Samaria was located between Judea on the south and Galilee on the north. It was occupied by remnants of the northern tribes, and they used the Pentateuch for scripture. The Jews despised them.
3. It seems ironic that Jewish persecution of the church led to its moving into the rest of the world.

Questions for Reflection

1. Can you think of modern examples of how persecution of the church has strengthened it?

2. Would you go into an area hostile to your faith to spread the good news?

Distinguishing Magic from Miracles: Acts 8:9-25

(9) But a certain man, named Simon, was in the city before, using sorcery, and bewitching the people of Samaria, saying that he was some great one; (10) to whom all gave heed, from the least to the greatest, saying: This man is the great power of God[8:10]. (11) And to him they gave heed, because for a long time they were bewitched by his sorceries. (12) But when they believed Philip publishing the good news concerning the kingdom of God and the name of Jesus Christ, they were immersed, both men and women. (13) And Simon also himself believed; and having been immersed, he continued with Philip, and wondered, beholding the miracles and signs which were wrought.

(14) And the apostles in Jerusalem, hearing that Samaria has received the word of God, sent to them Peter and John; (15) who, having come down, prayed for them, that they might receive the Holy Spirit; (16) for he had not yet fallen upon any of them; but they had only been immersed in the name of the Lord Jesus. (17) Then they laid their hands on them, and they received the Holy Spirit.

(18) And Simon, seeing that through the laying on of the apostles' hands the Holy Spirit was given, offered them money, (19) saying: Give me also this power, that on whomsoever I lay hands, he may receive the Holy Spirit. (20) But Peter said to him: Thy money perish with thee; because thou didst think to obtain the gift of God with money: (21) Thou hast no part nor lot in this matter; for thy heart is not right in the sight of God. (22) Repent therefore of this thy wickedness, and pray the Lord, if perhaps the thought of thy heart shall be forgiven thee. (23) For I perceive that thou art in the gall of bitterness, and the bond of iniquity.

(24) And Simon answering, said: Pray ye to the Lord for me, that none of the things which ye have spoken come upon me.

(25) They, therefore, having testified and spoken the word of the Lord, were returning to Jerusalem, and publishing the good news to many villages of the Samaritans.

<u>Compare:</u>

Acts 13:6-12

Acts 19:13-20

<u>Notes</u>

1. This is the first of three instances in Acts where there is careful distinction between magic and miracles.
2. Philip breaks down religious barriers and fulfills expectations for Samaritans established in Luke. (Luke 10:30-37 and Luke 17:11-19)
3. The medieval crime of 'simony' (trying to buy a church office) is derived from this scripture.

<u>Questions for Reflection</u>

1. Do you understand that magic sometimes involve the occult? Explain why.

2. In the larger sense are miracles a kind of magic, in the sense of the mysteries of God?

<u>Philip's Witness: Acts 8:26-40</u>

(26) But an angel of the Lord spoke to Philip, saying: Arise, and go down to the south, to the way that goes down from Jerusalem to Gaza. This is desert.

(27) And he arose and went. And behold, a man of Ethiopia, a eunuch, an officer of state of Candace queen of the Ethiopians, who was over all her treasure, and had come to Jerusalem to worship, (28) was returning, and sitting in his chariot; and he was reading the prophet Isaiah. (29) And the Spirit said to Philip: Go near, and join thyself to this chariot. (30) And Philip ran thither, and heard him reading Isaiah the prophet. And he said: Understandest thou then what thou art reading? (31) And he said: How could I, except some one should guide me? And he entreated Philip to come up, and sit with him.

(32) And the contents of the Scripture which he was reading was this:

He was led as a sheep to the slaughter;

And as a lamb dumb before his shearer,

So he opens not his mouth.

(33) In his humiliation his judgment was taken away;

And his generation[8:33] who shall fully declare?

For his life is taken away from the earth.

(34) And the eunuch answering said to Philip: I pray thee, of whom does the prophet speak this? Of himself, or of some other man? (35) And Philip opened his mouth, and beginning from this Scripture, made known to him the good news of Jesus. (36) And as they went along the way, they came to a certain water. And the eunuch said: See, here is water; what hinders that I should be immersed? (37) [8:37]And Philip said: If thou believest with all thy heart, thou mayest. And answering he said: I believe that Jesus Christ is the Son of God. (38) And he commanded that the chariot should stop. And they went down both into the water, both Philip and the eunuch; and he immersed him. (39) And when they came up out of the water, the Spirit of the Lord caught

away Philip; and the eunuch saw him no more, for he went on his way rejoicing. (40) But Philip was found at Azotus; and passing through, he published the good news to all the cities, till he came to Caesarea.

<u>**Notes**</u>

1. Candace was the title given to the queen of the Ethiopians.
2. Since a eunuch could not become a proselyte, this passage evidently envisions fulfillment of Isaiah 56:3-5.
3. Reading scriptures aloud was customary in the ancient world, so Philip heard him. He is reading Isaiah 53:7-8.
4. The baptism of the Ethiopian eunuch breaks both social and ritual barriers. Ethiopia was considered to be located 'at the ends of the Earth.'
5. Philip's journey proceeds from Gaza through Azotus (modern Ashdod) to Caesarea, the location of the Roman governor and an important seaport.

<u>**Questions for Reflection**</u>

1. Have you ever witnessed a person's conversion firsthand? If so, please describe it.

2. What are your feelings about leading people to Christ? Do you have a desire to do so? Why

I am surrendered to You, Gracious God, just as I am. I need your help to create, grow, and multiply more faithful disciples who are born again. I am relying on You to save me from my sins, Lord Jesus. I am grateful for the opportunity to serve You in Christ's name for His glory, and I pray in His name. Amen.

Saul Becomes Paul: Acts 9:1-19a

BUT Saul, yet breathing threatening and slaughter against the disciples of the Lord, went to the high priest, (2) and asked of him letters to Damascus to the synagogues, that if he found any of this way, whether they were men or women, he might bring them bound to Jerusalem.

(3) And as he journeyed, he came near Damascus. And suddenly there flashed around him a light from heaven; (4) and he fell to the earth, and heard a voice saying to him: Saul, Saul, why persecutest thou me? (5) And he said: Who art thou, Lord? And the Lord said: I am Jesus, whom thou persecutest. (6) But arise, and go into the city, and it shall be told thee what thou must do.

(7) And the men who journeyed with him were standing speechless, hearing the voice, but seeing no one. (8) And Saul arose from the earth; and his eyes being opened, he saw nothing; and leading him by the hand, they brought him into Damascus. (9) And he was three days without sight, and neither ate nor drank.

(10) And there was a certain disciple at Damascus, named Ananias; and to him the Lord said, in a vision, Ananias! And he said, Behold, I am here, Lord. (11) And the Lord said to him: Arise, and go into the street which is called Straight, and inquire in the house of Judas for one called Saul of Tarsus. For, behold, he prays; (12) and in a vision he saw a man named Ananias coming in, and putting his hand on him, that he might receive sight.

(13) And Ananias answered: Lord, I have heard from many concerning this man, how great evils he did to thy saints at Jerusalem. (14) And here he has authority from the chief priests to bind all that call on thy name. (15) But the Lord said to him: Go; for he is to me a chosen vessel, to bear my name before Gentiles, and kings, and the sons of Israel; (16) for I will show him how great things he must suffer for my name's sake. (17) And Ananias went, and entered into the house; and putting his hands on him, he said: Brother Saul, the Lord has sent me, Jesus who appeared to thee in the way thou camest, that thou mayest receive sight, and be filled with the Holy Spirit. (18) And immediately there fell off from his eyes as it were scales; and he received sight, and arose, and was immersed; (19) and having taken food, he was strengthened.

Compare

Acts 22:4-16

Acts 26:9-18

Galatians 1:13-17

Notes

1. Luke tells of Paul's conversion more than once in Acts in order to stress its importance.
2. 'The Way' was a phrase that referred to Christianity, but it is not known where this expression started.
3. There are similarities of this story to those of calling prophets in the Old Testament.
4. Jesus tells Paul that when he persecutes Christians, he is persecuting Him.
5. Ananias is evidently one of the leaders of The Way in Damascus. Acts does not tell us how Christianity came to be in Damascus.
6. The 'street Called Straight' is the name for Darb el-Mostakim, an east-west street in the old city of Damascus today.
7. Like the prophets, Paul is chosen by God for a specific purpose.

Questions for Reflection

1. Do you see individual Christians today that you believe as having a particular calling by God? Describe them.

2. Do you believe that God has given you a sense of purpose in your life? Explain.

Damascus to Jerusalem: Acts 9:19b-31

And Saul was certain days with the disciples at Damascus. (20) And straightway he preached Jesus, in the synagogues, that he is the Son of God. (21) And all that heard him were amazed, and said: Is not this he who destroyed in Jerusalem those who call on this name? And he came hither for this purpose, that he might bring them bound to the chief priests.

(22) But Saul was more strengthened, and confounded the Jews who dwelt at Damascus, proving that this is the Christ.

(23) And when many days were completed, the Jews took counsel to kill him. (24) But their lying in wait became known to Saul. And they were watching the gates day and night to kill him. (25) But the disciples took him by night, and let him down through the wall, lowering him in a basket.

(26) And Saul, having come to Jerusalem, attempted to join himself to the disciples; and all were afraid of him, not believing that he was a disciple. (27) But Barnabas took him, and brought him to the apostles, and related fully to them how he saw the Lord in the way, and that he spoke to him, and how he preached boldly at Damascus in the name of Jesus. (28) And he was with them, going in and out at Jerusalem, (29) and speaking boldly in the name of the Lord Jesus; and was speaking and disputing against the Grecian Jews; but they were attempting to slay him. (30) And the brethren, learning it, brought him down to Caesarea, and sent him forth to Tarsus.

(31) The church therefore, throughout all Judaea and Galilee and Samaria, had peace, being built up, and walking in the fear of the Lord, and in the consolation of the Holy Spirit, was multiplied.

Notes

1. Paul's immediate preaching in the synagogues is the beginning of a pattern for Paul.
2. (Verses 24-25) In 2 Corinthians 11:32-33 Paul speaks of fleeing from the ethnarch Aretas IV, who was king of the Nabateans. Ethnic conflicts were often stirred by religious debates in the ancient world.
3. Barnabus intercedes upon Paul's behalf. In Galatians 1:18-19 Paul claims to have only seen Peter and James, the brother of Jesus. James is not considered an apostle in Acts.

Questions for Reflection

1. Is there someone in your life that has played the role of a Barnabus, giving you encouragement?

2. Do you have the opportunities to share the story of your coming to Christ? Do you create such witnessing opportunities?

Peter goes to Lydda and Joppa: Acts 9:32-43

(32) And it came to pass that Peter, going through them all, came down also to the saints who dwelt at Lydda. (33) And there he found a certain man named Aeneas, who had lain upon a pallet eight years, who was palsied. (34) And Peter said to him: Aeneas, Jesus the Christ makes thee whole; arise, and make thy bed. And

immediately he arose. (35) And all that dwelt at Lydda and Saron saw him; and they turned to the Lord.

(36) And there was at Joppa a certain disciple named Tabitha, which interpreted is called Dorcas. This woman was full of good works, and of alms, which she did. (37) And it came to pass in those days, that she was sick, and died. And having washed her, they laid her in an upper chamber. (38) And as Lydda was near to Joppa, the disciples, having heard that Peter was there, sent to him two men, entreating that he would not delay to come to them.

(39) And Peter arose and went with them. When he was come, they brought him into the upper chamber; and all the widows stood by him weeping, and showing coats and garments which Dorcas made, while she was with them. (40) But Peter put them all forth, and kneeled down, and prayed; and turning to the body, he said: Tabitha, arise. And she opened her eyes; and seeing Peter, she sat up. (41) And he gave her his hand, and raised her up; and calling the saints and widows, he presented her alive. (42) And it became known throughout all Joppa; and many believed on the Lord.

(43) And it came to pass, that he remained many days in Joppa, with one Simon, a tanner.

Notes

1. Lydda was northwest of Jerusalem between Azotus and Caesarea and about 11 miles southeast of Joppa. There are already believers in both of these cities, possibly due to the activity of Philip, as learned in the previous section.
2. Joppa, now known as Jaffa, is about 30 miles south of Caesarea.
3. Peter's lodging with a tanner, who would be ceremonially unclean.

Questions for Reflection

1. Have you ever spent the night or an extended period of time with someone that did not keep himself or herself clean?

2. Have you ever shared your faith with someone whose appearance was offensive to you?

> I give all that I am and have to You, gracious heavenly Father. I pray for my friends and neighbors. Some of them can be difficult to love, so help me to love each of them as You teach me to do. You have shown me how to serve You on Your terms, in Your way. Thank You. Forgive my sometimes-clumsy efforts. I offer this prayer to Your power and divine love in Jesus' name. Amen.

Conversion of Cornelius: Acts 10:1-48

THERE was a certain man in Caesarea named Cornelius, a centurion of the band called the Italian band; (2) devout, and one that feared God with all his house, giving many alms to the people, and praying to God always. (3) He saw in a vision, distinctly, about the ninth hour of the day, an angel of God coming in to him, and saying to him: Cornelius! (4) And fixing his eyes on him, he was afraid, and said: What is it, Lord? And he said to him: Thy prayers and thine alms are come up for a memorial before God. (5) And now send men to Joppa, and call for Simon, who is surnamed Peter. (6) He lodges with one Simon a tanner, whose house is by the seaside.

(7) And when the angel who spoke to Cornelius was gone, he called two of his household servants, and a devout soldier of those who waited on him; (8) and having told them all these things, he sent them to Joppa.

(9) On the morrow, as they were journeying, and drawing near to the city, Peter went up upon the house-top to pray, about the sixth hour. (10) And he became very hungry, and desired to eat. While they now were making ready, there fell upon him a trance; (11) and he beholds heaven opened, and a certain vessel descending upon him, as a great sheet, bound by four corners, and let down upon the earth; (12) wherein were all the fourfooted beasts and creeping things of the earth, and birds of the air. (13) And there came a voice to him: Arise, Peter; slay, and eat. (14) But Peter said: Not so, Lord; for I never ate anything common or unclean. (15) And a voice came to him again, the second time: What God cleansed, call not thou common. (16) This was done thrice; and the vessel was taken up again into heaven.

(17) And while Peter was doubting in himself what the vision might be which he saw, behold, the men who were sent from Cornelius, having made inquiry for Simon's house, came and stood before the gate; (18) and calling they asked, whether Simon, who is surnamed Peter, lodges here.

(19) While Peter was earnestly considering the vision, the Spirit said to him: Behold, men are seeking thee. (20) But arise, and go down, and go with them, making no scruple; because I have sent them.

(21) Peter went down to the men, and said: Behold, I am he whom ye seek. What is the cause for which ye are here? (22) And they said: Cornelius, a centurion, a just man, and one that fears God, and of good report among all the nation of the Jews, was warned from God by a holy angel to send for thee to his house; and to hear words from thee.

(23) He called them in, therefore, and lodged them. And on the morrow Peter went forth with them, and certain brethren from Joppa went with him. (24) And on the morrow after, they entered into Caesarea. And Cornelius was expecting them, having called together his kinsmen and near friends. (25) And as Peter was coming in, Cornelius met him, and fell down at his feet, and did reverence to him. (26) But Peter raised him, saying: Stand up; I myself also am a man. (27) And while talking with him, he went in, and found many that were come together. (28) And he said to them: Ye know that it is unlawful[10:28] for a Jew to keep company with, or come to, one of another nation; but God showed me that I should not call any man common or unclean. (29) Wherefore I also came without delay, when sent for. I ask therefore for what reason did ye send for me?

(30) And Cornelius said: Four days ago I was fasting unto this hour, and at the ninth hour was praying in my house; and, behold, a man stood before me in bright clothing, (31) and said: Cornelius, thy prayer was heard, and thine alms were remembered before God. (32) Send therefore to Joppa, and call for Simon, who is surnamed Peter; he lodges in the house of Simon a tanner, by the sea-side; who, when he comes will speak to thee. (33) Immediately therefore I sent to thee; and thou didst well in coming hither. Now therefore we are all present before God, to hear all things that are commanded thee from the Lord.

(34) And Peter opened his mouth, and said: Of a truth I perceive that God is not a respecter of persons; (35) but in every nation he that fears him, and works righteousness, is acceptable to him. (36) The word which he sent to the sons of Israel, publishing glad tidings of peace through Jesus Christ (he is Lord of all) , (37) ye know; the thing which was done throughout all Judaea, beginning from Galilee, after the immersion which John preached; Jesus of Nazareth, (38) how God anointed him with the Holy Spirit and with power; who went about doing good, and healing all that were oppressed by the Devil; because God was with him. (39) And we are witnesses of all things which he did both in the country of the Jews, and in Jerusalem; whom they slew, hanging him on a tree. (40) Him God raised on the third day, and showed him openly; (41) not to all the people, but to witnesses before appointed by God, to us, who ate and drank with him after he rose from the dead. (42) And he

commanded us to preach to the people, and to testify that it is he who has been appointed by God to be Judge of the living and dead. (43) To him all the prophets bear witness, that through his name every one who believes on him shall receive remission of sins.

(44) While Peter was yet speaking these words, the Holy Spirit fell on all who heard the word. (45) And those of the circumcision who believed, as many as came with Peter, were astonished, that on the Gentiles also was poured out the gift of the Holy Spirit. (46) For they heard them speaking with tongues, and magnifying God.

Then answered Peter: (47) Can any one forbid the water, that these should not be immersed, who received the Holy Spirit even as we also? (48) And he commanded that they should be immersed in the name of the Lord. Then they entreated him to remain certain days.

<u>Compare:</u>
Luke 7:1-10

<u>Notes</u>
1. This story is crucial to the Book of Acts because it asserts the inclusion of Gentiles in the community, and says this is directed by God.
2. Cornelius worshiped God but had not been circumcised. The presence of a devout soldier suggests that some of those under him shared his sense of Jewish piety.
3. 3:00 PM was the time of afternoon prayers.
4. Although in Mark 7:14-19 Jesus declared all foods clean, that teaching is not included in Luke's gospel, making it all the more important here for Luke's Gentile readers.
5. By inviting them in, Peter is willing to associate with Gentiles, but in terms of his Jewish background is grounds for being ritually unclean.
6. The circumcised believers saw the speaking in tongues as indication that the Holy Spirit had come upon believers before baptism.

<u>Question for Reflection</u>
➢ What are some indicators for you that people who says they are Christians really are followers of Jesus and try to be like Him?

I am humbled by the work of the Holy Spirit, and so offer glory and honor to Jesus. Please help my church's members share the gospel this week and see more conversions, Lord God. You alone know how often we all have sinned in wandering from Your ways. I worship You, and humble myself before You. Thank You for hearing my prayer in Jesus' name. Amen.

<u>**Defending Gentile Baptism: Acts 11:1-18**</u>

AND the apostles, and the brethren throughout Judaea, heard that the Gentiles also received the word of God. (2) And when Peter went up to Jerusalem, they that were of the circumcision contended with him, (3) saying: Thou wentest in to men uncircumcised, and didst eat with them.

(4) But Peter rehearsed the matter to them in order, from the beginning, saying: (5) I was in the city of Joppa praying; and in a trance I saw a vision, a certain vessel descending, as a great sheet, let down out of heaven by four corners; and it came even to me. (6) On which fixing my eyes, I considered, and saw fourfooted beasts of the earth, and wild beasts, and creeping things, and birds of the air. (7) And I heard a voice saying to me: Arise, Peter; slay and eat. (8) But I said: Not so, Lord; for nothing common or unclean ever entered into my mouth. (9) But a voice answered me a second time out of heaven: What God cleansed, regard not thou as common. (10) And this was done three times; and all were drawn up again into heaven.

(11) And, behold, immediately there stood three men at the house where I was, having been sent to me from Caesarea. (12) And the Spirit bade me go with them, making no scruple. And these six brethren also went with me, and we entered into the man's house. (13) And he told us how he saw the angel in his house, standing and saying to him: Send to Joppa, and call for Simon who is surnamed Peter; (14) who will speak to thee words, whereby thou shalt be saved, and all thy house.

(15) And as I began to speak, the Holy Spirit fell on them, as also on us at the beginning; (16) and I remembered the word of the Lord, how he said: John indeed immersed in water, but ye shall be immersed in the Holy Spirit. (17) If therefore God gave the like gift to them as to us, having believed on the Lord Jesus Christ, who then was I, that I could withstand God?

(18) When they heard these things, they held their peace, and glorified God, saying: So then, to the Gentiles also God gave repentance unto life.

<u>**Notes**</u>
1. News of Gentile baptism had reached Jerusalem.
2. The question is not whether Gentiles can be believers, but regarding association of Jews and Gentiles.
3. This 'Gentile Pentecost' was obviously an act of God, so the issue is settled for the moment, but the issue will resurface later in Acts.

<u>**Questions for Reflection**</u>
1. How do you decide whether something is an act of God in your life or in someone else's life?

2. Are there Christians you don't want to associate with? Why?

<u>**Greek Mission in Antioch: Acts 11:19-26**</u>

(19) Now they who were scattered abroad by the persecution that arose on account of Stephen, went as far as Phoenicia, and Cyprus, and Antioch, speaking the word to none but Jews. (20) But some of them were men of Cyprus and Cyrene, who, having come to Antioch, spoke to the Greeks, publishing the good news of the Lord Jesus. (21) And the hand of the Lord was with them; and a great number believed, and turned to the Lord. (22) But the report concerning them came to the ears of the church which was in Jerusalem; and they sent forth Barnabas, to go as far as Antioch. (23) Who having come, and seen the grace of God, rejoiced; and he exhorted all, that with purpose of heart they should cleave to the Lord. (24) For he was a good man, and full of the Holy

Spirit and of faith. And a great multitude was added to the Lord.

(25) And Barnabas departed to Tarsus, to seek for Saul; (26) and having found him, he brought him to Antioch. And it came to pass, that a whole year they came together in the church, and taught a great multitude; and the disciples were first called Christians in Antioch.

Notes

1. Antioch, which was the capital of the Roman province of Syria, included both Galilee and Judea. According to Josephus, the Roman historian, it was the third largest city in the empire after Rome and Alexandria.

2. Barnabus came from Cyprus, and there were Cypriots in Antioch. He expresses approval on behalf of the leaders in Jerusalem.

3. This was the beginning of an extended collaboration between Barnabus and Paul, as mentioned in Galatians.

4. The term 'Christian' means 'partisan for Christ.' Interestingly, the term occurs in only two other places in the Bible, in Acts 26:28 and 1 Peter 4:16, yet it became the term of preference for followers of Christ after the Biblical era.

Questions for Reflection

1. How would you feel if a Christian leader from another part of the world came and expressed approval of your church, expressing it on behalf of a church in another part of the world?

2. Do you consider yourself a partisan for Christ? How so?

Antioch Helps Jerusalem: Acts: 11:27-30a

(27) And in these days prophets came down from Jerusalem to Antioch. (28) And there stood up one of them named Agabus, and signified by the Spirit that there should be a great dearth over all the world; which came to pass in the days of Claudius Caesar. (29) And the disciples, according as any one was prospered, determined each of them to send relief to the brethren dwelling in Judaea; (30) which also they did, sending it to the elders by the hands of Barnabas and Saul.

Notes

1. According to Acts, prophets were numerous in the early church. According to I Corinthians 14:3-4, they teach and build up the church.

2. The famine was probably the one of 47 AD, described by Josephus the Roman historian. It was not worldwide but was highly destructive to the region.

3. Elders (in Greek, 'old men') as leaders are first mentioned here. It probably developed out of synagogue practice.

> I bask in Your glory and Your gracious divine love, heavenly Father. Forgive me, merciful God, for I don't seek Your presence and power enough throughout each day. Thank You for delivering me from evil threats, both visible and invisible. You have called me to serve You, and I gladly obey, empowered by the power of Jesus' name, and in His name I pray. Amen.

Persecution of the Apostles: Acts 11:30b to12:1-19

AND about that time, Herod the king stretched forth his hands to oppress [12:1] certain of the church. (2) And he slew James the brother of John with the sword. (3) And seeing that it pleased the Jews, he proceeded further to take Peter also; (then were the days of unleavened bread;) (4) whom he also seized and put in prison, delivering him to four quaternions of soldiers to keep him; intending after the passover to bring him forth to the people.

(5) Peter therefore was kept guarded in the prison; but earnest prayer was made by the church to God on his behalf.

(6) And when Herod was about to bring him forth, in that night Peter was sleeping between two soldiers, bound with two chains; and keepers before the door were guarding the prison. (7) And, behold, an angel of the Lord stood by him, and a light shined in the prison; and he smote Peter on the side, and raised him, saying: Rise up quickly. And his chains fell from off his hands. (8) And the angel said to him: Gird thyself, and bind on thy sandals; and he did so. And he said to him: Cast thy garment about thee, and follow me. (9) And he went out, and followed him; and knew not that what was done by the angel was true, but thought he saw a vision.

(10) And having passed the first and the second watch, they came to the iron gate that leads into the city, which opened to them of its own accord; and they went out, and passed on through one street, and immediately the angel departed from him.

(11) And Peter, having come to himself, said: Now I know truly, that the Lord sent forth his angel, and delivered me out of the hand of Herod, and from all the expectation of the people of the Jews. (12) And becoming fully conscious of it, he went to the house of Mary the mother of John, who was surnamed Mark, where many were gathered together, and praying.

(13) And as Peter knocked at the door of the gate, a maidservant came to hearken, named Rhoda.

(14) And recognizing Peter's voice, she opened not the gate for gladness, but ran in, and told that Peter was standing before the gate. (15) And they said to her: Thou art mad. But she confidently affirmed that it was even so. And they said: It is his angel.

(16) But Peter continued knocking; and opening the door they saw him, and were amazed. (17) And beckoning to them with the hand to be silent, he related to them how the Lord brought him out of the prison. And he said: Go tell these things to James, and to the brethren. And he departed, and went to another place.

(18) And when it was day, there was no small commotion among the soldiers, as to what was become of Peter. (19) And Herod, when he had sought for him, and found him not, after examining the keepers, commanded that they should be led away to death. And he went down from Judaea to Caesarea, and there abode.

Notes

1. This particular Herod was Herod Agrippa I, who was grandson of Herod the Great and nephew of Herod Antipas, the Herod mentioned in Luke's gospel. He was made King of Judea by Claudius Caesar in 41AD.
2. No replacement is made for James, son of Zebedee, who is martyred.

3. John Mark is mentioned elsewhere in the New Testament. Tradition without evidence identifies him as the author of the second gospel. According to Colossians 4:10 he is Barnabus's cousin.

4. A person's guardian angel (Verse 15) in those days was thought to resemble the person being guarded.

5. James, the brother of Jesus, now begins to emerge as a leader in the Jerusalem church.

Questions for Reflection

1. Have you ever gotten into trouble because of your faith? How so?

2. If you get into serious trouble because of being a follower of Christ, do you think you will be faithful? Explain

Death of a Herod: Acts 12:20-25

(20) And Herod was highly displeased with the Tyrians and Sidonians. But they came with one accord to him, and, having made Blastus the king's chamberlain their friend, desired peace; because their country was nourished by that of the king.

(21) And on a set day Herod, arrayed in royal apparel, sat upon his throne, and made a speech to them. (22) And thereupon the people shouted: The voice of a god, and not of a man! (23) And immediately an angel of the Lord smote him, because he gave not glory to God; and he was eaten by worms, and expired.

Notes

1. Josephus gives a similar account Herod being stricken with a fatal disease after flatters address him as a god, and Herod dies after five days of pain. He acknowledges the false acclamation and accepts his fate.

2. Herod's death occurs in 44AD, approximately the time of the famine.

Ceremony at Antioch: Acts 12:24-13:3

(24) But the word of God grew and multiplied. (25) And Barnabas and Saul returned from Jerusalem, having performed the service, taking with them also John, who was surnamed Mark.

Acts 13: AND there were at Antioch, in the church that was there, prophets and teachers; Barnabas, and Simeon who was called Niger, and Lucius the Cyrenean, and Manaen the foster-brother of Herod the tetrarch, and Saul. (2) And while they were ministering to the Lord, and fasting, the Holy Spirit said: Set apart for me Barnabas and Saul, unto the work to which I have called them. (3) Then, having fasted and prayed, and laid their hands on them, they sent them away.

Notes

1. After making their famine relief trip Barnabas and Paul return to Antioch with John Mark.

2. Prophets and teachers were crucially important to the leadership of the early church.

3. The Holy Spirit initiates new developments as is typical in Acts.

<u>**Question for Reflection**</u>

> Have you had hands laid on you to commission you for church work, done so for someone else, or witnessed it in a worship setting?

True freedom is mine as I walk by faith in You, glorious God. The constitution guarantees us freedom of religion, but there are those who would persecute Christians because we declare the joys of our faith. Thank You for providing for me even as You deliver me from evils around me. I offer myself again in service to You as I pray in Jesus' name. Amen.

On to Cyprus: Acts 13:4-12

(4) They therefore, being sent forth by the Holy Spirit, came down to Seleucia; and from thence they sailed away to Cyprus. (5) And having come to Salamis, they preached the word of God in the synagogues of the Jews; and they had also John as an assistant.

(6) And having gone through the island to Paphos, they found a certain Magian, a Jewish false prophet, whose name was Bar-jesus; (7) who was with the proconsul of the country, Sergius Paulus, an intelligent man. He, having called for Barnabas and Saul, desired to hear the word of God. (8) But Elymas the Magian (for so his name is interpreted) , withstood them, seeking to turn away the proconsul from the faith.

(9) Then Saul (who is also called Paul) , filled with the Holy Spirit, fixed his eyes on him, (10) and said: O full of all deceit and all wickedness, child of the Devil, enemy of all righteousness, wilt thou not cease to pervert the right ways of the Lord? (11) And now, behold, the hand of the Lord is upon thee, and thou shalt be blind, not seeing the sun for a season. And immediately there fell on him a mist and darkness; and going about, he sought persons to lead him by the hand.

(12) Then the proconsul, seeing what was done, believed, being astonished at the teaching of the Lord.

Notes

1. Salamis was an important port and was the capital city at the eastern end of the island.
2. Paul begins his missionary activity in the local synagogue, as is typical according to Luke.
3. Sergius Paulus is a Roman officer favorable to Christianity.
4. From this point on Saul begins to identify himself as Paul. He used Saul to indicate his Jewish origins, and he used Paul to assert his Roman name as part of his missionary activity.

Journey Inland: Acts 13:13-52

(13) And Paul and his companions, having put to sea from Paphos, came to Perga in Pamphylia; and John departing from them returned to Jerusalem. (14) But they, going on from Perga, came to Antioch in Pisidia; and entering into the synagogue on the sabbath day, they sat down. (15) And after the reading of the law and the prophets, the rulers of the synagogue sent to them, saying: Men, brethren, if ye have any word of exhortation for the people, speak.

(16) And Paul arose, and beckoning with the hand, said: Men of Israel, and ye that fear God, hearken. (17) The God of this people of Israel chose our fathers; and he exalted the people in their sojourn in the land of Egypt, and with a high arm he brought them out of it. (18) And about the time of forty years he nourished them[13:18] in the wilderness. (19) And having destroyed seven nations in the land of Canaan, he gave them their land as a possession, (20) about four hundred and fifty years. And after that, he gave judges, until Samuel the prophet. (21) And afterward they desired a king; and God gave them Saul the Son of Kish, a man of the tribe of Benjamin, for forty years. (22) And having removed him, he raised up for them David to be their king; to whom also he gave testimony, saying: I found David the son of Jesse, a man after my own heart, who will do all my will.

(23) Of the seed of this man, God, according to promise, raised up to Israel a Savior, Jesus; (24) John having first preached, before his entrance, the immersion of repentance to all the people of Israel. (25) Now as John was finishing his course, he said: Whom do ye suppose me to be? I am not he. But, behold, there comes one after me, the sandal of whose feet I am not worthy to loose.

(26) Men, brethren, children of the race of Abraham, and whoever among you fears God, to you the word of this salvation was sent forth. (27) For they who dwell at Jerusalem, and their rulers, not knowing him, nor the voices of the prophets which are read every sabbath day, fulfilled them in condemning him. (28) And though they found no cause of death, they demanded of Pilate that he should be slain. (29) And when they had fulfilled all the things written of him, they took him down from the tree, and laid him in a tomb. (30) But God raised him from the dead. (31) And he was seen for many days by those who came up with him from Galilee to Jerusalem, who are now his witnesses unto the people. (32) And we declare to you glad tidings of the promise made to the

fathers, (33) that God has fulfilled this to us their children, in raising Jesus; as also it is written in the second psalm [13:33]:

Thou art my Son; I this day have begotten thee.

(34) And that he raised him up from the dead to return no more to corruption, he has thus spoken: I will give to you the holy, the sure promises of David. (35) Wherefore also in another psalm he says: Thou wilt not suffer thy Holy One to see corruption. (36) For David, having served his own generation according to the purpose of God, fell asleep, and was added to his fathers, and saw corruption. (37) But he, whom God raised, saw not corruption.

(38) Be it known to you therefore, men, brethren, that remission of sins through this man is announced to you; (39) and by him all that believe are justified from all things, from which ye were not able to be justified by the law of Moses.

(40) Beware therefore, lest that come upon you, which is spoken in the prophets:

(41) Behold, ye despisers, and wonder, and perish; Because I work a work in your days,

A work which ye will not believe, Though one should fully declare it to you.

(42) And as they were going out, they besought that these words might be spoken to them on the next sabbath. (43) And when the congregation was broken up, many of the Jews and of the proselyte worshipers followed Paul and Barnabas; who, speaking to them, persuaded them to continue in the grace of God.

(44) And on the next sabbath day, almost the whole city came together to hear the word of God. (45) But the Jews, seeing the multitudes, were filled with indignation, and spoke against the things said by Paul, contradicting and blaspheming.

(46) Then Paul and Barnabas spoke boldly, and said: It was necessary that the word of God should first be spoken to you; but since ye thrust it from you, and judge yourselves not worthy of the eternal life, lo, we turn to the Gentiles. (47) For so has the Lord commanded us:

I have set thee for a light of the Gentiles,

That thou shouldst be for salvation to the end of the earth.

(48) And the Gentiles hearing it rejoiced, and glorified the word of the Lord; and as many as were appointed unto eternal life believed. (49) And the word of the Lord was spread abroad throughout all the region.

(50) But the Jews stirred up the devout and honorable women, and the chief men of the city, and raised persecution against Paul and Barnabas, and drove them out from their borders. (51) And they, having shaken off the dust of their feet against them, came to Iconium. (52) And the disciples were filled with joy, and with the Holy Spirit.

Notes

1. Since the mid-19th century Bible teachers have spoken of Paul's three missionary journeys. This is only a teaching tool, and it is truly part of the New Testament.
2. When in synagogue, one lesson each from the law and the prophets was customary.
3. A survey of Biblical history sets up the fulfillment lesson that Paul offers in his sermons.
4. The resurrection is the heart of the gospel throughout Acts.
5. 'set free' or 'justified' (verse 39) is the only place in Acts where Paul defends the concept of justification by faith rather than works.

<u>Questions for Reflection</u>

1. If you had an opportunity to witness to a totally non-Christian group, what would you say how would you respond? Explain.

2. If you need to explain why Jesus is so important to you, would you approach the subject in the same way as Paul did? Why?

> Is there anyone like You, Lord? You are the God of mighty acts and divine love. Empower the preaching of Your Word in my community of faith, that it be biblically careful and Holy Spirit infused. Thank You for fulfilling Your promises in Jesus. Glory, praise, and worship can only be about You and Your divine love. I offer this prayer in the power of Jesus' name. Amen.

<u>Missions and Return to Antioch: Acts 14:1-28</u>

AND it came to pass in Iconium, that they went together into the synagogue of the Jews, and so spoke, that a great multitude both of Jews and Greeks believed. (2) But the Jews who disbelieved stirred up and embittered the minds of the Gentiles against the brethren. (3) They spent a long time, therefore, speaking boldly in the Lord, who gave testimony to the word of his grace, granting signs and wonders to be done by their hands.

(4) But the multitude of the city was divided; and part held with the Jews, and part with the apostles. (5) And when a movement was made, both of the Gentiles and Jews with their rulers, to abuse and stone them, (6) they, being aware of it, fled to the cities of Lycaonia, Lystra and Derbe, and the region around; (7) and there they were publishing the good news.

(8) And there sat a certain man at Lystra, impotent in his feet, being lame from his mother's womb, who never walked. (9) This man was listening to Paul as he spoke; who, fixing his eyes on him, and perceiving that he had faith to be healed, (10) said with a loud voice: Stand upright on thy feet. And he leaped up, and walked.

(11) And the multitudes, seeing what Paul did, lifted up their voices, saying in the speech of Lycaonia: The gods are come down to us in the likeness of men. (12) And they called Barnabas, Jupiter; and Paul, Mercury, because he was the chief speaker. (13) And the priest of Jupiter, that was before the city, having brought oxen and garlands to the gates, would have offered sacrifice with the people. (14) But the apostles, Barnabas and Paul, hearing of it, rent their clothes, and rushed forth to the multitude; crying out, (15) and saying: Sirs, why do ye these things? We also are men of like nature with you, bringing you glad tidings, that ye should turn from these vanities to the living God, who made heaven, and earth, and the sea, and all things that are therein; (16) who, in the ages past, suffered all nations to walk in their own ways; (17) although he left not himself without witness, in that he did good, giving you rain from heaven, and fruitful seasons, filling your hearts with food and gladness.

(18) And with these sayings they hardly restrained the people from sacrificing to them. (19) But there came thither Jews from Antioch and Iconium; and having persuaded the people, and stoned Paul, they drew him out of the city, supposing that he was dead. (20) But the disciples having gathered around him, he rose up, and came into the city; and on the morrow he departed with Barnabas to Derbe. (21) And having published the good news to that city, and made many disciples, they turned back to Lystra, and Iconium, and Antioch; (22) confirming the souls of the disciples, exhorting them to continue in the faith, and that we must through much affliction enter into the kingdom of God.

(23) And having appointed for them elders in every church, they commended them, with prayer and fasting, to the Lord, on whom they believed. (24) And after passing through Pisidia, they came to Pamphylia. (25) And having spoken the word in Perga, they went down to Attalia; (26) and thence they sailed away to Antioch, from whence they had been commended to the grace of God for the work which they accomplished.

(27) And having come, and gathered the church together, they reported how great things God wrought with them, and that he opened to the Gentiles a door of faith. (28) And they spent no little time with the disciples.

<u>Notes</u>

1. In other places the term 'apostles' refers to the twelve. Here it seems to indicate emissaries of the church in Antioch.
2. In Acts, persecution always leads to new opportunities.
3. As in other places in Acts, Paul seems to duplicate the experiences of Peter.
4. According to a myth of the region (verses 11-12), the gods Zeus and Hermes visited Baucis and Philemon in human form and rewarded their hospitality. Paul, as chief speaker, was hailed as the messenger of the gods.
5. Tearing one's clothes was a sign of horror and dismay.
6. In Acts Paul's churches are ruled by elders (Greek: 'presbyters'). They are the only places where Paul himself uses the term.

<u>Questions for Reflection</u>

1. Do any of the people you know worship other gods? By name?

2. Have others ever become visibly upset when you have witnessed to your faith? Would that bother you?

> I am thankful that you, the Almighty and divinely loving God, have given me eyes to see Your light and fill my life with Your light. My prayer is that the leaders of my spiritual community stay above reproach and avoid temptation, complacency, idolatry, and worldliness. Restore the joy of Your salvation in me and sustain me with Your bountiful Spirit. I cherish You, thank You, and I pray in the name of Jesus. Amen.

Jerusalem Affirms Gentile Christians: Acts 15:1-35

AND certain men, coming down from Judaea, taught the brethren: Except ye are circumcised after the custom of Moses, ye can not be saved. (2) Paul and Barnabas having therefore had no little dissension and discussion with them, they determined that Paul and Barnabas, and certain others of them, should go up to Jerusalem to the apostles and elders, about this question.

(3) They therefore, having been sent forward by the church, passed through Phoenicia and Samaria, declaring the conversion of the Gentiles; and they caused great joy to all the brethren. (4) And having come to Jerusalem, they were gladly received by the church, and the apostles and elders; and they reported how great things God wrought with them. (5) But there arose some of those from the sect of the Pharisees who believed, saying: It is necessary to circumcise them, and to command them to keep the law of Moses.

(6) And the apostles and the elders came together to consider this matter. (7) And when there had been much discussion, Peter arose, and said to them: Men, brethren, ye know that a long time ago God made choice among us, that by my mouth the Gentiles should hear the word of the glad tidings and believe. (8) And God who knows the heart bore them witness, giving to them the Holy Spirit, as also to us; (9) and made no difference between us and them, purifying their hearts by faith.

(10) Now therefore why do ye tempt God, by putting a yoke upon the neck of the disciples, which neither our fathers nor we were able to bear? (11) But, through the grace of the Lord Jesus, we believe that we shall be saved, in the same manner as they also.

(12) And all the multitude became silent, and listened to Barnabas and Paul, narrating how great signs and wonders God wrought among the Gentiles through them.

(13) And after they were silent, James answered, saying: Men, brethren, hearken to me. (14) Simeon narrated how at first God visited the Gentiles, to take out of them a people for his name. (15) And with this agree the words of the prophets; as it is written:

(16) After this I will return,

And will rebuild the tabernacle of David, which is fallen down;

And I will rebuild the ruins thereof, and will set it up again;

(17) that the rest of men may seek after the Lord,

And all the Gentiles, upon whom my name has been called,

Saith the Lord, who does these things[15:17].

(18) Known to God are all his works from the beginning of the world.

(19) Wherefore my judgment is, that we trouble not those who from among the Gentiles are turning to God; (20) but that we write to them, that they abstain from pollutions of idols, and from fornication, and from what is strangled, and from blood. (21) For Moses of old time has in every city those who preach him, being read in the synagogues every sabbath.

(22) Then the apostles and the elders, with the whole church, resolved, having chosen men from themselves, to send them to Antioch with Paul and Barnabas; namely, Judas surnamed Barsabas, and Silas, leading men among the brethren. (23) And they wrote by them thus:

The apostles and the elders and the brethren, to the brethren from the Gentiles throughout Antioch and Syria and Cilicia, greeting: (24) Forasmuch as we heard, that some who went out from us troubled you with words, subverting your souls, saying that ye must be circumcised and keep the law[15:24], to whom we gave no commandment; (25) it seemed good to us, having become of one mind, to choose men and send them to you, with our beloved Barnabas and Paul, (26) men who have hazarded their lives for the name of our Lord Jesus Christ.

(27) We have sent therefore Judas and Silas, who will themselves also by word tell you the same things. (28) For it seemed good to the Holy Spirit, and to us, to lay upon you no further burden except these necessary things; (29) that ye abstain from things offered to idols, and from blood, and from what is strangled, and from fornication; from which if ye keep yourselves, ye will do well. Farewell.

(30) They therefore, being dismissed, came to Antioch; and assembling the multitude they delivered the

letter. (31) And having read it, they rejoiced for the consolation. (32) And Judas and Silas, also themselves being prophets, exhorted the brethren with many words, and confirmed them.

(33) And having remained a while, they were dismissed with peace from the brethren to the apostles. (34) But it pleased Silas to abide there still. (35) Paul also and Barnabas continued in Antioch, teaching and publishing the glad tidings of the word of the Lord, with many others also.

Notes

1. Paul identifies the pharisees (verse 5) as false believers in Galatians 2:4.
2. The issue of Gentile Christians supposedly settled in chapter 11 now resurfaces.
3. In chapter 2 of Galatians Paul reports that this meeting included a contentious debate which is not included here in Acts.
4. Peter takes a more conservative approach to food sacrificed to idols than does Paul in I Corinthians 10:27-29.
5. The list in verse 20 may be quite practical, such as avoiding non-kosher food and fornication.

Questions for Reflection

1. Assuming that for you there are things you will not give into, how do you go about setting those limits?

2. Do you make a distinction regarding those who say they are Christians and those who live the life? How do you make that distinction?

Paul Revisits Some Churches: Acts 15:36-16:5

(36) And some days after, Paul said to Barnabas: Let us return now, and visit the brethren in every city where we preached the word of the Lord, and see how they do. (37) And Barnabas determined to take with them John, who was surnamed Mark. (38) But Paul thought it proper not to take with them him who departed from them from Pamphylia, and went not with them to the work. (39) And there arose a sharp contention, so that they parted one from the other, and Barnabas took Mark, and sailed to Cyprus. (40) And Paul, having chosen Silas, went forth, being commended by the brethren to the grace of God. (41) And he went through Syria and Cilicia, confirming the churches.

Acts 16

AND he came down to Derbe and Lystra. And, behold, a certain disciple was there, named Timothy, the son of a believing Jewish woman, but whose father was a Greek; (2) who was well reported of by the brethren in Lystra and Iconium. (3) Him Paul wished to go forth with him, and took and circumcised him on account of the Jews who were in those places; for they all knew that his father was a Greek.

(4) And as they journeyed through the cities, they delivered to them the decrees to keep, that were ordained by the apostles and elders who were in Jerusalem. (5) The churches, therefore, were established in the faith, and increased in number daily.

Notes

1. The disagreement and resulting departure of John Mark is reported by Paul in Galatians 2:11-13.
2. Barnabus and Mark revisit Cyprus, discussed in chapter 13.

3. Paul now sets out as a solo missionary {40}.

4. Paul's letters indicate that Timothy was a more important traveling companion for Paul than Acts seems to suggest.

5. The Apostles as a group are now mentioned for the last time {16:4}

<u>Questions for Reflection</u>

1. How does one go about strengthening a church? Teaching? Encouragement? Prayer?

2. If you were wanting someone to partner with you in strengthening a church, would you want to make sure of your partner's faith? How?

> I am embracing the new pathway You are revealing to me, glorious divine Father in heaven. Increase my courage and strengthen my faith in You. I love You and want the courage to trust You, but my faith is often weak. Please forgive me and build up my faith. I remember how Your Son Jesus ordered the stormy sea to calm down with divine loving power. Thank You again for my salvation in Him. I pray in His name. Amen.

Journey to Troas: Acts 16:6-10

(6) And having gone through the region of Phrygia and Galatia, and being forbidden by the Holy Spirit to speak the word in Asia, (7) they came to Mysia, and attempted to go into Bithynia; but the Spirit of Jesus did not permit them. (8) And passing by Mysia, they came down to Troas.

(9) And a vision appeared to Paul in the night. There stood a man, a Macedonian, beseeching him, and saying: Come over into Macedonia and help us. (10) And when he had seen the vision, immediately we sought to go into Macedonia, concluding that the Lord had called us to publish the good news to them.

Notes:

1. They now journey through the interior of Asia Minor to the Aegean.
2. The Spirit of Jesus (Verse 7) is the equivalent of the Holy Spriit.
3. The 'we' passages begin in verse 10, adding vividness to the story telling. Many have speculated that this indicates Luke being a traveling companion of Paul.

Questions for Reflection

1. Have you ever felt restrained to not share your faith? If so, how confident were you that your restraint was from God?

2. Have you ever had a dream you felt you had to follow through on?

Journey to Philippi: Acts 16:11-40

(11) Therefore setting sail from Troas, we ran with a straight course to Samothrace, and on the following day to Neapolis; (12) and from thence to Philippi, which is a chief city of that part of Macedonia, a colony. And we continued in that city certain days.

(13) And on the sabbath, we went forth out of the gate by a river side, where was wont to be a place of prayer; and we sat down, and spoke to the women who came together.

(14) And a certain woman named Lydia, a seller of purple, of the city of Thyatira, who worshiped God, was listening; whose heart the Lord opened to attend to the things spoken by Paul. (15) And when she was immersed and her household, she besought us, saying: If ye have judged me to be a believer in the Lord, come into my house, and abide. And she constrained us.

(16) And it came to pass, as we were going to the place of prayer, a certain bondmaid having a spirit of divination met us, who brought her masters much gain by soothsaying. (17) She, having followed Paul and us, cried, saying: These men are the servants of the most high God, who announce to us the way of salvation.

(18) And this she did many days. But Paul, being indignant, turned and said to the spirit: I command thee in the name of Jesus Christ to come out from her. And he came out the same hour.

(19) And her masters, seeing that the hope of their gain departed, laid hold of Paul and Silas, and drew them into the market-place before the rulers. (20) And having brought them to the magistrates, they said: These men, being Jews, greatly disturb our city; (21) and teach customs, which it is not lawful for us to receive, or to observe, being Romans.

(22) And the multitude rose up together against them; and the magistrates rent off their clothes, and commanded to beat them with rods. (23) And having laid many stripes on them, they cast them into prison, charging the jailer to keep them safely; (24) who, having received such a charge, thrust them into the inner prison,

and made their feet fast in the stocks.

(25) And at midnight Paul and Silas prayed, and sang praises to God; and the prisoners listened to them. (26) And suddenly there was a great earthquake, so that the foundations of the prison were shaken; and immediately all the doors were opened, and the chains of all were loosed. (27) And the jailer, awaking out of sleep, and seeing the prison doors open, drew his sword, and was about to kill himself, supposing that the prisoners had fled. (28) But Paul cried with a loud voice, saying: Do thyself no harm; for we are all here. (29) And calling for lights, he sprang in, and trembling fell down before Paul and Silas; (30) and having brought them out, he said: Sirs, what must I do to be saved? (31) And they said: Believe on the Lord Jesus Christ, and thou shalt be saved, and thy house. (32) And they spoke to him the word of the Lord, and to all that were in his house.

(33) And taking them along, the same hour of the night, he washed their stripes; and was immersed, himself and all his, immediately. (34) And having brought them up into his house, he set food before them, and rejoiced, with all his house, believing in God.

(35) And when it was day, the magistrates sent the sergeants, saying: Let those men go. (36) And the keeper of the prison reported these words to Paul: The magistrates have sent to let you go; now therefore depart, and go in peace.

(37) But Paul said to them: They beat us openly, uncondemned, being Romans, and cast us into prison; and now do they send us forth secretly? Nay verily; but let them come themselves and bring us out.

(38) And the sergeants reported these words to the magistrates; and they were afraid, when they heard that they were Romans. (39) And they came and besought them, and bringing them out, entreated them to depart out of the city.

(40) And they went out of the prison, and entered into the house of Lydia; and seeing the brethren they exhorted them, and departed.

Notes

1. Samothrace is an island in the northern Aegean, halfway between Troas and Neapolis, which was the seaport for Philippi.
2. Philippi was not the capital but was a Roman colony containing discharged soldiers who had received grants of land. Such colonies enjoyed freedom from taxation and were protected by Roman legal procedures.
3. Dependents always followed the head of the household in religious matters.
4. It was not lawful for Jews to make converts of Romans.
5. A Roman jailer who allowed a prisoner to escape had to forfeit his life.
6. The improvement of Paul's credentials (a Roman citizen) serves to demonstrate compatibility of Christianity with Roman life.

I join in the everlasting music and praise in heaven for You, my heavenly Father. I'm ashamed of my sins and grateful for being forgiven. I am grateful to you, Lord God, for providing Christian missionaries worldwide with words of hope and equipping them to love and serve those around them. May my prayers be used to give encouragement and protection as they spread the good news. In the power of Jesus' name, I pray. Amen.

Journey to Athens: Acts 17:1-15

AND passing through Amphipolis and Apollonia, they came to Thessalonica, where was the synagogue of the Jews. (2) And Paul, as his custom was, went in to them, and for three sabbaths reasoned with them from the Scriptures, (3) opening them, and setting forth that the Christ must suffer, and rise again from the dead; and that this is the Christ, Jesus whom I preach to you. (4) And some of them believed, and joined themselves to Paul and Silas; and of the devout Greeks a great multitude, and of the chief women not a few.

(5) But the Jews, moved with envy[17:5], having taken to them, of the idlers in the market-place, certain vicious men, and having gathered a crowd, set the city in an uproar; and assaulting the house of Jason, they sought to bring them unto the people. (6) And not finding them, they dragged Jason and certain brethren before the rulers of the city, crying: These that have turned the world upside down are come hither also. (7) Whom Jason has received; and all these are acting contrary to the decrees of Caesar, saying that there is another king, Jesus.

(8) And they troubled the people and the rulers of the city, when they heard these things. (9) And having taken security of Jason, and of the others, they let them go.

(10) And the brethren immediately sent away Paul and Silas by night to Beroea; who coming thither went into the synagogue of the Jews. (11) These were more noble than those in Thessalonica, in that they received the word with all readiness, and searched the Scriptures daily whether these things were so.

(12) Many of them therefore believed; and of honorable Grecian women and men, not a few. (13) But when the Jews of Thessalonica knew that also at Beroea the word of God was preached by Paul, they came, stirring up the people there also. (14) And then immediately the brethren sent away Paul to journey as upon the sea; but Silas and Timothy abode there still. (15) And they who conducted Paul brought him to Athens; and having received a command to Silas and Timothy to come to him as soon as possible, they departed.

Notes

1. Paul's custom was to start new missions in the local synagogue.
2. Taking bail from Jason made him financially and legally responsible for future good behavior.
3. Christianity is attracting people of high standing (verses 11-12) .

Questions for Reflection

1. Are people always receptive when you share your faith? How does their response affect you?

2. Have you ever had occasion to assist a missionary?

Mission in Athens: Acts 17:16-34

(16) Now while Paul was waiting for them at Athens, his spirit was stirred in him, when he saw the city full of idols. (17) Therefore he reasoned in the synagogue with the Jews and the devout persons, and in the market daily with those who met with him. (18) And certain philosophers of the Epicureans, and of the Stoics, were disputing with him. And some said: What would this babbler say? and others: He seems to be a proclaimer of foreign gods; because he made known to them the good news of Jesus and the resurrection. (19) And taking hold of him, they brought him upon Mars' Hill, saying: May we know what this new doctrine is, of which thou speakest? (20) For thou bringest certain strange things to our ears; we would know therefore what these things mean. (21) Now all Athenians, and the strangers residing there, spent their leisure for nothing else, but to tell or

to hear something new.

(22) And Paul, standing in the midst of Mars' Hill, said: Men of Athens, in all things I perceive that ye are very devout. (23) For as I passed by, and observed your objects of worship, I found also an altar with this inscription: TO AN UNKNOWN GOD. Whom therefore, not knowing, ye worship, him I announce to you. (24) The God who made the world and all things therein, he being Lord of heaven and earth, dwells not in temples made with hands; (25) nor is ministered to by human hands, as if needing anything more, himself giving to all life, and breath, and all things. (26) And he made of one blood every nation of men to dwell on all the face of the earth, having fixed the appointed seasons and bounds of their habitation; (27) that they should seek the Lord, if haply they might feel after him, and find him, although he is not far from every one of us; (28) for in him we live, and move, and have our being; as also some of your own poets have said: For his offspring also are we. (29) Being therefore God's offspring, we ought not to think that the Godhead is like to gold, or silver, or stone, graven by art and man's device. (30) The times of ignorance therefore God overlooked; but now, commands all men everywhere to repent. (31) Because he fixed a day, in which he will judge the world in righteousness, by the man whom he appointed, having given assurance to all by raising him from the dead.

(32) And when they heard of a resurrection of the dead, some mocked; and others said: We will hear thee again of this matter. (33) And thus Paul departed from among them.

(34) But certain ones, joining themselves to him, believed; among whom was also Dionysius the Areopagite, and a woman named Damaris, and others with them.

Notes

1. Paul is the first Christian philosopher, using both Stoic and Jewish arguments.

2. Paul recognizes both epicureans and stoics in his speech. Stoics felt that truth could be gained by denying all human emotions, and that virtue is sufficient for happiness. Epicureans felt that the purpose of life was to gain maximum pleasure and enjoyment.

3. God as creator is an idea common to Greeks as well as Jews.

Questions for Reflection

1. Why do you think many Christians associate guilt with pleasure?

2. Since Jesus said, 'I cam that you may have life and have it abundantly,' how do you connect that with enjoying life and having pleasure, or do you?

> Loving Father in heaven, I love You and find my greatest joy in You. I cannot make my things and pleasures my substitute gods. When I am following Jesus and trying to be like Him, You are zealous for me. I live in a world centered on pleasure, but as a Christian, I cannot be content to just experience You in worship. I can't just hold your hand, but I must seek your face. I surrender myself and offer my prayer in Jesus' name. Amen.

Paul Goes to Corinth: Acts 18:1-17

AFTER these things Paul departed from Athens, and came to Corinth. (2) And finding a certain Jew named Aquila, a native of Pontus, lately come from Italy, and Priscilla his wife (because Claudius had commanded all the Jews to depart from Rome) , he came to them; (3) and because he was of the same trade, he abode with them, and labored; for by their occupation they were tentmakers. (4) And he reasoned in the synagogue every sabbath, and persuaded both Jews and Greeks.

(5) And when Silas and Timothy came down from Macedonia, Paul was engrossed with the word, testifying to the Jews that Jesus is the Christ. (6) But they opposing themselves and blaspheming, he shook out his garments and said to them: Your blood be upon your own head; I am clean; from henceforth I will go to the Gentiles.

(7) And departing thence he entered into a certain man's house, named Justus, one who worshiped God, whose house was adjoining the synagogue. (8) And Crispus, the ruler of the synagogue, believed on the Lord with all his house; and many of the Corinthians hearing believed, and were immersed.

(9) And the Lord said to Paul, through a vision in the night: Be not afraid, but speak, and hold not thy peace; (10) for I am with thee, and no one shall assail thee to hurt thee; for I have much people in this city. (11) And he continued there a year and six months, teaching the word of God among them.

(12) And when Gallio was proconsul of Achaia, the Jews rose up with one accord against Paul, and brought him before the judgment-seat, (13) saying: This man persuades men to worship God contrary to the law.

(14) And as Paul was about to open his mouth, Gallio said to the Jews: If it were some injustice, or wicked misdeed, O Jews, with reason I would have borne with you. (15) But if it is a question about a word, and names, and your own law look to it yourselves; I will not be a judge of these things (16) And he drove them away from the judgment-seat.

(17) But having all seized upon Sosthenes, the ruler of the synagogue, they beat him before the judgment-seat. And Gallio cared for none of these things.

Compare:

I Corinthians 1-4

Notes

1. The old city was destroyed in 146 BC and rebuilt as a Roman colony by Julius Caesar in 44 BC. It was made a capital in 27 BC and quickly became a key commercial center because of its location.

2. Aquila and Priscilla worked with Paul according to Romans 16:3-5. Since the church met in their house, they were probably wealthy.

3. The baptism of Crispus by Paul is a special case indicated in I Corinthians 1:14.

4. L. Junius Gallio was proconsul of Achaia in 52 AD. This fact is essential to dating Paul's activity in the region and the dating of the rest of Paul's career.

5. Gallio voices one of the sub-themes of Acts, that Christianity is not a cause for concern to Rome at this time.

Questions for Reflection

1. Does knowing Paul's role in the context of Roman history help your faith and your understanding of the Bible? If so, how?

2. Does knowing the role of Corinth in the ancient world help in your understanding of Acts and of Paul's letters to the Christians in Corinth? Explain.

Travel Transition: Acts 18:18-23

(18) And Paul having remained yet many days, took leave of the brethren, and sailed thence to Syria, and with him Priscilla and Aquila; having shaven his head in Cenchrea, for he had a vow. (19) And they came to Ephesus, and he left them there but entering himself into the synagogue, he reasoned with the Jews. (20) And they desiring him to remain a longer time with them, he consented not; (21) but took leave of them, saying: [18:21][I must by all means keep the coming feast at Jerusalem; but] I will return again to you, if God will. And he sailed from Ephesus. (22) And having landed at Caesarea, and gone up and saluted the church, he went down to Antioch. (23) And after he had spent some time there, he departed, going through the country of Galatia and Phrygia in order, strengthening all the disciples.

Notes

1. After returning to Antioch Paul sets out again for Asia Minor. In the tradition of church school teaching since early in the 19th century, this is the end of the first missionary journey and the beginning of the second.
2. Paul had his hair cut as a temporary Nazirite vow. The specifications of Nazirite vows are found in Numbers 6:1-21. The rule was to cut the hair off at the end of the vow.
3. Ephesus, on the Aegean coast, was the capital of the Roman province of Asia.

Question for Reflection

➤ Do you find studying Acts easier when you think of Paul's work in terms of three missionary journeys? Why or why not?

Apollos in Ephesus: Acts 18:24-28

(24) And a certain Jew named Apollos, a native of Alexandria, an eloquent man, and mighty in the Scriptures, came to Ephesus. (25) This man was instructed in the way of the Lord and being fervent in spirit, he spoke and taught correctly the things concerning Jesus, knowing only the immersion of John. (26) And he began to speak boldly in the synagogue. But Aquila and Priscilla, having heard him, took him to them, and expounded to him the way of God more perfectly. (27) And he wishing to pass through into Achaia, the brethren wrote, exhorting the disciples to receive him; who, when he was come, contributed much to those who had believed through grace. (28) For he powerfully confuted the Jews in public, showing by the Scriptures that Jesus is the Christ.

Notes

1. Although Apollos was teaching accurately, he had not been baptized.
2. To read more about the activities of Apollos, see I Corinthians 1:12, 3:1-9, and 3:21-23.

<u>Questions for Reflection</u>

1. Have you known someone like Apollos? What were your impressions?

2. Have you known people with the boldness of Priscilla and Aquilla? If so, how have they influenced your faith?

3. Are you bold to express your faith? Why or why not?

> Can there be anyone like You, Lord? You are a God of mighty acts. Empower the preaching of Your Word in my community of faith. Thank You for fulfilling Your promises in Jesus. Glory, praise, and worship must only be about You – God the Father, God the Son, and God the Holy Spirit. I'm trying to be one who lives as well as prays in the power of Jesus' name. Yes! Amen.

Paul's Ministry in Ephesus: Acts 19:1-41

AND it came to pass, that, while Apollos was at Corinth, Paul having passed through the upper districts came to Ephesus. And finding certain disciples, (2) he said to them: Did ye receive the Holy Spirit when ye believed? And they said to him: Nay, we did not even hear whether there is a Holy Spirit. (3) And he said to them: Unto what then were ye immersed? And they said: Unto John's immersion. (4) Then said Paul: John indeed immersed with the immersion of repentance; saying to the people, that they should believe on him who should come after him, that is, on Jesus. (5) And when they heard this, they were immersed in the name of the Lord Jesus. (6) And Paul having laid his hands upon them, the Holy Spirit came on them; and they spoke with tongues, and prophesied. (7) And all the men were about twelve.

(8) And he went into the synagogue, and spoke boldly for three months, reasoning and persuading them of the things concerning the kingdom of God. (9) But when some were hardened, and believed not, speaking evil of the Way before the multitude, he departed from them, and separated the disciples, reasoning daily in the school of Tyrannus. (10) And this continued for two years; so that all who dwelt in Asia heard the word of the Lord, both Jews and Greeks. (11) And God wrought special miracles by the hands of Paul; (12) so that also there were carried from his body to the sick, handkerchiefs or aprons, and the diseases departed from them, and the evil spirits went out from them.

(13) Then some of the wandering Jewish exorcists took upon them to name, over those who had the evil spirits, the name of the Lord Jesus, saying: I adjure you by the Jesus whom Paul preaches. (14) And there were seven sons of one Sceva, a Jewish chief priest, who did this. (15) And the evil spirit answering said: Jesus I know, and Paul I well know; but who are ye? (16) And the man in whom the evil spirit was leaped on them, and overcame them, and prevailed against both, so that they fled out of that house naked and wounded. (17) And this became known to all, both Jews and Greeks, who dwelt at Ephesus; and fear fell on them all, and the name of the Lord Jesus was magnified. (18) And many of the believers came, confessing, and declaring their deeds. (19) Many of those also who practiced curious arts brought together the books, and burned them before all; and they counted the price of them, and found it fifty thousand pieces of silver. (20) So mightily grew the word of God and prevailed.

(21) When these things were ended, Paul purposed to go to Jerusalem, passing through Macedonia and Achaia; saying: After I have been there, I must also see Rome. (22) And having sent into Macedonia two of those who ministered to him, Timothy and Erastus, he himself stayed in Asia for a season.

(23) And about that time, there arose no small tumult concerning the Way. (24) For a certain man named Demetrius, a silversmith, who made silver shrines of Diana, brought no small gain to the craftsmen; (25) whom he called together, with the workmen of like occupation, and said: Sirs, ye well know that by this craft we have our wealth. (26) Moreover ye see and hear, that this Paul has persuaded and turned aside much people, not only of Ephesus, but of almost all Asia, saying that they are not gods, which are made with hands. (27) And there is danger to us, not only that this branch of business will come into disrepute, but also that the temple of the great goddess Diana will be accounted nothing, and her magnificence will be destroyed, whom all Asia and the world worship.

(28) And hearing it, they became full of wrath, and continued crying out, saying: Great is Diana of the Ephesians. (29) And the whole city was filled with confusion; and they rushed with one accord into the theatre, having seized Gaius and Aristarchus, men of Macedonia, Paul's companions in travel. (30) And Paul wishing to enter in unto the people, the disciples suffered him not. (31) And some also of the chiefs of Asia, being his friends, sent to him, entreating him not to adventure himself into the theatre.

(32) Some therefore were crying one thing, and some another; for the assembly was confused, and the greater part knew not wherefore they had come together. (33) And they brought forward Alexander out of the multitude, the Jews thrusting him forward. And Alexander beckoned with the hand, desiring to make his defense to the people. (34) But when they knew that he was a Jew, one voice arose from all, crying about two hours: Great is Diana of the Ephesians.

(35) And the town-clerk, having quieted the people, said: Men of Ephesus, what human being is there, who knows not that the city of the Ephesians is keeper of the great Diana, and of the image which fell down from Jupiter? (36) These things being therefore undeniable, ye ought to be quiet, and to do nothing rashly. (37) For

ye brought hither these men, who are neither robbers of temples, nor blasphemers of your goddess. (38) If therefore Demetrius, and the craftsmen with him, have a matter against any man, the law is open[19:38], and there are proconsuls; let them implead one another. (39) But if ye make any demand concerning other matters, it shall be determined in the lawful assembly. (40) For we are in danger of being called in question for this day's riot, there being no cause whereby we may give an account of this concourse. (41) And having thus spoken, he dismissed the assembly.

Notes

1. This covers roughly a two-year period, and it forms the background for the letters to the Corinthians.
2. Tyrannus was probably a local philosopher in Ephesus. There are inscriptions regarding him in the ruins that have been excavated by archaeologists.
3. Paul's audience continues to be a mixture of both Jews and Greeks.
4. The story in verses 15-16 makes it clear that this was not part of the realm of magic. Acts makes a clear distinction between Christian miracle working and the profiteering of religious charlatans.
5. Ephesus was a center of magic that was so well-known that books on magic were often referred to as Ephesian scripts.
6. The theater has been excavated and can seat at least 24,000.

Questions for Reflection

1. What is your attitude towards magic? Do you think of it as just entertainment? Why?

2. Have you ever witnessed a miracle? Why do you think of what happened in this way

> Whether or not I witness a miracle today, Lord, I am Yours. I ask for opportunities today to lead people to my Savior as I contribute to my spiritual community as best I can. Thank You for answering my prayers, even before I don't see Your answers. All that You do, You do perfectly. I praise You, I love You, and I pray this prayer in Jesus' name. Amen.

Final Visit to Greece: Acts 20:1-6

AND after the tumult ceased, Paul called to him the disciples, and having embraced them, departed to go into Macedonia. (2) And having gone through those regions, and given them much exhortation, he came into Greece. (3) And after he had stayed three months, a plot being laid for him by the Jews, as he was about sailing to Syria, it was resolved that he should return through Macedonia. (4) And there accompanied him unto Asia, Sopater, son of Pyrrhus, a Beroean; and of the Thessalonians, Aristarchus and Secundus; and Gaius of Derbe, and Timothy; and of Asia, Tychicus and Trophimus. (5) These, having gone forward, were waiting for us at Troas. (6) But we sailed forth from Philippi, after the days of unleavened bread, and came to them to Troas in five days; where we abode seven days.

Notes

1. Paul revisits the churches at Philippi, Thessalonica, and Beroea before going on to spend three months in Corinth.
2. The problems discussed in II Corinthians are not discussed in Acts.

Questions for Reflection

1. Why doyou suppose Paul had all of these traveling companions at this point?

2. If through prayer you came to understand that God wanted you to move to another community to serve Him there, would you go? Why?

Resurrection of Eutychus: Acts 20:7-12

(7) And on the first day of the week, we having come together to break bread, Paul discoursed to them (being about to depart on the morrow) , and continued the discourse until midnight. (8) Now there were many lights in the upper room, where we were assembled. (9) And there sat on the window a certain young man named Eutychus, being fallen into a deep sleep; and as Paul was long discoursing, he sunk down with sleep, and fell down from the third loft, and was taken up dead. (10) And Paul went down, and fell on him, and embracing him said: Do not lament, for his life is in him. (11) And having come up again, and broken the bread, and eaten, he talked a long while even till break of day, and so departed. (12) And they brought the young man living, and were not a little comforted.

Notes

1. Eutychus was a relatively common name meaning 'fortunate.'
2. The location, three stories tall, was a kind of tenement-style building.
3. Thia resurrection is vastly understated by Luke.

Questions for Reflection

1. Does Eutychus' falling asleep offer a setting for potential humor?

2. Why do you suppose Luke seems to play down this resurrection story?

3. If this happened in your own local community of faith, how would you react?

Travel & Speech to Ephesian Leaders: Acts 20:13-38

(13) And we, going forward to the ship, embarked for Assos, intending there to take in Paul; for so he had appointed, intending himself to go on foot. (14) And when he met with us at Assos, we took him in, and came to Mitylene. (15) And sailing thence, we came the following day over against Chios; and the next day we arrived at Samos; and having tarried at Trogyllium, we came the next day to Miletus. (16) For Paul had determined to sail past Ephesus, that he might not spend time in Asia; for he was hastening, if it were possible for him, to be at Jerusalem on the day of Pentecost.

(17) And from Miletus he sent to Ephesus, and called the elders of the church. (18) And when they were come to him, he said to them: Ye know, from the first day that I came into Asia, after what manner I have been with you the whole time; (19) serving the Lord with all lowliness of mind, and with tears, and trials which befell me by the plottings of the Jews; (20) how I kept back nothing that was profitable, that I should not announce it to you, and teach you, publicly and from house to house; (21) testifying, to both Jews and Greeks, repentance toward God, and faith toward our Lord Jesus Christ.

(22) And now, behold, I go bound in the spirit to Jerusalem, not knowing the things that shall befall me there; (23) save that the Holy Spirit witnesses to me in every city, saying that bonds and afflictions await me. (24) But none of these things move me, neither do I count my life dear to myself, so that I may finish my course with joy[20:24], and the ministry which I received from the Lord Jesus, to testify the good news of the grace of God.

(25) And now, behold, I know that all ye, among whom I went about preaching the kingdom of God, shall see my face no more. (26) Wherefore I testify to you this day, that I am pure from the blood of all; (27) for I shunned not to declare to you the whole counsel of God.

(28) Take heed therefore to yourselves, and to all the flock, in which the Holy Spirit made you overseers, to feed the church of the Lord, which he purchased with his own blood. (29) For I know this, that after my departure grievous wolves will enter in among you, not sparing the flock. (30) And from among yourselves will men arise, speaking perverse things, to draw away disciples after them. (31) Therefore watch, remembering that for the space of three years, night and day, I ceased not to warn every one with tears.

(32) And now, brethren, I commend you to God, and to the word of his grace, who is able to build you up, and to give you an inheritance among all the sanctified. (33) I coveted no one's silver, or gold, or apparel. (34) Ye yourselves know, that these hands ministered to my necessities, and to those who were with me. (35) In all ways I showed you that, so laboring, ye ought to assist the weak, and to remember the words of the Lord Jesus, that he himself said: It is more blessed to give than to receive.

(36) And having thus spoken, he kneeled down, and prayed with them all. (37) And they all wept sorely, and fell on Paul's neck, and kissed him; (38) sorrowing most of all for the word which he had spoken, that they should behold his face no more. And they accompanied him to the ship.

Notes

1. Paul's farewell address to the leaders of Ephesus is the only speech in Acts specifically addressed to people who are already followers of Christ.

2. The image of a shepherd leader is found not only in the Bible but also in the non-Biblical world

<u>Questions for Reflection</u>

1. What seems to be the purpose of Paul's address to the Christian leaders from Ephesus?

2. How would you feel if your pastor addressed you in this way?

3. If you must leave your community of faith, what would you need to say to them?

> Almighty God, strengthen me emotionally and spiritually as I walk with You. I dedicate myself to walk in faith with Jesus, wherever You lead me. Show me how to function in Your divine love. I know I'm still a sinner, yet I'm forgiven due to Jesus shedding His blood for me. You, Father, are glorious and amazing. In Jesus I pray. Amen.

Travel to Jerusalem: Acts 21:1-16

AND it came to pass, that after we had torn ourselves from them, and had put to sea, we came with a straight course to Coos, and the day following to Rhodes, and from thence to Patara. (2) And finding a ship crossing over to Phoenicia, we went aboard, and put to sea. (3) And bringing Cyprus in sight, and leaving it on the left hand, we sailed to Syria, and landed at Tyre; for there the ship was to unlade her burden. (4) And having found out the disciples, we remained there seven days; who said to Paul through the Spirit, that he should not go up to Jerusalem.

(5) And when we had completed the days, we departed and went our way; they all accompanying us, with wives and children, till we were out of the city; and we kneeled down on the beach, and prayed. (6) And having embraced one another, we went on board the ship; and they returned to their homes.

(7) And we, completing the voyage, came down from Tyre to Ptolemais; and having embraced the brethren, we remained with them one day. (8) And on the morrow we departed, and came to Caesarea; and entering into the house of Philip the evangelist, being one of the Seven, we abode with him. (9) And this man had four daughters, virgins, who prophesied.

(10) And while we were remaining several days, there came down from Judaea a certain prophet, named Agabus. (11) And coming to us, he took off Paul's girdle, and bound his own hands and feet, and said: Thus says the Holy Spirit: So will the Jews at Jerusalem bind the man, whose this girdle is, and will deliver him into the hands of the Gentiles. (12) And when we heard these things, both we, and they of that place, besought him not to go up to Jerusalem. (13) Then answered Paul: What mean ye, to weep and to break my heart? For I am ready not only to be bound, but also to die at Jerusalem, for the name of the Lord Jesus. (14) And when he would not be persuaded, we ceased, saying: The will of the Lord be done.

(15) And after those days, having packed up our baggage, we went up to Jerusalem. (16) There went with us also some of the disciples from Caesarea, bringing us to Mnason of Cyprus, an old disciple, with whom we should lodge.

Notes

1. Philip the evangelist had arrived in Caesarea some time before.
2. Agabus, like Hebrew prophets in the Old Testament, performs a symbolic act. Compare with 1 Kings 11:29-32 and Isaiah 20:2-6. His predictions are not entirely fulfilled in the chapters that follow.

Questions for Reflection

1. Have you ever witnessed either the giving or the fulfillment of a prophecy?

2. If this prophecy were offered to you, would you feel discouraged about the future? Why?

Paul Conforms to Judaism: Acts 21:17-26

(17) And when we were come to Jerusalem, the brethren received us gladly. (18) And on the following day, Paul went in with us to James; and all the elders were present. (19) And having embraced them, he recounted particularly what things God had wrought among the Gentiles through his ministry.

(20) And they, hearing it, glorified the Lord. And they said to him: Thou seest, brother, how many thousands of Jews there are who believe; and they are all zealots for the law. (21) And they were informed concerning thee, that thou teachest all the Jews who are among the Gentiles to forsake Moses, saying that they

should not circumcise their children, nor walk after the customs. (22) What is it therefore? A multitude must surely come together; for they will hear that thou hast come. (23) Do therefore this that we say to thee: We have four men who have a vow on them; (24) these take with thee, and purify thyself with them, and bear the charges for them, that they may shave their heads; and all will know that those things, of which they have been informed concerning thee, are nothing, but that thou thyself also walkest orderly, keeping the law. (25) But concerning the Gentiles who have believed, we wrote to them, deciding that they should observe no such thing, except that they keep themselves from things offered to idols, and from blood, and from what is strangled, and from fornication.

(26) Then Paul took the men, and the next day, having purified himself with them, entered into the temple, announcing the completion of the days of the purification, until the offering was brought for each one of them.

Notes

1. Paul takes a vow to avoid suspicion.
2. The Jerusalem church leaders show unity and accept Paul and his accomplishments.
3. Paul can demonstrate his faithfulness to the law by undergoing purification.

Questions for Reflection

1. Have you ever gone through a ritual to prove your faithfulness, either to yourself or to others?

2. Have you ever been falsely accused? How did you respond? Were you defensive?

Uproar and Arrest: Acts 21: 27-40

(27) And as the seven days were about to be completed, the Jews from Asia, having observed him in the temple, stirred up all the people, and laid hands on him, (28) crying out: Men of Israel, help. This is the man who teaches all, everywhere, against the people, and the law, and this place; and further also, he brought Greeks into the temple, and has polluted this holy place. (29) For they had before seen with him in the city Trophimus the Ephesian, whom they supposed that Paul brought into the temple. (30) And all the city was moved, and the people ran together; and laying hold of Paul, they dragged him out of the temple; and forthwith the doors were shut.

(31) And while they were seeking to kill him, a report came up to the chief captain of the band, that all Jerusalem was in an uproar; (32) who immediately took with him soldiers and centurions, and ran down to them; and they, seeing the chief captain and the soldiers, left off beating Paul. (33) Then the chief captain came near, and took hold of him, and commanded him to be bound with two chains; and inquired who he was, and what he had done. (34) And some cried one thing, some another, among the multitude; and not being able to know the certainty on account of the tumult, he commanded him to be led into the castle. (35) And when he came upon the stairs, so it was, that he was borne by the soldiers on account of the violence of the people. (36) For the multitude of the people followed after, crying: Away with him.

(37) And as he was about to be led into the castle, Paul says to the chief captain: May I speak to thee? And he said: Canst thou speak Greek? (38) Art thou not then the Egyptian, who before these days made an uproar, and led out into the wilderness the four thousand men of the assassins? (39) And Paul said: I am a Jew of Tarsus, a citizen of no obscure city of Cilicia; and I beseech thee, suffer me to speak to the people.

(40) And he having given him permission, Paul, standing on the stairs, beckoned with the hand to the

people. And a great silence ensuing, he spoke to them in the Hebrew tongue, saying:

Notes

1. It was a capital offense for non-Jews to pass beyond the Court of the Gentiles. Josephus the Roman historian confirms this.

2. A tribune commanded a cohort, a detachment of 1000 men. They were stationed in Antonia fortress.

3. Paul's case came into the hands of Roman, not Jewish authorities.

4. 'The Egyptian' was a false messiah who, with 1000's of followers, armed to take Jerusalem back from Rome.

Questions for Reflection

1. If you were falsely accused of a major offense, would you prefer to go before a civil judge rather than be tried before a religious body? Why?

2. Do you think Paul is being logical in the way he is handling his problem? How so?

> Holy God, in a crisis, sometimes I'm aware of my sinful thoughts that betray me. I offer all that I am to You, my merciful God. Thank You for being my deliverer and fortress against evil. As the world surrounds me with evil deceptions and uncertainty, please guide me and deliver me as I make my way into the future. In the name of Jesus, my Lord and Savior, I pray. Amen.

Defense and Custody: Acts: 22-1-29

BRETHREN, and fathers, hear my defense, which I now make to you. (2) And hearing that he spoke to them in the Hebrew tongue, they kept the more silence. (3) And he says: I am a Jew, born indeed in Tarsus of Cilicia, but brought up in this city, taught at the feet of Gamaliel, according to the strictness of the law of the fathers, being zealous for God, as ye all are this day. (4) And I persecuted this Way unto death, binding and delivering into prisons both men and women. (5) As also the high priest bears me witness, and all the eldership; from whom, moreover, I received letters to the brethren, and was journeying to Damascus, to bring also those who were there bound to Jerusalem, that they might be punished.

(6) And it came to pass, that as I journeyed, and came near to Damascus, about midday, there suddenly flashed around me a great light out of heaven. (7) And I fell to the ground, and heard a voice saying to me: Saul, Saul, why persecutest thou me? (8) And I answered: Who art thou, Lord? And he said to me: I am Jesus the Nazarene, whom thou persecutest. (9) And they who were with me beheld indeed the light, and were afraid; but the voice of him who spoke to me they heard not[22:9]. (10) And I said: What shall I do, Lord? And the Lord said to me: Arise, and go into Damascus; and there it shall be told thee concerning all things which it is appointed thee to do.

(11) And as I could not see, for the glory of that light, being led by the hand by those who were with me, I came into Damascus. (12) And one Ananias, a devout man according to the law, having a good report from all the Jews who dwelt there, (13) came to me, and standing by me said to me: Brother Saul, receive sight. And I, in that very hour, looked up upon him. (14) And he said: The God of our fathers appointed thee to know his will, and to see the Just One, and to hear a voice out of his mouth. (15) For thou shalt be a witness for him to all men, of what thou hast seen, and didst hear. (16) And now why tarriest thou? Arise, be immersed and wash away thy sins, calling on his name.

(17) And it came to pass, when I had returned to Jerusalem, and as I was praying in the temple, that I was in a trance, (18) and saw him saying to me: Make haste, and go forth quickly out of Jerusalem; for they will not receive thy testimony concerning me. (19) And I said: Lord, they well know that I imprisoned and beat in every synagogue those who believe on thee; (20) and when the blood of thy witness Stephen was shed, then I myself was standing by, and consenting, and keeping the garments of those who slew him. (21) And he said to me: Depart; for I will send thee far hence to the Gentiles.

(22) And they heard him unto this word, and then lifted up their voices, and said: Away with such a one from the earth; for it was not fit that he should live. (23) And as they were crying out, and throwing up their garments, and casting dust into the air, (24) the chief captain commanded him to be brought into the castle, and bade that he should be examined by scourging; that he might know for what charge they were thus crying out against him.

(25) And as they stretched him forth with the thongs[22:25], Paul said to the centurion who stood by: Is it lawful for you to scourge a man that is a Roman, and uncondemned? (26) The centurion, hearing it, he went and told the chief captain, saying: What art thou about to do? For this man is a Roman. (27) And the chief captain came, and said to him: Tell me, art thou a Roman? He said: Yes. (28) And the chief captain answered: For a great sum I obtained this freedom. And Paul said: But I was born free.

(29) Immediately, therefore, they departed from him who were about to examine him; and the chief captain also was afraid, after he knew that he was a Roman, and because he had bound him.

Notes

1. Defense of the gospel is the ongoing theme of the next three chapters.
2. What Ananias says here {14-15} is roughly equivalent to what is found in Acts 9:15.
3. The report of the vision {17-21} is not given in the other accounts of Paul's conversion.
4. Examination by flogging was to determine the truth.
5. In the early part of the reign of Claudius, citizenship could be purchased for a large sum.

<u>**Questions for Reflection**</u>

1. Would you value your citizenship differently if you had purchased it? Why?

2. Who purchased your citizenship in the kingdom of God?

3. Why do you see it this way?

<u>**Sanhedrin Trial: Acts: 22:30-23:11**</u>

(30) On the morrow, wishing to know the certainty, wherefore he was accused by the Jews, he released him, and commanded the chief priests and all the council to come together; and he brought Paul down, and set him before them.

Acts 23

AND Paul, earnestly beholding the council, said: Men, brethren, I have lived in all good conscience before God unto this day.

(2) And the high priest Ananias commanded those who stood by him to smite him on the mouth.

(3) Then Paul said to him: God will smite thee, thou whited wall. And dost thou sit to judge me according to the law, and command me to be smitten contrary to law?

(4) And they that stood by said: Revilest thou God's high priest?

(5) And Paul said: I knew not, brethren, that he is high priest; for it is written: Thou shalt not speak evil of a ruler of thy people.

(6) And Paul, knowing that the one part were Sadducees, and the other Pharisees, cried out in the council: Men, brethren, I am a Pharisee, the son of a Pharisee; for the hope of the resurrection of the dead I am now judged.

(7) And when he had said this, there arose a dissension between the Pharisees and the Sadducees; and the multitude was divided. (8) For Sadducees say that there is no resurrection, nor angel, nor spirit; but Pharisees acknowledge both.

(9) And there arose a great clamor; and the scribes of the party of the Pharisees arose, and contended, saying: We find no evil in this man; but if a spirit spoke to him, or an angel?

(10) And a great dissension arising, the chief captain, fearing lest Paul should be pulled in pieces by them, commanded the soldiery to go down, and to take him by force from among them, and to bring him into the castle.

(11) And the night following, the Lord stood by him, and said: Be of good courage; for as thou didst fully testify the things concerning me at Jerusalem, so must thou testify also at Rome.

<u>**Notes**</u>

1. The tribune's purpose is to gather evidence. He calls for an advisory meeting of the council.
2. Ananias was high priest during the reigns of Claudius and Nero. He was murdered by rebels in 66 AD.
3. Paul exploits the differences between the Sadducees and Pharisees by raising the issue of resurrection.
4. A vision provides assurance that martyrdom will not happen in Jerusalem.

> Merciful God, I confess that I could do more than I am currently doing. I love and adore You, eternal humbling God. I am thankful for the saints who have gone before me in heaven, my eternal home, and have created and built my spiritual community on Earth. Help all of us in my community of faith to be more like Our Savior and Lord. I humbly offer my prayers to Your perfect timing in Jesus' name. Amen.

<u>Transfer to Caesarea: Acts 23:12-35</u>

(12) And when it was day, the Jews banded together, and bound themselves under a curse, saying that they would neither eat nor drink till they had killed Paul. (13) And they were more than forty who made this conspiracy. (14) And they came to the chief priests and the elders, and said: We bound ourselves under a great curse, to taste nothing until we have slain Paul.

(15) Now therefore do ye, with the council, signify to the chief captain that he bring him down to you, as though ye would ascertain more exactly the matters concerning him; and we, before he comes near, are ready to kill him.

(16) And the son of Paul's sister, hearing of their lying in wait, went and entered into the castle, and told Paul. (17) Then Paul called one of the centurions to him, and said: Bring this young man to the chief captain; for he has something to tell him. (18) So he took him, and brought him to the chief captain, and said: Paul, the prisoner, called me to him, and asked me to bring this young man to thee, as he has something to say to thee.

(19) Then the chief captain took him by the hand, and went aside privately, and asked: What is that thou hast to tell me? (20) And he said: The Jews agreed to desire thee, that thou wouldst bring down Paul to-morrow into the council, as though they would inquire somewhat more exactly concerning him. (21) But do not thou yield to them; for of them more than forty men are lying in wait for him, who bound themselves with an oath, neither to eat nor to drink till they have killed him; and now they are ready, looking for the promise from thee.

(22) The chief captain therefore dismissed the young man, having charged him to say to no one, that thou didst show these things to me. (23) And calling to him two or three of the centurions, he said: Make ready two hundred soldiers to go to Caesarea, and seventy horsemen, two hundred spearmen, at the third hour of the night; (24) and let them provide beasts, that they may set Paul thereon, and bring him safe to Felix the governor.

(25) And he wrote a letter after this manner: (26) Claudius Lysias to the most excellent governor Felix, sends greeting. (27) This man was taken by the Jews, and was about to be killed by them; but I came upon them with the soldiery, and rescued him, having learned that he is a Roman. (28) And wishing to know the crime for which they were accusing him, I brought him down into their council; (29) whom I found to be accused concerning questions of their law, but having nothing laid to his charge worthy of death or of bonds. (30) And being informed that a plot was about to be laid against the man, I sent straightway to thee, having also commanded the accusers to say before thee what they had against him. Farewell.

(31) The soldiers, therefore, as was commanded them, took up Paul, and brought him by night to Antipatris. (32) But on the morrow, leaving the horsemen to go with him, they returned to the castle; (33) who, when they had entered into Caesarea, and delivered the letter to the governor, presented Paul also before him. (34) And having read it, he asked of what province he was. And learning that he was from Cilicia, (35) he said: I will hear thee fully, when thy accusers are also come. And he commanded him to be kept in the praetorium of Herod.

Notes

1. The attempt to kill Paul leads to his transfer.
2. Caesarea is the seat of the Roman Governor.
3. Paul's being educated in Jerusalem suggests that other family members were there, but we have no further evidence of his family.
4. The extent of the danger is reflected in the number of soldiers used to protect Paul.
5. Antonius Felix was the procurator of Judea from 52-56 AD.
6. The letter evidently casts the tribune in a better light and summarizes what had happened.

Questions for Reflection

1. If you learned of plot to kill you because of your faith in Jesus, would you defend your faith? How?

2. What are the most important things you might say in defending your faith?

Trial Before Felix: Acts: 24-1-27

AND after five days, the high priest Ananias came down with the elders and a certain orator named Tertullus, who informed the governor against Paul; (2) and he having been called, Tertullus began to accuse him, saying: Seeing that by thee we enjoy great quietness, and that very worthy deeds are done for this nation through thy providence, in every way and everywhere; (3) we accept it, most noble Felix, with all thankfulness.

(4) But, not to hinder thee too long, I pray thee that thou wouldst hear us of thy clemency a few words. (5) For we have found this man to be a pest, and exciting disturbance among all the Jews throughout the world, and a ringleader of the sect of the Nazarenes; (6) who also attempted to profane the temple; whom we took, and desired to judge according to our law. (7) But Lysias the chief captain came, and with great violence took him away out of our hands, (8) commanding his accusers to come before thee;] from whom thou canst thyself ascertain, by examination, concerning all these things whereof we accuse him. (9) And the Jews also joined in assailing him, saying that these things were so.

(10) Then Paul, the governor having beckoned to him to speak, answered: Knowing that thou hast been for many years a judge for this nation, I do the more cheerfully answer for myself; (11) inasmuch as thou mayest know, that there are not more than twelve days since I went up to Jerusalem to worship; (12) and neither in the temple did they find me disputing with any one, or causing a tumult of the people, nor in the synagogues, nor in the city; (13) nor can they prove the things whereof they now accuse me.

(14) But this I acknowledge to thee, that according to the way which they call a sect, so I worship the God of our fathers, believing all things which are written in the law and the prophets; (15) having a hope toward God, which these themselves also look for, that there will be a resurrection both of the just and unjust. (16) Therefore do I also myself strive to have always a conscience void of offense toward God and men.

(17) And after many years I came to bring alms to my nation, and offerings. (18) Amidst which they found me purified in the temple, not with a crowd, nor with tumult; but certain Jews from Asia [caused it], (19) who ought to be here before thee, and make accusation, if they had aught against me. (20) Or let these themselves say what crime they found in me, while I stood before the council, (21) except for this one voice that I cried, standing among them: Concerning the resurrection of the dead I am judged by you this day.

(22) And Felix put them off, knowing the things concerning the Way more accurately, saying: When Lysias the chief captain shall come down, I will fully inquire into your matters. (23) And he commanded the centurion that he should be guarded, and should have indulgence; and to forbid none of his acquaintance to minister to him.

(24) And after certain days, Felix came with his wife Drusilla, who was a Jewess, and sent for Paul, and heard him concerning the faith in Christ. (25) And as he reasoned of righteousness, temperance, and the judgment to come, Felix trembled, and answered: Go thy way for this time; when I have a convenient season, I will call for thee. (26) He hoped also that money would be given him by Paul; wherefore he sent for him the oftener, and conversed with him.

(27) But after two years, Felix was succeeded by Porcius Festus; and Felix, wishing to gain favor with the Jews, left Paul bound.

Notes

1. When Paul denies the charges, the governor postpones the case.
2. The term agitator amounted to a charge of sedition.
3. Resurrection {15} is common ground on which to speak.
4. Drusilla was the sister of Herod Agrippa and Bernice. She had left her husband Azizus, the king of Emesa, to marry Felix.
5. Although Felix is a mixture of both good and bad governance, his corruption comes through in keeping Paul in prison.
6. Porcius Festus was appointed procurator of Judea by Nero in 60 AD.

<u>Questions for Reflection</u>

1. What are some things about this trial that are different from those you have known through the media in this century?

2. Considering the reasons that Christ's resurrection is important to your faith that you previously stated, how does this trial speak to your faith?

> My glorious Father in heaven, I am accepting the new path you are pointing out to me. I pray that You strengthen my courage and faith in You. I have a strong love for You and I long to always trust You, but my faith is often lacking. Forgive me. I have a memory of your Son, Jesus, using His divine loving power to calm the stormy sea. I want to express my gratitude for my salvation in Him once more. My prayer is in His name. Amen.

<u>**Appeal to the Emperor: Acts 25:1-12**</u>

FESTUS, therefore, having come into the province, after three days went up from Caesarea to Jerusalem.

(2) And the high priest and the chief of the Jews informed him against Paul, and besought him, (3) asking for themselves a favor against him, that he would send for him to Jerusalem, preparing an ambush to slay him on the way. (4) But Festus answered, that Paul was to be kept a prisoner at Caesarea, and that he himself should soon go thither. (5) Let them therefore, said he, who are powerful among you, go down with me, and accuse this man, if there is any wickedness in him.

(6) And having tarried among them not more than eight or ten days, he went down to Caesarea; and on the morrow, sitting on the judgment-seat, he commanded Paul to be brought. (7) And when he was come, the Jews who had come down from Jerusalem stood around, bringing many and grievous charges, which they could not prove; (8) while Paul said in defense: Neither against the law of the Jews, nor against the temple, nor against Caesar, did I commit any offense.

(9) But Festus, wishing to gain favor with the Jews, answered Paul, and said: Wilt thou go up to Jerusalem, and there be judged concerning these things, before me? (10) And Paul said; I stand at Caesar's judgment-seat, where I ought to be judged. To Jews I did no wrong, as thou also very well knowest. (11) If then I am an offender, and have done anything worthy of death, I refuse not to die; but if there be none of the things whereof these accuse me, no man can give me up to them. I appeal to Caesar.

(12) Then Festus, having conferred with the council, answered: Thou hast appealed to Caesar; to Caesar thou shalt go.

Notes

1. Paul maintains that he is both a good Jew and a good Roman citizen.
2. The appeal becomes the means by which Paul goes to Rome.

<u>**Questions for Reflection**</u>

1. If you were on trial, would you prefer a church court or a civil court? Why?

2. Are you be willing to trust God with justice for you?

3. Are you willing to trust God with anything and everything?

> Heavenly Father, your word tells me that first century Christians faced challenges that I hope I never face. In my country, there is still freedom of religion, but there are those who oppose it. It brings me joy that you have not given up on me, offering your divine love and forgiveness. You are worthy of all praise and glory. In Jesus' name, I pray. Amen.

Paul Before Agrippa: Acts 25:13-26:32

(13) And after certain days, Agrippa the king, and Bernice, came to Caesarea to salute Festus. (14) And as they were spending some days there, Festus laid the case of Paul before the king, saying: There is a certain man left in bonds by Felix; (15) about whom, when I was at Jerusalem, the chief priests and the elders of the Jews made complaint, asking for judgment against him. (16) To whom I answered: It is not a custom for Romans to give up any man, before the accused has the accusers face to face, and has opportunity to answer for himself concerning the crime laid against him.

(17) When, therefore, they had come together here, without any delay on the morrow I sat on the judgment-seat, and commanded the man to be brought forth; (18) and standing up around him, the accusers brought no accusation of such things as I supposed; (19) but had certain controversies with him concerning their own religion, and concerning a certain Jesus who was dead, whom Paul affirmed to be alive. (20) And I, being perplexed in regard to the dispute about these things, asked whether he would go to Jerusalem, and there be judged concerning them. (21) But Paul having appealed, to be kept in custody for the decision of Augustus, I commanded him to be kept until I shall send him up to Caesar.

(22) And Agrippa said to Festus: I would also hear the man myself. To-morrow, said he, thou shalt hear him.

(23) On the morrow, therefore, Agrippa and Bernice having come with great pomp, and entered into the place of hearing, with the chief captains and principal men of the city, at Festus' command Paul was brought forth. (24) And Festus said: King Agrippa, and all men who are here present with us, ye see this man, about whom all the multitude of the Jews interceded with me, both at Jerusalem and here, Crying out that he ought not to live any longer. (25) But having found that he had committed nothing worthy of death, and he himself having appealed to Augustus, I determined to send him. (26) Of whom I have nothing certain to write to my lord. Wherefore I brought him forth before you, and specially before thee, king Agrippa, in order that, the examination having been made, I may have something to write. (27) For it seems to me unreasonable to send a prisoner, and not also signify the charges against him.

Acts 26

AND Agrippa said to Paul: Thou art permitted to speak for thyself. Then Paul stretched forth the hand, and answered for himself:

(2) I think myself happy, king Agrippa, because I shall answer for myself before thee this day, concerning all things whereof I am accused by Jews; (3) especially since thou art expert in all the customs and questions among Jews. Wherefore I beseech thee to hear me patiently.

(4) My manner of life, therefore, from my youth, which was from the beginning among my own nation at Jerusalem, all Jews know; (5) having known me from the first, if they were willing to testify, that according to the strictest sect of our religion, I lived a Pharisee. (6) And now I stand and am judged for the hope of the promise made by God to the fathers; (7) unto which our twelve tribes, earnestly serving day and night, hope to attain; concerning which hope, O king, I am accused by Jews.

(8) Why is it judged incredible with you, if God, raises the dead?

(9) I therefore thought to myself, that I ought to do many hostile things against the name of Jesus the Nazarene. (10) Which I also did in Jerusalem; and many of the saints did I myself shut up in prisons, having received authority from the chief priests; and when they were put to death, I gave my voice against them. (11) And punishing them often, throughout all the synagogues, I constrained them to blaspheme; and being exceedingly mad against them, I persecuted them also unto foreign cities.

(12) Whereupon, as I went to Damascus with authority and a commission from the chief priests, (13) at midday, O king, I saw in the way a light from heaven, above the brightness of the sun, shining around me and those who journeyed with me. (14) And we all having fallen to the earth, I heard a voice speaking to me, and saying in the Hebrew tongue: Saul, Saul, why persecutest thou me? It is hard for thee to kick against the goads. (15) And I said: Who art thou, Lord? And he said: I am Jesus, whom thou persecutest. (16) But arise, and stand upon thy feet; for I appeared to thee for this purpose, to appoint thee a minister and a witness both of the things which thou sawest, and of the things in which I will appear to thee; (17) delivering thee from the people, and the Gentiles, to whom I send thee, (18) to open their eyes, that they may turn from darkness to light, and from the power of Satan unto God, that they may obtain forgiveness of sins, and an inheritance among the sanctified, by faith in me.

(19) Wherefore, O king Agrippa, I was not disobedient to the heavenly vision; (20) but to those in Damascus first, and in Jerusalem, and unto all the region of Judaea, and to the Gentiles, I announced that they should repent and turn to God, doing works worthy of repentance.

(21) For these causes the Jews, seizing me in the temple, attempted to kill me. (22) Having therefore obtained help from God, I continue unto this day, witnessing both to small and great, saying nothing except those things which the prophets and Moses said should come; (23) whether the Christ should suffer, whether he, the first of the resurrection from the dead, shall show light to the people and to the Gentiles.

(24) And as he thus spoke for himself, Festus said with a loud voice: Paul, thou art mad; much learning makes thee mad.

(25) But he said: I am not mad, most noble Festus; but utter words of truth and soberness. (26) For the king knows well concerning these things, to whom also I speak boldly; for I am persuaded that none of these things are hidden from him; for this has not been done in a corner. (27) King Agrippa, believest thou the prophets? I know that thou believest.

(28) And Agrippa said to Paul: With little pains[26:28a] thou persuadest me to become a Christian. (29) And Paul said: I could pray God, that with little or much[26:29], not only thou, but also all that hear me this day, may become such as I am, except these bonds.

(30) And the king rose up, and the governor, and Bernice, and they who sat with them. (31) And having withdrawn, they talked together, saying: This man does nothing worthy of death or of bonds. (32) And Agrippa said to Festus: This man could have been set at liberty, if he had not appealed to Caesar.

Notes

1. Paul's speech is intended to provide a model defense of Christianity in general, not just himself.
2. Presiding is Herod Agrippa II, who was in power from 53-93 AD.
3. 'Nothing deserving death' is the repeated conclusion by Roman authorities.
4. Only is this account of his conversion does Paul say his commission comes directly from Jesus.

Questions for Reflection

1. How would you defend your faith against those who do not believe in God or believe there is no God?

2. Do the Roman authorities surprise you with their support for Paul? Why?

3. If you get into serious legal trouble, would you have the support of your family and friends?

> Forgive me, Lord Jesus, when I focus on my struggles and not on Your blessings. Whether in the heat of summer or the frost of winter, Lord, thank You for providing glorious and amazing life for me. Please help me to continue growing in my faith in You. I can face anything today, Lord Jesus, because You are my strength, and my prayers are in Your name. Amen.

Shipwrecked: Acts 27:1-44

AND when it was determined that we should sail to Italy, they delivered Paul and certain other prisoners to a centurion named Julius, of the Augustan band. (2) And entering into a ship of Adramyttium, about to sail along the coasts of Asia, we put to sea, Aristarchus, a Macedonian of Thessalonica, being with us. (3) And on the second day we landed at Sidon. And Julius treated Paul humanely, and permitted him to go to his friends and receive their care. (4) And thence having put to sea, we sailed under Cyprus, because the winds were contrary, (5) And having sailed over the sea along Cilicia and Pamphylia, we came to Myra, a city of Lycia. (6) And there the centurion found a ship of Alexandria sailing to Italy; and he put us on board of it. (7) And sailing slowly many days, and having come with difficulty over against Cnidus, the wind not suffering us to put in[27:7], we sailed under Crete, over against Salmone; (8) and coasting along it with difficulty, we came to a certain place called Fair Havens, near to which was the city Lasa.

(9) And much time having been spent, and the voyage being now dangerous, because also the fast had already passed by, Paul exhorted them, (10) saying: Sirs, I perceive that the voyage will be with violence and much loss, not only of the lading and the ship, but also of our lives. (11) But the centurion believed the master and the owner of the ship, more than the things spoken by Paul. (12) And as the haven was not well situated for wintering, the greater number advised to sail thence also, if by any means they might reach Phoenix, a haven of Crete, looking toward the southwest and northwest, and there winter.

(13) And a south wind beginning to blow moderately, supposing that they had obtained their purpose, they weighed anchor, and coasted along close by Crete. (14) But not long after, there struck against it a tempestuous wind, called Euracylon. (15) And the ship being caught, and unable to face the wind, we yielded to it, and were driven along. (16) And running under a certain small island called Clauda, we were hardly able to come by the boat; (17) which when they had taken up, they used helps, undergirding the ship; and, fearing lest they should be cast away on the quicksand, they lowered the sail, and so were driven.

(18) And we being violently tempest-tossed, the next day they lightened the ship; (19) and the third day we cast out with our own hands the tackling of the ship. (20) And neither sun nor stars appearing for many days, and no small tempest lying on us, thenceforward all hope that we should be saved was utterly taken away. (21) But after much abstinence, then Paul, standing up in the midst of then, said: Sirs, ye should have hearkened to me and not put to sea from Crete, and so have escaped this violence and loss. (22) And now I exhort you to be of good cheer; for there shall be no loss of life among you, but only of the ship. (23) For there stood by me this night an angel of God, whose I am, and whom I serve, (24) saying: Fear not, Paul; thou must stand before Caesar; and, lo, God has given thee all those who sail with thee. (25) Wherefore, sirs, be of good cheer; for I believe God, that it will be even so, as it has been told me. (26) But we must be cast away upon a certain island.

(27) And when the fourteenth night was come, as we were driven onward in the Adriatic sea, about midnight the seamen suspected that they were near to some country; (28) and sounding, they found twenty fathoms; and having gone a little further, they sounded again, and found fifteen fathoms. (29) Then fearing lest we should fall upon rocks, they cast four anchors out of the stern, and wished for day.

(30) And as the seamen were seeking to flee out of the ship, and had let down the boat into the sea, under color as if they were about to extend anchors out of the foreship, (31) Paul said to the centurion and to the soldiers: Except these abide in the ship, ye can not be saved. (32) Then the soldiers cut off the ropes of the boat, and let it fall off.

(33) And while the day was coming on, Paul besought them all to take food, saying: This day is the fourteenth day that ye have waited, and continued fasting, having taken nothing. (34) Wherefore I pray you to take food; for this is for your safety; for there shall not a hair fall from the head of one of you.

(35) And having thus spoken, he took bread, and gave thanks to God in presence of them all; and having broken it, he began to eat. (36) Then were they all of good cheer, and they also took food. (37) And we were in all in the ship two hundred and seventy-six souls. (38) And when they had eaten enough, they lightened the ship, casting out the grain into the sea.

(39) And when it was day, they knew not the land; but they perceived a certain creek, having a beach, on which they determined, if they were able, to drive the ship ashore. (40) And cutting the anchors entirely away,

they abandoned them to the sea, at the same time unfastening the bands of the rudders; and hoisting the foresail to the wind, they made toward the beach. (41) And falling into a place where two seas met, they ran the ship aground; and the prow sticking fast remained immovable, but the stern was broken by the violence of the waves. (42) And it was the plan of the soldiers, that they should kill the prisoners, lest any one should swim out, and escape. (43) But the centurion, wishing to save Paul, kept them from their purpose; and commanded that those who could swim should cast themselves first into the sea and get to land, (44) and the rest, some on boards, and others on some of the pieces from the ship. And so it came to pass, that all escaped safe to land.

Notes

1. There was a unit named The Augustan Cohort stationed in Syria in the first century.
2. Sailing was dangerous from September to mid-November, then things were relatively calm until March.
3. The fast for the Day of Atonement would occur in September or October.
4. There being 276 people on board was quite possible although crowded.
5. The details supplied by Luke reflects his intelligence and education.

Questions for Reflection

1. Would you be frightened if you were on the ocean in a major storm?

2. Would your faith play a role in how you handled the storm?

3. Have you experienced other kinds of storms in your life, and if so, what was your faith's role, if any?

> Glorious God, please forgive me when I am tempted with extreme responses to evil which could be as bad as the evil I witness. Thank You for being my shield and fortress that shelter me from the storms of life. Grant me, I pray, the wisdom to respond effectively to the many needs around me. Use me for Your glory, I ask in Jesus' name. Amen.

<u>On Malta: Acts 28:1-10</u>

AND having escaped, they then learned that the island is called Melita. (2) And the barbarians showed us no little kindness; for they kindled a fire, and received us all, because of the present rain, and because of the cold.

(3) And Paul having gathered a bundle of sticks, and laid them on the fire, there came out a viper from the heat, and fastened on his hand. (4) And when the barbarians saw the animal hanging from his hand, they said among themselves: No doubt this man is a murderer, whom, though escaped from the sea, justice suffered not to live. (5) He, however, shaking off the animal into the fire, suffered no harm. (6) But they were expecting that he would become inflamed, or suddenly fall down dead; but after looking a great while, and seeing no harm befall him, they changed their minds, and said that he was a god.

(7) In the region around that place, there were lands of the chief man of the island, whose name was Publius, who received and entertained us kindly three days. (8) Now it happened, that the father of Publius was lying sick with a fever and a bloody flux; to whom Paul entered in, and having prayed, laid his hands on him and healed him. (9) And this having been done, the others also, who had diseases in the island, came and were healed; (10) who also honored us with many honors; and when we put to sea, they loaded us with such things as were necessary.

<u>Notes</u>

1. Malta is an island controlled at that time by the Romans south of Sicily. It was considered significant for travel within the Roman Empire.
2. Natives could be literally translated 'barbarians' because they were non-Greek.
3. At that time on the island, justice is a god.

<u>Question for Reflection</u>

➢ How would you react if you saw a stranger be bitten by a snake but be unaffected? Why?

<u>Travel to Rome: Acts 28:11-16</u>

(11) And after three months, we put to sea in a ship of Alexandria, which had wintered in the island, whose sign was Castor and Pollux. (12) And landing at Syracuse, we remained three days. (13) And from thence, making a circuit[28:13], we came to Rhegium. And after one day, a south wind arose, and we came on the second day to Puteoli; (14) where we found brethren, and were entreated to remain with them seven days; and so we went toward Rome. (15) And from thence, the brethren, having heard of us, came to meet us as far as Appii Forum, and the Three Taverns; whom when Paul saw, he gave thanks to God, and took courage.

(16) And when we came to Rome, the centurion delivered the prisoners to the commander of the camp; but Paul was suffered to dwell by himself, with the soldier who guarded him.

<u>Notes</u>

1. Three months is probably an approximation since it would be too soon to continue to Rome.
2. There are already Christians in Rome.
3. Evidently Paul had private quarters.
4. Once again, note the details supplied by Luke.

Question for Reflection

> ➢ Since this is Paul's first trip to Rome, how do you think Christianity got established there?

Jewish Dialogue: Acts 28:17-28

(17) And it came to pass, that after three days Paul called together those who were the chief men of the Jews; and when they were come together, he said to them: Men, brethren, though I had done nothing against the people, or the customs of our fathers, yet I was delivered a prisoner from Jerusalem into the hands of the Romans; (18) who, when they had examined me, wished to release me, because there was no cause of death in me. (19) But as the Jews spoke against it, I was compelled to appeal to Caesar; not that I have anything to charge against my nation. (20) For this cause therefore I called for you, to see and to speak with you; for on account of the hope of Israel I am compassed with this chain.

(21) And they said to him: We neither received letters from Judaea concerning thee, nor did any one of the brethren that came, report or speak any evil concerning thee. (22) But we desire to hear from thee what thou thinkest; for concerning this sect, we know that everywhere it is spoken against.

(23) And having appointed a day for him, they came to him in greater numbers to his lodging; to whom he expounded, testifying fully the kingdom of God, and persuading them of the things concerning Jesus, both from the law of Moses and the prophets, from morning till evening. (24) And some believed the things spoken, and some believed not. (25) And disagreeing among themselves, they departed, after Paul had spoken one word: Well did the Holy Spirit speak through Isaiah the prophet to our fathers, (26) saying:

Go to this people, and say;

With the hearing ye will hear, and will not understand,

And seeing ye will see, and will not perceive.

(27) For the heart of this people is become gross,

And their ears are dull of hearing,

And their eyes they have closed;

Lest haply they see with their eyes,

And hear with their ears,

And understand with their heart,

And turn, and I shall heal them.

(28) Be it known to you, therefore, that to the Gentiles the salvation of God was sent; they, moreover, will hear.[28:29 not included in this translation.]

Notes

1. Even as a captive Paul maintains his pattern of speaking to the Jewish community first.
2. The hope of Israel's future is now bound up with Christianity.
3. The reaction to his presentation was mixed as usual.
4. Verse 29 reads, 'And when he had said these words the Jews departed, arguing vigorously among themselves.' This verse is not found in the oldest manuscripts.

<u>**Questions for Reflection**</u>

1. Why do you suppose Paul does not mention here the charges against him?

2. How do you suppose the Jews felt when they heard an ancient prophecy applied to them?

Lord God, I surrender to Your power and truth. May it guide me and lead me towards living for Jesus. Thank you for the vision to perceive Your will, for the faith to believe in all that You reveal to me, and for the courage I need to always fully trust You. I am not yet sure where You are leading me. I trust You and pray in the power of Jesus' name. Amen.

<u>Conclusion: Acts 28:30-31</u>

(30) And Paul remained two whole years in his own hired house, and gladly received all that came in to him; (31) preaching the kingdom of God, and teaching the things concerning the Lord Jesus Christ, with all confidence, no one hindering him.

<u>Notes</u>

1. Though under house arrest Paul preached without hindrance for two whole years.
2. Although church tradition says Paul was executed, there is no historical evidence to support that tradition.
3. There are churches in Portugal, Spain, and Great Britian that say Paul established them.
4. Whether or not Paul was martyred or went on to Spain, those two years provided enough time for the two books, *Luke* and Acts, to be written.

<u>Question for Reflection</u>

➢ Do you think Paul was martyred after the two-year period, or do you think he went on to do further missionary activity as He planned?

<u>Other Bible Study Workbooks Available on Amazon</u>

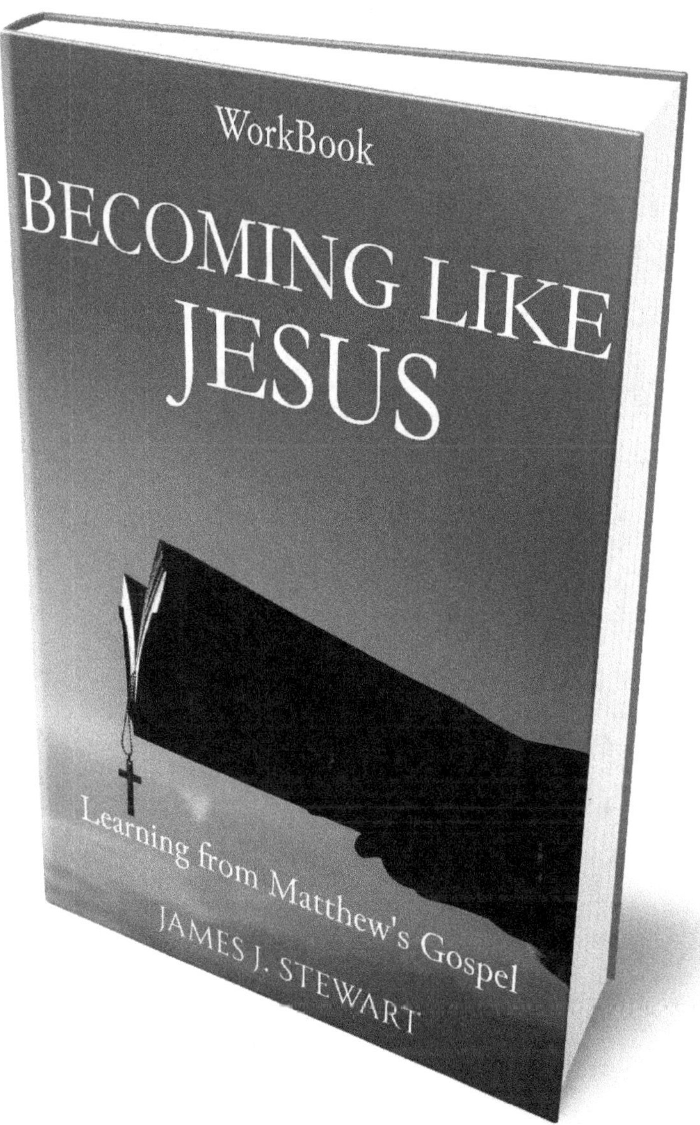

In this workbook, the emphasis is upon learning more from the Christ of faith and becoming faithful disciples of Jesus. Then, while faithfully following Jesus and trying to be like Him, you can actually become more like Him. Although there are almost always women present when Jesus speaks, Matthew's gospel is focused upon a primarily male audience. Along with the other three canonical gospels, it constitutes the heart of the faith of Christians during those first centuries after Christ's birth. In the years just before Christ's birth, Jews throughout the Roman Empire were praying fervently for the coming of the Messiah [Hebrew] or Christ [Greek]. Matthew testifies to how people responded to the Jesus of history, and how Jesus truly is the promised Messiah.

The Gospel of John is the most intimate portrayal of Jesus that we have in the Bible. If you want to follow Jesus and try to be like him, the gospel of John is a good beginning. John's Gospel records fewer incidents of Jesus' public teaching and more meetings of Jesus with individuals and small groups. As the gospel proceeds, we can observe his followers as they experience our savior's holiness and grow towards holiness. We too can grow in holiness.

This workbook is designed for individuals, couples, and small groups. A selection from the Book of Acts is often followed by notes for clarification, and then there are questions for reflection, discussion, and prayer.

<u>Another Bible Study available on Amazon</u>

Living for Jesus

A Biblical Focus for
Relating to God's Son

James J. Stewart

<u>Living for Jesus: A Biblical Focus for Relating to God's Son</u>

Being a Christian involves more than accepting some beliefs and trying to practice those beliefs. Unlike other religions, Christianity centers upon having a relationship with God through Jesus Christ. In our quest to know God more deeply the Bible is our primary resource, and this course is no exception. Unlike most Bible studies, however, this seven-week study does not focus either upon events in the life of Jesus or upon his teachings. Instead, it looks at some of those events from a few different perspectives. It is designed for small group study. It examines how Jesus related to individuals with His compassion, truth, humility, and authority. Secondly, it examines how those individuals responded to Jesus' impact on their lives. These situations will uncover the nature and character of Jesus and His will for each of us. Simply stated, this study focuses upon Jesus himself. The Gospel of John focuses on the person of Jesus that he knew, watching Jesus conversing with people one on one. The other gospels focus more upon his public teachings, though they also give us some glimpses of Jesus' character. Following Jesus is a lifetime pursuit. These seven sessions are intended to give Christians a fresh or new start in that pursuit.

<u>A Picture Book with Christian Poetry</u>
<u>Available on Amazon</u>

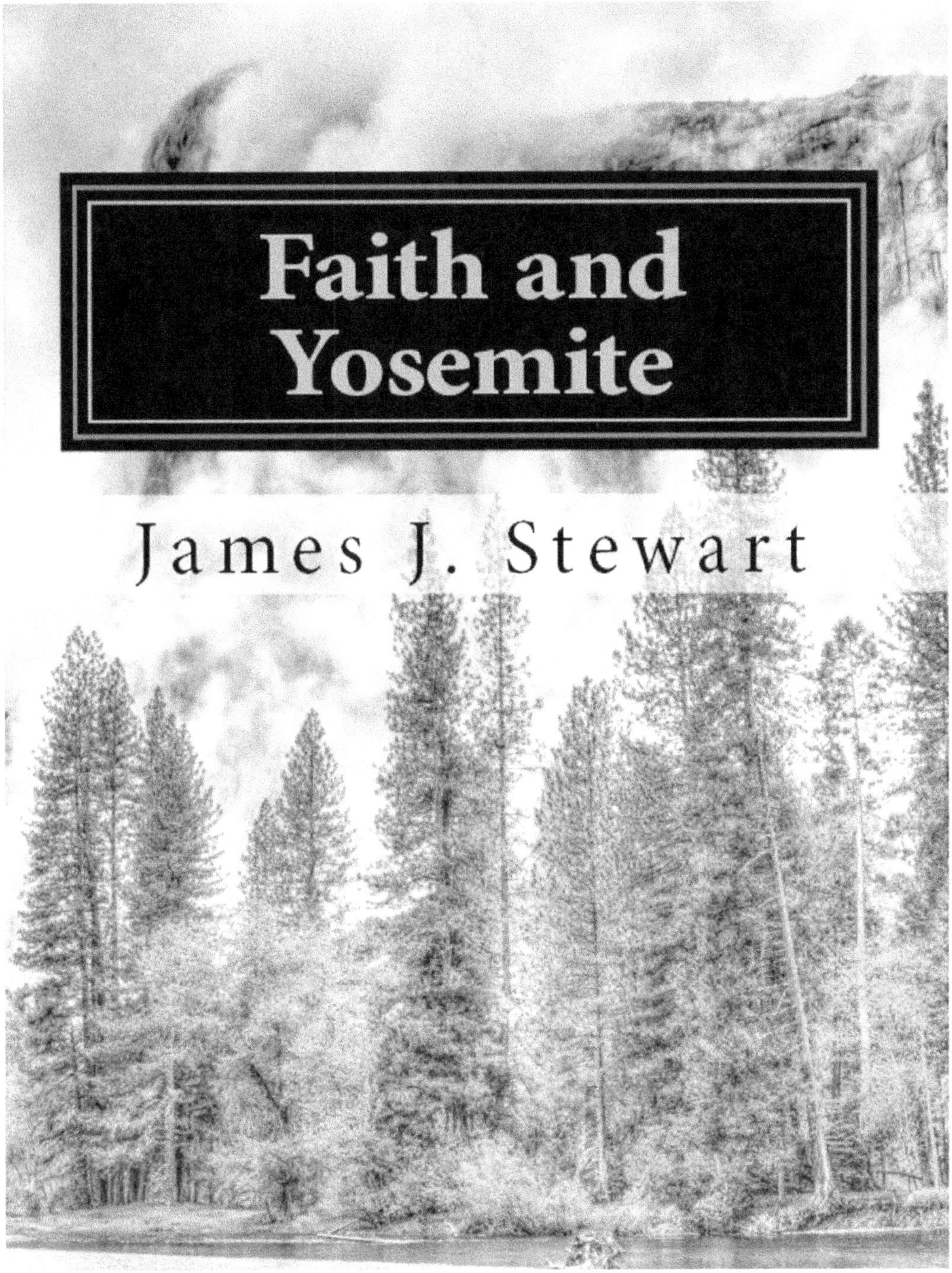

As with the previous editions, this beautiful book provides pictures of Yosemite National Park by a man who has been photographing this natural treasure for more than sixty years. With each picture is a poem about the Christian faith written by the photographer. This new edition provides pictures and some newer poetry not in previous editions as well as some of the same poems.

Fiction by this Author
Available on Amazon

In the Bible's Book of Judges, Deborah (1107-1067 BC) was a prophetess for the God of Israel, the only woman judge mentioned in the Bible. Deborah told the Bible's Barak that God commanded him to lead an attack against Jabin, the king of Canaan and his army. Barak would only go into battle against Jabin if Deborah went with him.Now, thirty-two hundred years later. California's Deborah is prophesying for the God of the Christians and Jews. Deborah tells Jethro, a brilliant hacker, God wants him to force the President of the United States out of office, along with other corrupt politicians, using dark web resources. Jethro will only take on President Dough and political corruption with Deborah joining him in the fight. She agrees, and she tells him that he will never get any of the credit for bringing John Dough down because it is God who makes all things possible. Deborah becomes a footnote in history books, but for Christians and Jews it is God who gets the glory.

A clean Christian romance, Jimmy is born just before the end of World War II. Growing up, he becomes a concert pianist. When working on his masters degree, Jimmy meets Carol, who is learning to play carillon bells, and they fall in love. As a couple living just outside of Yosemite, God begins putting miracles into their lives. When their three children are born, God brings miracles into their lives as well.

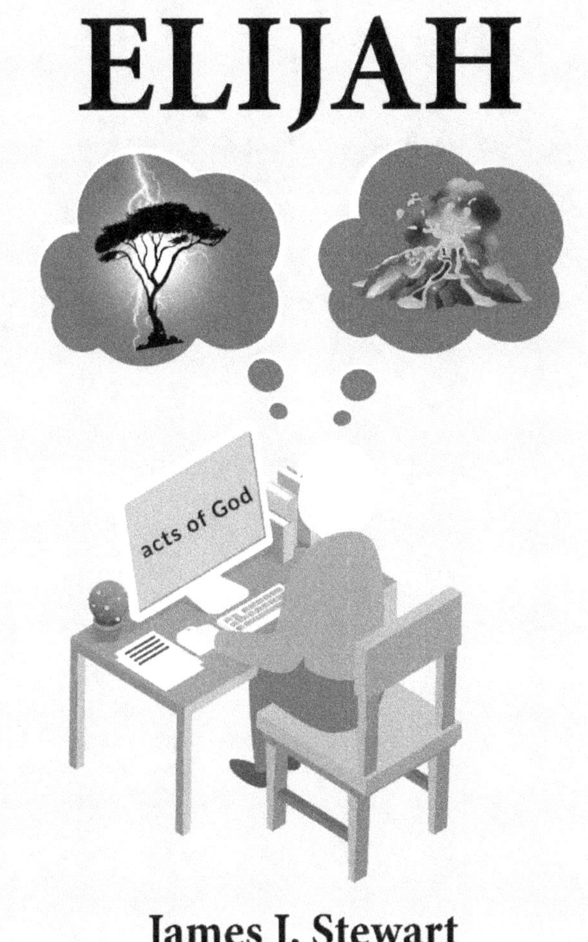

When Elijah retired as the pastor of a church in Texas, God began to use him in unexpected ways. When Elijah prayed, God gave Elijah images of what was taking place or about to take place. Then he sat down with his laptop and responded with his blog entries for the Internet. His longstanding blog began to be prophetic, but he avoided publicity and praised God. When his life adventure meant leaving behind his wife of more than forty years in a plane crash, God had another wife prepared for Elijah, along with more amazing adventures, including a nuclear winter that develops because of a super volcano.

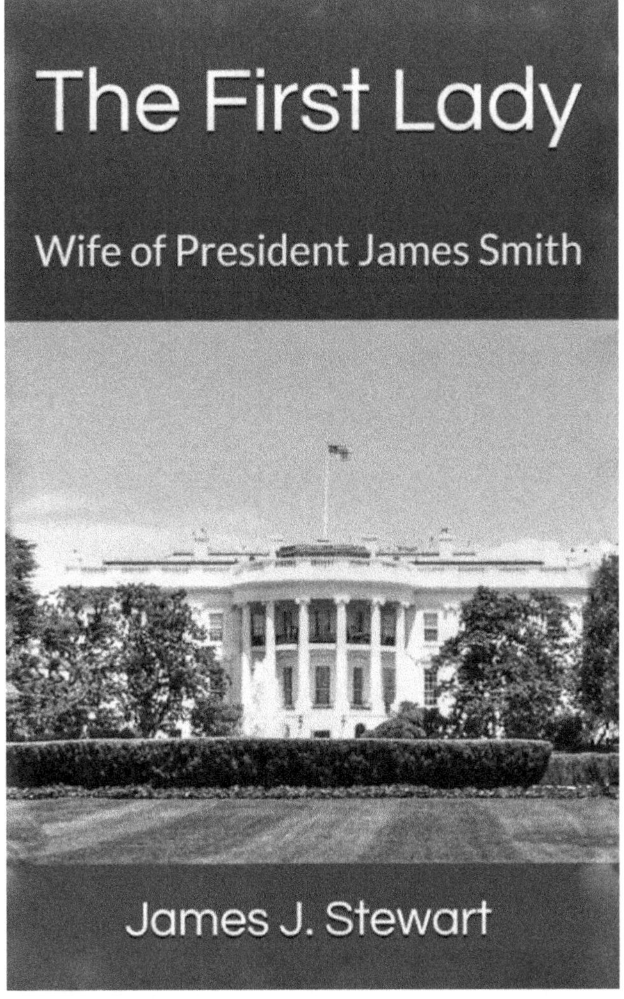

A brilliant musician and an equally brilliant astrophysicist fall in love, have a family, and stumble into politics. They innovate with everything they do, and they write new chapters of history politically and scientifically.

At an airport, a terrorist appears wearing a bomb. Joe curses the terrorist, and the suicide bomber disappears into the floor. Later that day, he meets a woman more than a generation younger than he is. It is love at first sight, but this second miracle is only the beginning. A series of miracles marks their lives together. These miracles shape the course of their adventures with each other.

An architect finds a large kitten hiding in the bushes near his home. It is a cheetah/puma cross-breed. It understands English, and it adopts the man. When a world-famous actress first sees the cat, she falls in love, first with the cat, and then with the man.

Frank Frazee has over 40 years of experience as a tenth-generation pastor. Before his first wife passes away due to diabetes complications, she introduces him to the woman she wants him to marry after she dies. The resulting gossip is vicious. Frank and his second wife are given the opportunity to serve God by building a church from scratch hundreds of miles away. As Frank Frazee tells his story, the reader witnesses the many ups and downs of serving a community in Jesus' name. There are also a few miracles along the way. After Frank dies at the age of one hundred and three, his second wife describes him in an epilogue to Frank's story. "Frank saw his purpose in life as helping people have a solid relationship with Jesus. He rescued people from time to time, and he did some charity work even beyond his role as a pastor. He preferred, however, to help people help themselves, so that they didn't need him to rescue them." Frank Frazee's story is that of great Christian love.

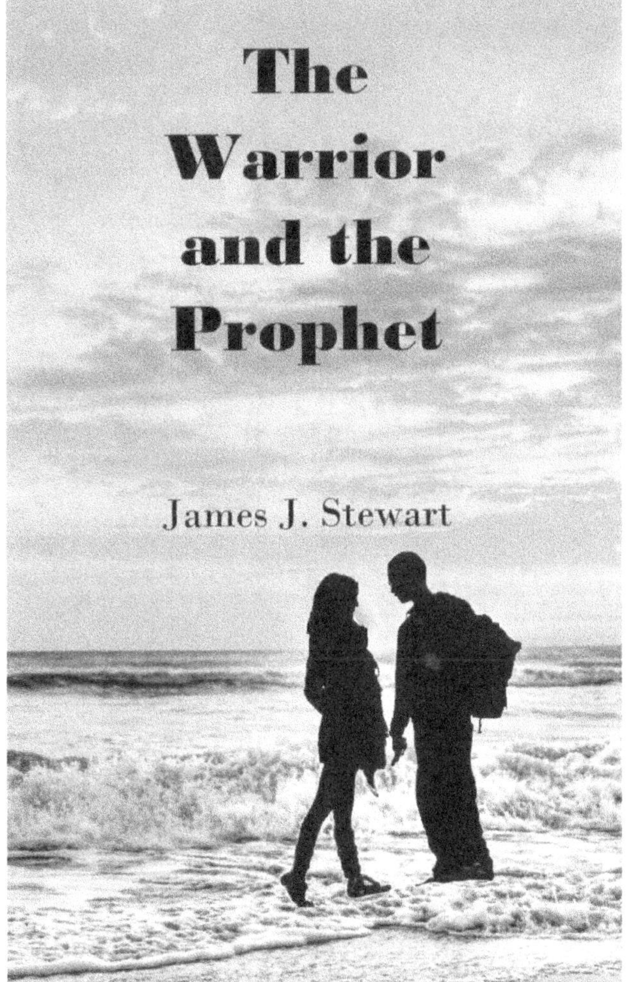

This saga began with "Casting Lots." It was followed by "Prayer Warriors" and "This World Is Not My Home." Each story stood on its own. Now, the year is 2062. Tonia is almost thirty. She grew up in the shadow of famous parents, both professional musicians and prophets. She does not plan to follow in her parents' footsteps, either as a musician (drummer) or as a prophet. She simply wants to spend her life with Toby and raise a family. Toby has just turned thirty. He is a ninth-generation prayer warrior. He is looking forward to spending the rest of his life with Tonia, who is both photogenic on the outside and beautiful on the inside. He plans to be an administrator like his Dad. The Creator of the Universe has big surprises and amazing blessings prepared for them.

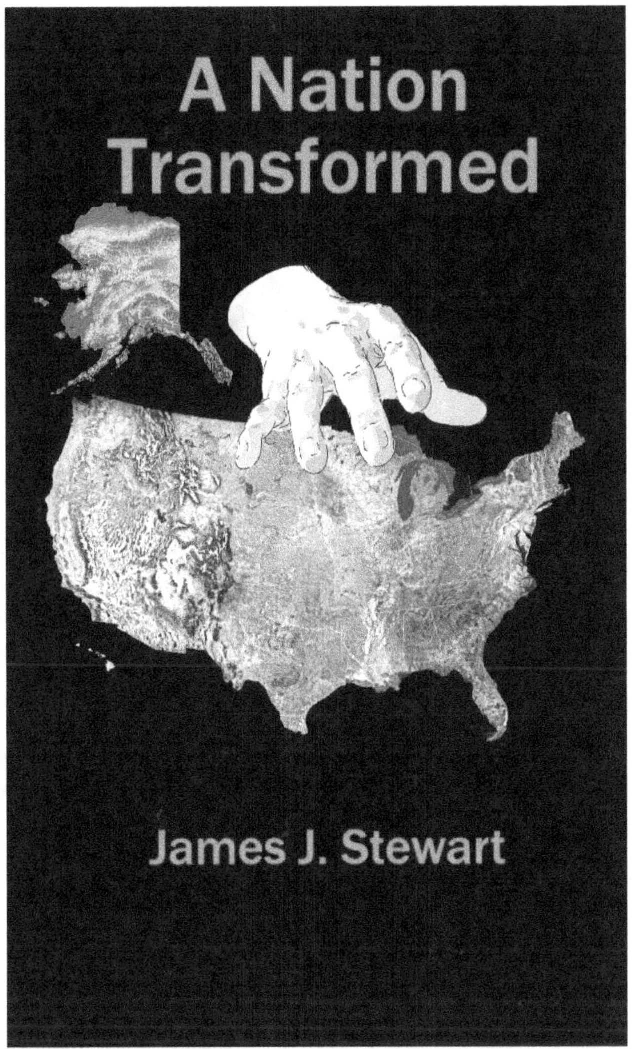

In 2042, it's been more than a decade since the six-year nuclear winter occurred. Although Christianity is still present in American culture, authentic Christ-centered living has become mostly a counter-cultural trend. Almost everyone associates love with sexual activity. Fun is often mistaken for joy. Relationships are prone to conflict. It's uncommon to have patience, genuine kindness is newsworthy, and self-control is often dismissed.

This is the account of a few individuals who have been struggling for years to be faithful in a society that is mostly faithless. Two prophets are seen as celebrities, except among those who really know them. Prayer warriors often witness answers to prayers that no one else is privy to. Although these people is appreciated by a few in positions of power, most political and social power is corrupt.

Transformation has started now that the Creator of the Universe has heard the prayers of the faithful for deliverance.

Both Carla and Ernie are young adults with a passion for photography. Ernie and his family in Germany have one of the biggest optics businesses in the world. Carla reviews photographic equipment and leads photo tours of Yosemite National Park and the Sierra Nevada Mountains.

They meet on the top of one of Yosemite's famous monoliths, Half Dome. There is instant friendship with a potential for much more. They open a local business together, and their friendship deepens.

This is a clean Christian romance mixed with adventure, and there are a few surprises along the way.

This is the mostly fictional autobiography of Brianan Tudor, who might be living with his current wife in Northern California today. If so, he is more than four hundred years old. He is the illegitimate son of King James VI of Scotland, who later became King James I of the Scottish and English Crowns. Brianan is an honest and honorable man, who tells of his impossibly long life.

Just how much of Brianan's story is not fictional, the reader must decide. Is this a string of biographical sketches strung together under the guise of one man? Why is there a steady supply of gemstones to support him throughout his life?

Most of the dates that are offered seem to be authentic in terms of history. Brianan's memories of conversations with his first wife in Scotland are foggy. His memories of his other wives during his extensive lifetime are vivid. Brianan was (is?) a loving, sensitive, and passionate Christian man, and he is gifted with many languages.

Judy Cunningham is a waitress. She grew up in Towne, a small community in the Sierra Nevada mountains of California. In high school she was homecoming queen and got straight A's, but she wasn't interested in going to college. She works at Bill's Bar and Grill, and has been there several years.

"Big John" Simmons is tall and muscular, and he's as big as a football linebacker. He moved to Towne to get away from heartache and to work on his thesis for a Ph.D. in Computer Engineering.

When Judy and John meet, they are both caught off guard by each other, and the seeds of romance are planted. Along comes an earthquake and other challenges, and they are thrown together more than either of them had planned.

Soul Mates is a sweet Christian romance that unfolds in the life of a typical small town.

In the Old Testament times of the Bible, was it gambling when a priest would cast lots to determine God's will? Technically, casting lots to reveal the will of God is called Cleromancy, and in much of the Old Testament, it was practiced. In the New Testament, there is only one example, when the followers of Jesus cast lots to determine who should replace Judas.

In Scandinavia, people engaged in the practice on through the ninth century. In Pietist tradition, Moravians extensively cast lots for many purposes, but the practice was discontinued in the late nineteenth century. In the Eastern Orthodox Church, the practice has continued to be used up until today on special occasions.

Two teenagers, who are musical prodigies, get married when they graduate from high school. They set out on their first concert tour, and they begin casting lots to determine God's will. They knew that God had gifted them musically, but then they discovered that they have the gift of prophecy. When they successfully predict a world-wide disaster, they learn that everything has a spiritual dimension.

A short story written for fun in the winter of 2000 is the foundation for The Gaardian Saga. Under several titles, that first novel became the first of four novels in the saga.

1. *Life Before Conception* tells of A bachelor ready to retire becomes friends with a three-legged man with yellowish-green skin and a tiger-like female with a human face. The pastor gets a second life as an intergalactic policeman called a Gaardian. Now apparently 30 again, the man is romanced by a famous actress.

2. *Starlight Adventures* tells of two extremely gifted scientists who are anonymously helped by the former pastor. He and other Gaardians help them deal with the media, a corrupt politician, and others

3. *The Still Small Voice* tells of beings from other planets becoming prophets who cause a change for the inhabitants of several worlds in unexpected ways.

4. The final novel, entitled *Stepping Beyond*, tells of god-like beings that pose a threat to thousands of planets. Equal in power to the Gaardians, the threat is very real, but so is God.